Praise fo

"In our anxious, fractured, post-pandemic world, the book
Mend offers pathways to hope and healing through poetry. Broken into
eighteen dynamic chapters presented by teacher poets, each chapter offers
a practical entry into poetry as a healing force. By opening their hearts and
sharing their own poetry, each teacher poet reinforces the gossamer
threads of our humanity. From self, to student, to the wider community,
Words That Mend offers the possibility of kinship and connection that has
the power to transform the world." ~**Ann Burg**, poet and author of *Force
of Nature, Flooded, Unbound, Serafina's Promise, and All the Broken Pieces*

"Important insight into specific methods and practices educators can
employ to bring poetry into their communities, their classrooms, and their
own lives. The educators here share their own experiences with writing
poetry as a form of much-needed healing in a difficult world. This hands-
on book will get not only students writing and appreciating poetry, but
will instill a love of poetry in the adults guiding them as well."
~**Kip Wilson**, award-winning author of *White Rose*

"As I read through *Words That Mend*—a book about writing poetry in
community like no other in its purpose and scope--the 2024 election season
was heating up. True to how that season has recently been unfolding,
words were launched as weapons meant to wound and only wound. This
book arrived as a salve, covering me whole cloth in poetry. Written by
teachers for teachers, with exemplar poems from teachers and students,
this collection will help us heal while we create that which can sustain us
for years to come." ~**Crag Hill**, poet and Oklahoma Writing Project Site
Director

"I will be recommending *Words That Mend*, to all my English teacher
friends. I was energized by each chapter, authored by a different teacher,
who courageously shared her vulnerabilities by participating in the poetry
writing process. I am motivated to guide more poetry lessons with my
students. Thanks to *Words That Mend*, I have lots of practical lessons at my
fingertips." ~**Sally Donnelly**, NBCT, Middle School Reading Coach,
Arlington Public School, VA

"The beauty our classrooms need—real, raw, and refreshing, like life itself.
This book celebrates the incredible healing power of words, revealing
profound truths and breathing life into those who embrace poetry. Its
impact is far-reaching, touching hearts and minds, and highlighting the
essential role of poetry in our lives." ~**Tracy Hunt**, Instructional Facilitator
for ELA Media Mid-Del Public Schools, Oklahoma

Praise for *Words That Mend*

"An emotion-evoking collection of works that blends together personal, meaningful teacher experiences grounded in reliable, research-based framework. It is brought to life through the inclusion of poetry by both teachers and students, along with detailed explanations of how the writing poetry activities can be replicated by other educators to build genuine relationships with their students and help supporting each other." ~**Kristina Bankston**, Hammond High Magnet School, LA, IBCP Service Learning & Reflective Project Coordinator

"Especially with poetry, many students ask, 'Why do we need to know this?' *Words That Mend* provides concrete examples of poetry's power in everyday living. From coming to terms with one's deepest emotions to sharing life's experiences with others, this book allows teachers to offer compelling, expedient answers to their students. " ~**Tina Smith Mckeen**, Spanish Teacher & Foreign Language Department Head, Highland HS, Medina, Ohio

"A hub and haven for English teachers who want to learn how to incorporate poetry writing into their classrooms and lives. Teachers can use this resource for instruction and inspiration as they envision and create classrooms where every student's voice–and their own –is heard and healed." ~**Jason Stephenson**, poet and Program Manager of Secondary Education, Oklahoma State Department of Education

"A beautiful book for English Language Arts teachers. I was touched by the vulnerability of all the authors as they shared how poetry has helped them and how they use poetry as SEL and for healing with their students. This is a great read for anyone wanting to bring more meaning to their poetry instruction and has the added benefit of helping the reader find some healing through writing, as well." ~**Gallit Zvi**, Principal at McKinney School in Richmond, British Columbia, and co-author of *The Genius Hour Guidebook.*

"An invaluable resource for teachers who wish to provide meaningful and out-of-the-box learning experiences. The practical "Your Turn" sections allow teachers to gain tried-and-true insights, strategies, and activities that can be immediately implemented in their classroom. These not only encourage students to fall in love with creative writing, but the most magical byproduct is that every member of the class gets to know one another on deep and authentic levels." ~**Kelly Koehler**, Middle School Gifted ELA Teacher, North Ridgeville, Ohio

Words That
MEND

**The Transformative Power of Writing Poetry
for Teachers, Students, and Community Wellbeing**

Sarah J. Donovan with

Susan Ahlbrand • Tamara Belko • Barb Edler

Wendy Everard • Kim Johnson • Jennifer Guyor Jowett

Denise Krebs • Leilya Pitre • Margaret Simon

Seela Books
Stillwater, OK 74075
www.ethicalela.com

ISBN: 978-0-9998768-5-5

Editors: Sarah J. Donovan
with Jennifer Guyor Jowett and Denise Krebs

Cover art: Owen Jowett

CONTENTS

For teachers
And always for students

Welcome

An Introduction

BY SARAH J. DONOVAN

INTRODUCTION

What a Poem Can Build
Sarah J. Donovan

What a Poem Can Build
by Susan Ahlbrand

I see the world through poet eyes
feel it through a poet heart.
Maybe that's why
my eyes see such sadness
and my heart feels so much pain.

A poem can't
feed a hungry child,
make a parent provide,
or pull someone out of poverty.

A poem can't
convince us to put the screens down,
engage with others face-to-face,
or relish in eye contact.

A poem can't
hold a therapy session,
do marriage counseling,
or prevent trauma in the first place.

A poem can't
start the chemotherapy line,
perform CPR,
or create a new vaccine.

A poem can't
enact legislation to make it harder to own a gun,
intervene and stop the trigger from being pulled,
or stem the pain that makes a person want to.

A poem can't

right the world's wrongs
but it can complete people
and fill empty hearts.

It can build
empathy
and compassion
and awareness.

And those things
can prevent the wrongs
from happening
in the first place.

This poem was written by Susan Ahlbrand in response to a poetry prompt on the Ethical ELA website, where we—teacher poets—have a five-day Open Write poetry writing each month. In April, the blog welcomes VerseLove, a thirty-day celebration of poetry, when teachers from across the world compose poems responding to a provided inspiration by the event hosts. Ethical ELA, founded by Sarah Donovan, began in May of 2015 as a space to share resources, experiences, begin conversations, connect with and support teachers.

On day 29 of 30 days of writing poetry together, Glenda Funk, Idaho high school English teacher of over 30 years, knew that our month-long endeavor was coming to an end. She had selected a mentor text and crafted a prompt for us that drew on her deep knowledge of teacher and literature. She suggested, "Darius V. Daughtry's magnificent poem '*what can a poem do?*' which begins with a series of litotes naming myriad things a poem can't do and concludes by imagining what poetry can do and does. It's these possibilities poems offer that bring me hope." Glenda included an excerpt from Daughtry's poem:

a poem cannot save a life
cannot Luke Cage your skin
fend off a dark alley attack
cannot make you less woman
or less poor
or less Black
and

thus
treated equally....

Each prompt and mentor text is followed by an invitation to write: "Think about the issues that concern you. Perhaps make a list. Next, choose a form for your poem. Daugherty names the sonnet, but maybe you prefer a villanelle, a free verse, or some other form."

Susan, a middle school teacher of 35 years in Indiana, wrote the above poem, and later, she shared Daugherty's poem with her students. Teachers are like that—we are always looking for good teaching ideas.

Susan's poem speaks to our collective lives as teachers. What teacher among us has not bought a student lunch because they "forgot" theirs (again), not needed marriage counseling, not known a colleague who needs sick day donations for their chemo? Yes, this poem speaks to teachers in its specifics and universal truths. And yet we know there are not many teachers among us who would name themselves Poet. So this book also serves as advocacy for writing poetry—for teachers, for students.

There was a time when we did not write poetry, were honestly intimidated by poetry, resisted invitations to write a stanza even for students during National Poetry Month's requisite poetry unit. The idea of writing poetry was far from joyful let alone healing. As an English teacher, it may feel like a betrayal to say so, but there it is. Poetry—as it was taught in secondary classrooms (and not taught in teacher preparation programs)—seemed to have very little to do with writing poetry, little to do with serving the writer at all. There was little conversation in our classrooms about what a poem can do. In fact, poetry in the textbooks (and TeachersPayTeachers lesson plans) was about interpretation, a correct reading, and, yes, sometimes a way of learning about a time period (e.g., Owen's war poetry, Hughes' Harlem Renaissance). In some secondary classrooms, the only writing assigned is in the service of literary analysis or research. Five-paragraph templates and state assessment rubrics tend to measure sentence variety and conventions—not too much healing or wellbeing goals there. Reading poetry specifically or writing, broadly speaking, had very little to do with the life of the student. Young adult literary poetry was not a thing during most of our teacher preparation programs. In fact, writing was not a process of meaning making nor an act of agency to uncover what writing can do for students and the things they care about. The classroom was not a place where we considered what a poem can do. And when we ask what a poem can do, aren't we really asking what we can do?

Most of the chapter authors and the teacher-poets cited throughout met celebrating National Poetry Month. Some of us started in 2019 while others joined in subsequent years. The April writing experience we call VerseLove extended to monthly Open Writes in the summer of 2020 when teachers were still isolating during the pandemic. Writing poetry has become a lifeline for many of us, and it didn't seem healthy to cut another lifeline when April ended, so we began the Open Write: five days of writing poetry, which typically begins the third Saturday of each month. As we write this chapter, it is 2024, and the monthly writing is still going strong. We began writing because it was National Poetry Month and Sarah initiated a teacher challenge to write a poem a day online. It was 2019, and together we wrote about 1500 poems and responses. Then, in 2020, during COVID-19, we wrote nearly 6000. Teachers from across the country, isolated during remote emergency teaching, found their way to poetry. And now three years later, we are still writing with over 9000 poems and responses written in April 2023.

We began writing this book together in the summer of 2023. Maybe that was because we were all coming out of our COVID-19 fog, or maybe we found ourselves closer to acceptance in the stages of grief. As a group of English language arts teachers, we began to recognize that our writing was a form of healing, a way of listening and reciprocating, finding ourselves once again after we had been lost for so long. Poetry is a living form, a way of bringing words and writers to life, and in our writing and responses we were resurrecting.

Among us, we know the reason we write is because writing poetry serves our hearts and minds, makes us feel connected, seen, valued for our whole being, but we also conducted a study to hear why other teachers write poetry.

What This Book Is (and Isn't)

But we are getting ahead of ourselves. Ending that anecdote with quantitative data undermines the mending we are here to offer, especially considering that we haven't explained to you why writing poetry matters and what sort of mending we are talking about. We plan to be as authentic and clear as possible throughout this book, but we also think it is important not to undersell the transformative potential inherent in poetic writing for teachers, students, and communities. With that in mind, what exactly is poetic writing, and what are you getting yourself into with this book?

While a detailed explanation of poetry as it is situated in the larger field of poetry writing instruction and its benefits takes up much of Chapter 1, here is a brief definition that might prove helpful at the outset: if you are asking students to write about their lives for purposes like getting to know our students, helping them get to know one another, showing them how different forms of writing evoke different ways of thinking about language beyond "for a test" or "for a grade," if you're asking students to stretch from concrete to abstract ways of thinking about their world and beyond, you're engaging in some form or poetic writing experience.

Let's look at that definition in the context of Glenda's poem prompt. First, she offers several possibilities for writing through Daugherty's poem. The invitation is to write a poem about poems — okay, so that seems like a narrow order much like telling students to write an essay about their summer. But then we see she teaches us litotes, which is to begin with the negative of its contrary, which is a sophisticated word and move, but seems possible the way Daughtery shows us. Then, there is the question of form—and Glenda offers us Daughtery's but also any other form we may know. Maybe we always resist form and structure and want to go our own way. This prompt says "yes, you can try Daughtery's way or reject that and try something new." So poetic writing recognizes that poets make a lot of choices—so far, there is topic, craft, and form.

Once we begin to read the excerpt from Daughtery, we see that he is doing something that doesn't happen in school, right, and certainly not during professional development meetings with teachers. This poem is an invitation to write about our life, the way we see the world. It isn't really about poetry, though it could be. This poem is an argument for equality, draws on the writer's prior knowledge of comics, perhaps witnessing or lived experiences with injustice in his context, from his perspective of what a poem can and can't do for him. And so, Susan takes up this prompt and Daughtery's poem, and his craft of litotes but she structures it into stanzas, different line breaks or scenes, and she draws on her lived experiences as a teacher to say something about what a poem can and can't do for her as a teacher.

In many secondary English language arts classrooms, poetry is read with some mnemonic device (TPCAST, 5Ts, SMILE) or, step-by-step approach to analyzing a poem that undermines or restricts what a poem can do. In this way, reading poetry is for the teacher or for a grade to decipher the text rather than serving the writer, i.e., a poem in the service of a poet, a writer. *Words That Mend* is asking for teachers to offer poetry in the service of you, the teacher, of our students, the poets, and of the community in desperate need of more poetry and healing. We are asking that we cultivate learning spaces that invite our literature and writing to position students to do authentic, meaningful work in a way that heals their hearts and offers space to engage with, comment on, and dialogue about what they are witnessing, living, wanting to live.

So that is what poetic writing is and what it can do in its most introductory form. What exactly can you expect to find in this book?

To begin, this isn't the right place to visit if you are looking for poetry theory. Theory is valuable and necessary, and we are not opposed to theory. In fact, we wish teacher preparation programs would include poetry courses for teachers and that more conferences would include poetic theory and traditions to deepen and demystify common understandings about what poetry is and can do. As a teacher educator, Sarah works regularly with preservice teachers and writing workshops to help teachers articulate the connection between theory and practice in order to understand why and how strategies are worth using, especially as they advocate for authentic and agentive writing practices in their schools. Theory matters, and we haven't avoided our responsibility in explaining it here, but we have always been drawn more toward books that speak directly to and alongside teachers, with practical experience contextualized and storied.

And this book is not a collection of poetry forms. There are plenty of those that have helped us to expand our knowledge of poetry and create prompts. Those exist. We are thinking of *Poems Are Teachers: How Studying Poetry Strengthens Writing in All Genres* (VanDerwater, 2017), *The Write Thing: Kwame Alexander Engages Students in Writing Workshop (And You Can Too!)* (Alexander, 2018), and *Lightning Paths: 75 Poetry Writing Exercises* (Vaughn, 2018)

So this is not a theory book nor a book about poem forms.

This book is an invitation to sit alongside us as we revisit the poetic writing experience that has been a balm specifically during the last few years. As teachers we're navigating implications of the enduring pandemic while 36 states launched 317 legislative actions broadly censoring conversations about race and gender identities (see "Legislation of Concern in 2023") denying experiences of historical marginalized people and their literary representations in schools also limiting readers' rights (see NCTE) and teacher autonomy in choosing the literature their learners need in their particular learning contexts. Teachers are feeling the harm from all angles while also (and always have been) taking care of their own families, bodies, and minds. We will say more about this in the next chapter and throughout as we share teachers' stories and results from our survey of teachers.

Many existing texts speak to skills-development and do so strictly from the deficit lens of closing some reading gap or making up lost learning, but what we've found that is missing from the existing literature is a text that helps teachers heal. We need to name or acknowledge explicitly the need for ongoing healing for ourselves to then support our students and communities. We hesitate to use this cliché metaphor, but it is apt: we must put on our oxygen masks. The time for white knuckling our way through the school year has to end. No more—just get to Thanksgiving. Just get to Christmas break. If I can only hold on until Memorial Day. Counting our sick days.

States have recognized that our students need trauma-informed instruction. In just two years, from 2017 to 2019, the number of states with policies requiring trauma-informed teacher training in schools increased from nine to thirty (Donovan, 2022), thus codifying trauma or making trauma-informed training binding on each public school and district within the state. This training is typically adverse childhood experiences (ACES) focusing on regulating dysregulation of emotion and behaviors seen in students. But what about teachers? We've been able to point to texts about trauma-informed education for students, and several books for adults related to burnout. However, what seemed to be missing from the professional conversation among secondary English teachers was a text establishing poetic writing as a valuable humanizing approach for a wide range of learning goals, including wellbeing, accompanied by descriptions of easily modified poetic writing engagements. What is missing is dedicated pages to teachers from teachers about their whole being and how nurturing their writing life in and of itself is valuable practice, and that in doing that work and showing students the benefits, we can nurture students' literary and lived lives through poetry.

A Brief Word about Structure

This book is divided into three parts: teacher, student, and community. In each part, we offer a series of chapters with a variety of poetic writing scenes, including prompts, mentor texts, suggested methods, and an invitation to write with us. The best use of this book is to write with us in the teacher section before or while you are writing with students to the degree that you can actively experience the benefits of writing in a community of teachers. While we know that writing poetry can be a salve, we also know that writing poetry with others engages reciprocity, an opportunity to cultivate a supportive community.

Across the book, we include full poems written by teachers and students. These poets have given their permission for their full poems to be published. In some cases, we were not able to contact the poet or there were copyright concerns, so we used only excerpts of poems. We lovingly cite other educators and students who have inspired us throughout.

What we hope sets this book apart is that it is, at heart, a book about *writing* poetry. We take up poetry writing forms in ways we hope are serious and helpful to your instructional practices. We've made this book easy to navigate, so you can find specific ideas in each chapter. But this is, first and foremost, a book that celebrates community and the opportunities writing with others presents for your students to do writing that matters. This may seem counter-intuitive. Many people say being a writer can be lonely or isolating, but we haven't found that to be the case because we share our poetry and volunteer to be listeners of others' poetry. And there is comfort in knowing that your words serve yourself and others.

To begin, some necessary organizational information: Chapter 1 provides an overview of poetic healing and the concept of writing for autobiographical expression. Soter (2016) says that poetry gives voice to "whatever is too large, too incomprehensible to express in any other way" (p. 2). We explore writing as nurturing empathic and nonjudgmental self-listening and how the process of sharing one's lived experience in the form of autobiographical poetic writings can be "joyful, sad, revealing, exciting and occasionally painful" (Custer, 2013, p. 1), We consider why all these possibilities are worth experiencing in the secondary English classroom.

Further, we conducted a study of 50 teachers who write poetry to explore the potential healing benefits, and we share our findings as a way of grounding this work in teachers' stories but also to make an argument for this book as a lifeline in our schools.

Part I includes chapters from each of us. The role of these chapters is to introduce you to poetic inspiration and share the ways writing poetry has served us in similar and different ways. This should help you start thinking about what you can do with poetic writing in your own life, and we hope you will join us in our live online space to write with us on www.ethicalela.com.

For anyone intimidated by the thought of writing poetry in public online spaces, we also wanted to start with these examples to encourage you to start writing poetry in a paper or digital notebook to see what it feels like to write your poetic experiences alongside ours. To notice the choices you make with topic, craft, form, and in sharing.

We begin each chapter with a scene from our experiences. We know story has the power to connect and surface universal experiences in the specific. We continue each chapter with poems that inspired our poetic engagements with permission from the poets, and, in the spirit of reciprocity, we share our first draft poetry writing with you to show what we wrote, how, and why. In student (Part II) and community chapters (Part III), we share poetry with permission from our students, families, and community members. So there is a lot of poetry in this book, from people we know and love and have healed alongside.

Part II includes chapters from a few of our classrooms so that you can see how our personal experiences writing poetry live in new ways with students. We do this to show you the impact on students—the way centering our students as poets over the text, centering writing over interpretation of poetry can shift toward humanizing ways of being together. We include testimony from teachers in our study to show the ways they have used poetry writing with students, too.

In Part III, we extend our work beyond the walls of the classroom to imagine how our poetry can live in public and digital spaces to serve others. We feel such joy when our poetry can serve others, and by turning our lines and verses over to an anthology publication or a spoken word event or a public poetry celebration, we can witness the poetic healing in new spaces. If you are looking for small and large-scale ways to try poetic writing that's engaging and authentic, your own community likely has a wide range of spaces, so we share our experiences to help you imagine possibilities with others.

At the end of the book, we offer you an appendix. In this section, we will include a chart with an overview of all the contents, including the poem forms, topics, and craft moves so that you can adapt them for you, your writing group, your students, your community. We also include documents that were useful in our writing process or lesson planning. In addition, we have developed quite a few protocols for supporting students in sharing and responding to poetry, so we offer these for you to try and adapt. Finally, poetry stirs hearts and minds, so we do think teachers should continue reading about what poetry can do including poetry as part of trauma-informed education and also ways to work with your school social worker or psychologist should the need arise. We offer a list of resources. And, yes, one more: We share a list of our favorite inclusive-affirming poetry anthologies to support your ongoing exploration of what a poem can do.

We think what makes our book extra beneficial is that we are writing from across the country with you. You will get to know us in our chapters and poetry, and we hope to get to know you, too. We zoom into scenes of our poetic experiences, and then we zoom out to offer commentary on our process and the insights we had when we first wrote the poems or first taught a poetic prompt. Sometimes we draw on a little theory or a favorite poet's insight to help us understand what about our experience made it so significant, and we tell you when we are uncertain or still contemplating meaning.

Finally, we close each chapter with an invitation for you to write and share your poem with us. We hope you will join us.

We understand that there are various states that have legislation against social emotional learning and some are opposed to community engagement because community sounds a lot like communist (as one Oklahoma Senator told Sarah). We know that there are lingering effects of COVID-19 that are still surfacing. We know that there are schools with scripted curriculum that fiercely protect their scope and sequence with little if any poetry writing. Our vision for writing poetry to have a place in the classroom could actually prove to be a catalyst by which students can be encouraged to engage with traditional content but through more honest, authentic, and humanizing methods that situate our content as serving students' hearts and minds rather than the reverse.

The next chapter offers some insight into research upon which *Word that Mend* is grounded. We encourage you to draw on this rationale for uncovering reasons to start writing poetry for your own wellbeing and for carving time during class for students to discover what writing poetry can do for themselves and alongside one another. As you read this book, we encourage you to be gentle with yourself. Open and close the book as you need to. Skim, slow down, or skip as the writing signals you to do so. So let's see what a poem can do.

One More Thing: Copyright

The authors of these chapters and the poems within belong to the authors who have agreed to share their poems in this book and online under the Creative Commons license CC-BY-NC-SA: Attribution- NonCommercial- ShareAlike. This allows others to remix, adapt, and build upon the work non-commercially, as long as they credit the creator and license their new creations under the identical terms.

This book is an Open Educational Resource (OER). OER are educational materials that are freely accessible and openly licensed for anyone to use, adapt, and redistribute. They aim to reduce costs and improve access to education. However, we have made available a paperback version of this book that is available in libraries and bookstores for no profit to us. We have priced this book at $0, but the provider or store will charge the cost of printing and any mark-up they wish. That is not within our control. We are doing our best to keep the cost down for teachers. A free Google doc and PDF are available on the website Ethical ELA or if you email any of the authors and request a copy.

How OER Work Within Copyright

1. Licensing: Creators of OER use licenses to specify how others can use their work. The most common licenses are from Creative Commons (CC).
2. Creative Commons Licenses: The license for this book and the poems within is the following. CC-BY-NC-SA: Attribution- NonCommercial- ShareAlike. Allows others to download, print, remix, adapt, and build upon the work

non-commercially, as long as they credit the creator and license their new creations under the identical terms.

Benefits of Using OER

1. Cost Reduction: Freely accessible educational materials reduce the cost of educational resources for students.
2. Adaptability: Educators can adapt and customize OER to better suit their teaching needs and local contexts.
3. Collaboration: Facilitates collaboration and sharing among educators and institutions.

Ensuring Compliance

1. Attribution: Always give appropriate credit, provide a link to the license, and indicate if changes were made.
2. Understand License Terms: Be sure to understand and follow the terms of the specific Creative Commons license applied to the OER.
3. Respect Non-OER Content: Be cautious with incorporating non-OER content that may have stricter copyright protections.

By understanding and utilizing Creative Commons licenses, educators and content creators can share their work more freely and contribute to the growing body of OER, thereby enhancing educational access and equity.

So please share these stories and poems widely.

References

Custer, D. (2014). Autoethnography as a transformative research method. *The Qualitative Report, 19,* 1–13.

Donovan, S. (2022). Reading trauma: Uncovering trauma paradigms in young adult literature. In E. Dutro's (Eds.), *English Journal Special Issue, 2.* NCTE. ISBN: 9780814145036

Soter, A. O. (2016). Reading and writing poetically for wellbeing: Language as a field of energy in practice. *Journal of Poetry Therapy: The Interdisciplinary Journal of Practice, Theory, Research and Education, 29*(3), 161–174.

CHAPTER 1

Writing Poetry Foundations & Framework
Sarah J. Donovan

Teachers know that the summers are rarely restful. We have professional development and summer institutes. The new school year begins, and we are still tired from the previous year. Still, we have a fresh start. Call it the Octobers or The October Slump or the October Slip, but by October, we are exhausted again. I don't remember a December holiday break when I wasn't looking for another job—other than teaching or in another school where the proverbial grass was greener. I think the idea of a change was a boost of hope I needed to get me through the school year. This idea of "getting through" or white-knuckling our way until winter break, then spring break, then summer, frames the work of a teacher as unsustainable.

But teaching now feels somehow even harder if that is possible. Of course, the state of teaching may not be fraught with tension for everyone. Some teachers are finding their stride. Still, there are contextual factors discussed below that are pressing on all teacher and personal lifespan events that can impact a teacher at any time.

Burnout remains a major issue, with teachers citing heavy workloads, lack of respect, and insufficient compensation as key factors. Teacher salaries have remained relatively stagnant compared to other professions requiring similar levels of education, which contributes to the "teacher pay penalty" and exacerbates feelings of undervaluation. Teachers' annual evaluation based on the students' standardized test scores adds to the stress and burnout. Additionally, efforts to improve teacher wellbeing often fall short, with superficial solutions like casual dress days or pep talks (even lectures of self-care) failing to address deeper systemic issues.

The state of teaching post-COVID-19 has been marked by significant challenges, particularly regarding teacher burnout and the impact of anti-teacher policies. The pandemic exacerbated existing issues, such as workload stress and inadequate support, leading to increased teacher burnout. Many teachers struggled with adapting to and from online learning, navigating acute and chronic health concerns, and maintaining educational standards under difficult circumstances.

Anti-teacher policies and legislation have further strained the profession. For example, in states like Florida, laws such as the "Don't Say Gay" bill and the Stop WOKE Act have created a hostile environment for educators, particularly those addressing LGBTQ+ issues and race. These policies limit teachers' ability to provide comprehensive education and support to students, leading to higher resignation rates and a worsening teacher shortage.

Research has shown that strong teacher unions can help mitigate some of these stresses by advocating for better pay, improved working conditions, and advocacy paths for teachers. However, anti-union laws in certain states have increased teacher stress and reduced the efficacy of these organizations.

Teacher Wellbeing

I was a social worker for seven years before I became a teacher. As a social worker, I learned about family dynamics, active listening, individual and group therapy, and how to manage my own compassion fatigue, secondary trauma, and burnout while nurturing my own emotional wellbeing. These are not things that I learned in my teacher training, and over the years, I have been amazed to witness how teachers balance their personal lives with the life of being a teacher, a life which, year after year, is responsible for the cognitive and emotional wellbeing of other people's children. Now, some may say that teachers are not responsible for the social and emotional learning and development of students, but I think any teacher will tell you that they cannot teach content without attending to the physical, social, and emotional needs of students. And few teachers are trained to do that. Rather, they figure it out. They draw on their capacity for care to attend to their students while, at times, setting aside their own needs.

Burnout is common—even by October—characterized by emotional exhaustion, depersonalization, and a reduced sense of personal accomplishment. It is prevalent among teachers due to the demanding nature of the job, especially when compounded by external pressures such as policy changes and social issues or personal lifespan events like marriage, divorce, birth, death, illness. Many teachers themselves have histories of adverse childhood experiences (ACEs) which can influence their susceptibility to burnout and secondary trauma. Understanding and addressing these personal histories can help in providing more targeted support and professional development.

Understanding Compassion Fatigue and Trauma

Compassion fatigue refers to the emotional and physical exhaustion that can affect individuals who care for others, particularly in high-stress environments like teaching. It can result from the continuous demand to provide empathy and support to students, which can drain teachers' emotional reserves over time. This phenomenon is compounded by the increasing emotional needs of students, particularly in the aftermath of the COVID-19 pandemic and other societal stressors.

Teachers and students experience various forms of trauma that impact their wellbeing in and out of school:

- **Acute Trauma:** Acute trauma refers to a single, isolated event that is extremely stressful or disturbing, such as the sudden loss of a loved one. Teachers need to be equipped with trauma-informed practices to support students immediately following such events.
- **Chronic Trauma:** Chronic trauma results from prolonged exposure to distressing events, such as ongoing abuse or persistent bullying. This can lead to long-term psychological effects and requires consistent support from teachers and mental health professionals.
- **Historical Trauma:** Historical trauma encompasses the cumulative emotional harm of an individual or generation caused by a traumatic experience or event, such as systemic racism or war. Understanding this type of trauma is essential for teachers working in historically marginalized communities. Historical trauma can include **intergenerational** trauma, which is carrying the effects of war and displacement, for example, genetically.
- **Contextual Trauma:** School shootings have a profound impact on the entire school community. Schools need comprehensive crisis response plans, mental health support systems, and preventative measures to address the potential for such events and their aftermath. Natural disasters disrupt the school environment and can cause significant trauma for students and staff. Schools need to have

emergency preparedness plans and provide ongoing support for affected individuals to rebuild a sense of safety and normalcy. Political issues such as anti-critical race theory (CRT) legislation and book banning create a contentious atmosphere that can undermine teachers' autonomy and educational goals. These policies can increase stress and burnout among teachers while also limiting students' access to diverse and inclusive curricula.

Teachers experiencing trauma from and through their work may show symptoms of vicarious traumatization (VT). VT is a transformation in the inner experience of the teacher resulting from empathetic engagement with students' trauma. A gift so many wonderful teachers have is empathy. You may identify as an empath yourself. VT, however, involves changes in teachers' core beliefs about themselves, others, and the world, often leading to a sense of hopelessness or heightened cynicism. With extended exposure to students enduring trauma because of a local event (fire, tornado, shooting) or personal acute trauma (domestic abuse), empathic teachers can burnout sooner, leaving the profession. While less common, teachers can absorb the trauma experienced by students. Secondary traumatic stress (STS) systems are similar to those of PTSD and include intrusive thoughts, emotional numbing, and hyperarousal. This can severely impact teachers' ability to function both professionally and personally.

Building empathetic relationships is crucial but challenging, especially under the strain of external stressors. Teachers who successfully navigate these relationships often exhibit higher levels of emotional intelligence and resilience, but they also need support systems to manage the emotional labor involved.

Again, as a social worker, I was trained to notice compassion fatigue, VT, and STS in our peers and intervene with support. There was support from a lead social worker and therapeutic resources, including mental health days.

Teachers' emotional wellbeing is essential for effective teaching and personal health. Strategies to enhance wellbeing include professional development focused on stress management, peer support networks, and institutional policies that promote a healthy work-life balance.

What Poetry in Community Can Do

Writing poetry can have profound effects, both personally and universally. Here's a breakdown of what writing poetry can do, emphasizing its healing power, self-healing benefits, and the various aspects of autobiographical writing, relational poetics, witnessing, and reciprocity.

The graphic illustrates the interconnected components of writing for healing and connection. Each element is linked to the others, showing how aspects like self-healing, autobiographical writing, connection to shared human experiences, the healing power of the language arts, and relational poetics through witnessing and reciprocity are interrelated and contribute to a holistic approach to writing and healing.

Language Arts as Healing

The research (Baker & Mazza, 2004; Custer, 2014; Donovan & Boutelier, 2023; Donovan et. al., 2024; Jacobs, 2016; Mazza, 2003) highlights the transformative and healing power of poetry and writing. In addition, a survey we conducted confirms the research.

We write poetry, but we wanted to hear from teachers who write poetry beyond our writing group. We wanted to be sure our stories live in other spaces and with teachers more broadly. We sent a survey through social media inviting teachers to share ways they use poetry in their classrooms and ways that writing poetry has helped them and their students beyond purely academic pursuits. We were looking for evidence of healing even if temporary. We were looking for evidence of teachers turning toward or to writing poetry to assuage their pain or process an experience.

Sixty teachers completed the survey. We found that these teachers often find that poetry serves as a powerful medium for healing, not just for themselves but also for their students and communities. Their definitions of healing through poetry encompass three main themes: processing and acknowledging the past, emotional and creative expression, and restoration and moving forward. By acknowledging past traumas and integrating them into their identities, teachers view healing as a reconciliation with history without allowing it to dictate their present and future. Emotional and creative expression through poetry allows them to process complex emotions, providing psychological relief and personal insight. Finally, restoration and moving forward emphasize the journey of overcoming pain and regaining a sense of balance and strength. These themes illustrate the multifaceted nature of healing, highlighting how poetry can serve as a therapeutic tool to navigate and transcend personal and collective challenges.

Through autobiographical writing and poetry, individuals can process their emotions, gain self-understanding, and find new meaning in their experiences. The historical and cultural significance of this practice underscores its enduring relevance in fostering emotional and psychological healing. As educators and therapists continue to explore and utilize these tools, the profound impact of poetry and writing on human wellbeing becomes increasingly evident.

Poetry allows individuals to express deeply personal experiences in ways that resonate universally. Through metaphors, imagery, and emotion, personal stories can evoke similar feelings and experiences in others, fostering empathy and connection. This universality from the personal can bridge cultural, social, and personal divides, creating a shared human experience.

Engaging in creative arts, including poetry, can be therapeutic. The process of writing poetry helps individuals process complex emotions and experiences, leading to emotional catharsis and psychological relief. Language arts provide a medium to explore and articulate feelings that might otherwise remain unexpressed, aiding in mental health and wellbeing.

Baker and Mazza (2004) emphasize that writing methods have historically been used to process life experiences and make sense of them. They highlight that writing brings "greater self-understanding, clarification, resolution, and control" (p. 144). This process of writing about life incidents allows individuals to handle their feelings better, leading to personal growth and transformation (Mazza, 1979, 2003).

Jacobs (2016) further elaborates that writing is an effective method for exploring and accepting one's emotions. It helps individuals to reach into the darker corners of their consciousness, bringing hidden thoughts and feelings to light. This exploration is essential for healing, as it allows individuals to confront and understand their emotions more deeply.

A significant theme in the responses from teachers in our survey is the idea of healing as a process of acknowledging and coming to terms with the past without letting it dominate one's present or future identity. Teachers express that understanding and accepting past traumas is essential for healing.

The responses from teachers reveal that healing through poetry involves processing and acknowledging past traumas, using creative expression as a therapeutic outlet, and striving for restoration and forward movement. These themes underscore the multifaceted nature of healing, where understanding the past, expressing emotions, and rebuilding strength are all integral to the journey. Through poetry, teachers and students alike can find a powerful tool for navigating and overcoming their personal challenges.

Autobiographical Writing

Writing autobiographical poetry allows individuals to delve into their own life stories, providing a structured way to reflect on and make sense of past experiences. This can be particularly healing as it encourages self-awareness and personal growth, helping individuals to understand and reconcile with their own histories.

Survey Themes: How teachers understand healing

Processing and Acknowledging the Past. These statements highlight the importance of reconciliation with past experiences as a crucial step in the healing process. This theme aligns with concepts in trauma-informed care, where acknowledging and processing trauma is a key component of healing.

- "Being healed means understanding and acknowledging the past without letting it control or shape my identity."
- "Healing means closing a wound and not reopening it. This can be both physical and emotional. I like the idea that we should settle up with the past and then live in the present and future."
- "Healing, to me, means coming to terms with what you can and cannot change."

Emotional and Creative Expression. Poetry provides a way to articulate complex feelings and experiences that might be difficult to express otherwise. This creative process can lead to emotional release and psychological relief, which are essential aspects of self-healing.

- "The expansion of creativity is healing. The trapping or controlling creativity is prison."
- "Healing is just a way to process your emotions in that moment."
- "By writing poetry, I can be honest in dealing with the reality, the struggle, and desire to live with that as a moment to shape me for the better."

Restoration and Moving Forward. This idea of restoration includes regaining a sense of balance, strength, and resilience. Healing is seen as a journey towards recovery, where individuals learn to cope with and overcome their struggles, ultimately leading to a renewed sense of self.

- "Healing is working through pain that has been caused. It makes something that hurts emotionally not hurt quite so bad."
- "Healing means gaining strength in mind and body to better handle stress in a positive way."
- "To heal is to physically or emotionally forgive and forget. A healed heart is made whole by loving even after it's been broken."

Autobiographical poetry is particularly effective in providing a platform for self-reflection and healing. Custer (2014) describes the process of sharing one's lived experiences through autobiographical writings as "joyful, sad, revealing, exciting, and occasionally painful" (p. 1). This multifaceted process allows individuals to process their emotions and gain new insights into their experiences.

Willis (2002) refers to autobiographical poems as "poetized reflections" that illuminate and crystallize experiences (p. 7). Kreuter (2009) highlights that this reflective process helps individuals find new meaning in life by encouraging inward reflection and outward expression with courage (p. 165). Writing poetry can help individuals explore relationships and interactions, both with themselves and others, fostering a deeper understanding and empathy within personal relationships.

Of course, English language arts teachers are very familiar with the personal narrative or personal essay — foundational writing assignments in school. Teachers and students discover the agentive power of telling a story as you remember and know it, of reflecting on a formative experience that you can only understand now that you are a little older. Writing in reflection is possible even for students writing just a year or less from a memory or experience.

And there is art and craft in engaging language and form to express the stories of our lives. That may be why you became a teacher in the first place.

As articulated thus far, poetry, in particular, offers a unique avenue for expression and healing. Soter (2016) argues that poetry gives voice to emotions that are too large or incomprehensible to express in any other way. This capacity of poetry to capture intense human experiences is also noted by Raingruber (2004), who states that the complexity and beauty of language within poetry allow for the expression of deep emotional experiences.

Writing poetry can help individuals explore relationships and interactions, both with themselves and others, fostering a deeper understanding and empathy within personal relationships.

Poetry is particularly effective in addressing trauma. Akhtar (2000) notes that poetry acts as a witness to traumatic experiences, providing a medium to recount and share private anguish. Raingruber (2004) states that poetry's fluid nature allows individuals to mourn and master challenges simultaneously. By transforming passive suffering into a creative act, poetry enables individuals to process and heal from trauma.

Berger (1984) encapsulates this healing power by stating that while poetry cannot repair loss, it defies the space which separates. This defiance fosters connection and understanding, making poetry a powerful tool for healing both personal and communal traumas.

In the survey, teachers reported writing poetry as a powerful tool for healing by helping individuals and communities process grief and loss, providing emotional and psychological relief, and fostering connections and support. Through poetry, they can articulate deep feelings, honor their experiences, and contribute to collective healing. These themes illustrate the multifaceted role of poetry in educational and communal contexts, emphasizing its therapeutic potential and its ability to unite and heal.

Survey Themes: How teachers use poetry as a path to healing

Processing Grief and Loss. Many teachers use poetry to navigate and process intense emotions related to grief and loss, both personally and within their communities. This theme underscores poetry's role in dealing with death, separation, and other forms of significant personal loss.

- "When my dad passed, I wrote some poems about him and about my mom dealing with the loss, and they definitely helped me process his death in a more healthful way."
- "I wrote a poem for Lucas at the beginning of this year... He was killed in an auto accident, and there was a void where his goofy loving optimism had been."
- "When my daughter was in the NICU, the poem I wrote helped me by acknowledging the pain I was in."
- "My daughter read it at his visitation in the gymnasium of our school. His parents put it on his tombstone as a tribute..."

Emotional and Psychological Healing. Teachers often use poetry as a tool for emotional and psychological healing, allowing them to explore and articulate complex emotions. This theme involves poetry as a means to understand, express, and heal from emotional pain.

- "As a teenager, I wrote poetry to heal from emotional issues."
- "I wrote a few poems that represented how I felt watching my mother in a helpless state."
- "I've written a couple of poems about my parents' divorce. And although it was amicable, it was still something that blindsided me as a 18 year-old headed to college. I thought that (divorce) couldn't happen to my parents. So writing about it and finding out a few details here and there have helped me come to terms with it."

Expressive Writing. By writing about their experiences and feelings, teachers find a therapeutic outlet that helps them process and make sense of their emotions, childhood, and past.

- "I wrote a poem about my name during OSUWP as an example. Until then I had a very negative connection to my name. Working through those feelings has made me see that it is not me with a problem but those who don't have enough respect for me to pay attention and say my name correctly."

- "I had my students write a poem in the fashion of Patrick Roche's "21" and wrote with them. It ended up being one I didn't share with them, but it helped me process my fears of relationships and marriage because of my own history of growing up in a domestically violent home, witnessing my sister's victimization at the hands of a domestically violent husband when I was a teen, and being a victim of sexual assault as a small child from a trusted family friend. Writing it was horrible--I cried a lot but demanded I be honest. However, it helped me to verbalize the fears I had refused to acknowledge and come to a place of hope that one day I will trust someone enough to build a life with them."

- "I had a miscarriage my first year into college and I was DEVASTATED. Years later I wrote a poem from the POV of the fetus questioning why she/he did not live to be born. It was well received and printed and framed for a female clinic in Weatherford, where I went to college. It was healing for me from my rainbow baby, and some interpreted it as an aborted fetus, some as a miscarried fetus. It just depended on the reader's frame of reference. It could be easily interpreted as both."

Facilitating Connection and Community Support. Poetry acts as a bridge, fostering connections among individuals and communities by sharing personal stories and collective experiences. This theme highlights poetry's role in building empathy, understanding, and support within a community.

- "I wrote a poem to try to bring some sense of comfort to our school community as we grieved."

- "My students and I were let down in a major way by one of our own; in the end, he was expelled. When they asked me to write a spring poem about them, I was sorely tempted to leave Mr. Expulsion out of the poem. In the end, I included him. I felt better for having honored his being a part of us. The students thanked me for not leaving him out. When he eventually saw it, he thanked me as well."

> • "One that really sticks out is the poem I wrote in Hungarian as I processed saying goodbye and the different aspects of life I would miss after living and working there for three years. That was a way to deal with grief, say farewell, and acknowledge the important pieces of my former life that I missed and hoped to return one day."

Relational Poetics

The foundational (to be redundant, essential) component of the chapters in this book is the relational qualities of writing poetry. The relational work is what we found to be most healing and humanizing.

We are moved by and learn through reading poetry — cognitively and affectively. Rowe (2000) asserts that poetry strikes the reader with its first word and resonates much longer than prose, creating a vivid and poignant picture of lived experiences. This evocative nature of poetry makes it a powerful tool for both the poet and the reader, fostering a sense of presence and prompting reflection (Connelly, 1999).

Relational poetics emphasizes the connections between the poet and the reader, as well as between different parts of the poet's own life. There are two key elements that we emphasize in this book: witnessing and reciprocity.

Witnessing with Reciprocity

Witnessing as we talk about it here means attending to another person's poem by reading it carefully and mirroring back to the writer your reading experience so that their sharing is not in the void, so there is evidence of a listener. To witness, the poet must know there is or will be a reader. We think of a person reading our poetry as the witness. When they read and respond to our poetry, it validates personal and collective experiences. The poem bridges the poet and the reader. The poem can serve as a form of witnessing, where individuals document and bear witness to their own and others' experiences. This can be particularly powerful for marginalized voices, providing a platform for stories that might otherwise go unheard. Sometimes our students feel invisible. And, yes, sometimes teachers feel invisible. Witnessing through poetry validates these experiences and can be a crucial step in the healing process. To be clear, poetry as witnessing needs not only be to or about trauma. It will be the joys like foods, places like the desert or ranches in the backyard, falling in like way before heartbreak, and noticing an animal shape in the clouds. All of this can be poetry.

Reciprocity means that we witness and allow others to witness our lives. In this exchange, that is not transactional though can be characterized as such, there is potential for mutual healing and a certain kind of empathy that is shared — not piled on or something we carry alone. Teachers can do this for one another in ways we can't with our students or even our families. For example, we cannot ask our students to carry our personal traumas though there may be poems from our life beyond the classroom students need to read-witness to validate their own, maybe permission to explore their lives through poetry. And teachers may hesitate to share personal poetry with spouses or children, poems that only a teacher might understand.

Teachers are selfless or try to appear so. We struggle to ask for help. And may try not to bring our teacher-life home. Teacher-families are often starving for attention from a teacher-parent always grading papers or lesson planning. Our families are already aching for our attention; they are not ready to hear our pain or struggles with one more school story.

In sum, reciprocity works best when the poet and reader are peers. The act of sharing poetry can create a reciprocal relationship between the poet and the reader. No one is selfish or self-indulgent because after one listens or bears witness, the other does, too. The writer experiences healing through the process of creation and expression, while readers may find solace and connection in the shared experiences and emotions. This reciprocity can lead to a mutual sense of understanding and healing..."when we benefit from the relationships that we share with others, then we too are responsible for paying those benefits forward to others" (p. 47).

In our writing group and in some of our classes, we use this simple template to get us started in witnessing and reciprocity. In the Introduction, we shared how the Open Write and VerseLove work. On the writing day, a teacher-host posts a prompt with a mentor text, and then the teacher-writers scroll to the comment section on the post and write the poem. In the chapters that follow, you will see that the teacher-poet approaches and experiences these prompts in a variety of ways. Then, the teacher-poet posts their poem (in response to the host's prompt). (Note: the writer is always invited to reject the prompt and write whatever they need that day and in any form.)

The writing group is expected to read and respond to at least three other poems by offering a readerly mirror to the poet. This simply means that we show the reader what it was like for us to read the poem in an observational and celebratory tone, sometimes a curious tone, too. We may respond by sharing a memory that surfaced for us as we read the moment. We may respond to a phrase that was unexpected or some revelation about the topic. And we may respond to the poet's craft: a clever line, a vivid word, an unfamiliar metaphor, the use of an ellipses or colon or semicolon that we see working as a metaphor. See image.

Conclusion

Throughout this book, you will see up-close accounts of *Words That Mend*, various poems, writing experiences, and connections along a path toward healing. Writing poetry transcends the personal to touch the universal, offering significant healing powers through the arts. It promotes self-healing by allowing autobiographical exploration, fostering relational poetics, bearing witness to experiences, and enabling reciprocal connections. Through these processes, poetry can be a powerful tool for emotional wellbeing and personal growth.

Complimenting writers: Be sure to use their names in your response to them. Below are three perspectives you might consider when crafting your compliments:

From the heart (pathos)	From the mind (logos)	From the writer in me (ethos)
Respond by sharing a memory that surfaced for you. Did you have a similar experience? Did this remind you of something from your life?	What did the writer say that you liked, learned from, never considered before this moment? Did you like the way the writer pointed out (something)?	What did you like about how it was written? Sound: rhyme, repeating lines, alliteration. Pace: short phrases, long phrases, one word. Imagery: a verb, image, pun, simile, metaphor, sensory detail (color, texture of objects).
• I can relate to the phrase "..." because.... • When you wrote "...," I felt/was reminded ...because... • Your words "..." really moved me/resonated with me because...	• The phrase "..." got me thinking about...because... • Until I read/heard your words "...," I had not considered...in this way. Now I see... • I see or understand ...in a new way after reading ...because... • I think the heart of this piece is in the line "..." because	• I noticed you used the technique of ...in the phrase/stanza...: it's effect is... • A vivid word is... because... • A clever line is ...because... • Your use of ... gives the effect...

Adapted from Donovan, S.J. (2015). 3 perspectives improve peer-to-peer response. *Middle Web*.
https://www.middleweb.com/24247/3-perspectives-can-improve-peer-to-peer-response/

References

Akhtar, S. (2000). Mental pain and the cultural ointment of poetry. *International Journal of Psychoanalysis, 81*, 229–243.

Baker, K. C., & Mazza, N. (2004). The healing power of writing: Applying the expressive/creative component of poetry therapy. *Journal of Poetry Therapy: The Interdisciplinary Journal of Practice, Theory, Research and Education, 17*(3), 141–154.

Bateson, M. C. (1989). *Composing a life*. New York: Grove Press.

Berger, J. (1984). *And our faces, my heart, brief as photos*. New York: Pantheon Books.

Connelly, J. (1999). Being in the present moment: Developing the capacity for mindfulness in medicine. *Academic Medicine, 74*, 420–424.

Custer, D. (2014). Autoethnography as a transformative research method. *The Qualitative Report, 19*, 1–13.

Donovan, S. & Boutlier, S. (2023). Human-centered Poem-ing: The care of teacher-writers online.[2] *Writing & Pedagogy*. International. https://doi.org/10.1558/wap.24337 [3]

Donovan, S., Guyor-Jowett, J., Krebs, D., Daley, M. (2024). Relational poetic practice: High school English teachers' experiences during COVID-19.[4] *Research in the Teaching of English, 58*(3).

Eisner, E. (1985). *Beyond creating: The place for art in America's schools*. Los Angeles: Getty Center for Education in Art.

Furman, R. (2004b). Using poetry and narrative as qualitative data: Exploring a father's cancer through poetry. *Families, Systems, & Health, 22*(2), 162–170.

Jacobs, B. (2016). The creative journal: The art of finding yourself. *Journal of Poetry Therapy: The Interdisciplinary Journal of Practice, Theory, Research and Education, 29*(3), 183–184.

Janeczko, P. B. (Ed.). (2002). *Seeing the blue between: Advice and inspiration for young poets*. Cambridge: Candlewick Press.

Koch, K. (2000). *Wishes, lies, and dreams: Teaching children to write poetry*. New York: Harper Perennial.

Kreuter, E. A. (2009). Catalyzing the inner spirit of the type-A professional through poetic expression. *Journal of Poetry Therapy: The Interdisciplinary Journal of Practice, Theory, Research and Education, 22*(3), 165–171.

O'Reilly, M. R. (1993). *The peaceable classroom: Essays toward a pedagogy of nonviolence*. Portsmouth: Boyton-Cook.

Raingruber, B. (2004). Using poetry to discover and share significant meanings in child and adolescent mental health nursing. *Journal of Child and Adolescent Psychiatric Nursing, 17*(1), 13–20.

Reece, R. L. (2000). Preserving the soul of medicine and physicians: A talk with David Whyte. *The Physician Executive, 26*(2), 14–19.

Roberts, S. K. (2007). Composing a peaceful classroom through poetry writing. *Journal of Poetry Therapy, 20*(2), 103-109. https://doi.org/10.1080/08893670701394424

Rowe, R. C. (2000). Poetry and verse: An ideal medium for scientific communication. *Drug Discovery Today, 5*(436), 437.

Sharma, D. (2019). Being alive with poetry: Sustaining the self by writing poetry. *Journal of Poetry Therapy, 32*(1), 22-36. https://doi.org/10.1080/08893675.2019.1548728

Soter, A. O. (2016). Reading and writing poetically for wellbeing: Language as a field of energy in practice. *Journal of Poetry Therapy: The Interdisciplinary Journal of Practice, Theory, Research and Education, 29*(3), 161–174.

Tannen, D. (1998). *The argument culture: Moving from debate to dialogue.* New York: Random House.

Tompkins, G. E. (2004). *Teaching writing: Balancing process and product* (4th ed.). New York: Pearson.

Willis, P. (2002). Poetry and poetics in phenomenological research. *Indo-Pacific Journal of Phenomenology, 2*, 1–19.

Links

[1] https://www.epi.org/blog/teachers-unions-reduce-teacher-stress-anti-union-laws-significantly-increase-it/

[2] https://drive.google.com/file/d/1gyllDgs-P9gKqekiidB8gEVhkYr-rnQc/view

[3] https://doi.org/10.1558/wap.24337

[4]

https://drive.google.com/file/d/1i7ELoIdp0LzTIPGvi3W_hy1jLFmd2fhz/view

Part I

why we write poetry

Part I: Teacher Healing

Part I invites readers to witness the teachers' experiences of healing through writing. In this section, each of us writes a story of how words mend various traumatic and tragic events and explains how the process of writing poetry alongside others—witnessing, reciprocity—helped us find comfort, support, and energy to move toward recovery. We have been writing for a while together. While responding to various prompts, we realized that much of our writing was transformative, for us, so we have narrated memorable poetic moments. As an extension of our stories, we invite you to join us in some writing. At the end of each chapter, we provide an invitation to try the prompt yourself or with your students.

"Ten Reasons to Continue" by Jennifer Guyor Jowett. This chapter introduces readers to the world of teachers overwhelmed with students' struggles while desperately trying to help and support them. Finding hope and healing turns into a long journey. Jennifer's poem included in this chapter is written in free verse.

"No Small Thing: A Convergence of Parenting, Teaching and Poetry" by Tammi Belko. In this chapter, the author presents a story of writing poetry using colors to express anxiety and worries of motherhood as her daughter goes on a trip without a parent for the first time. Tammi's poem is written in free verse.

"When We Lose a Student" by Barbara Edler. This chapter offers a story of an unexpected student loss and the process of grieving in the classroom alongside other students. Barb's poem is written in free verse.

"Piano Lessons, Terzanelles, & Changing Schools" by Sarah J. Donovan. In this chapter, the author focuses on centering herself in a new place while greatly missing the old one. To work through this troubling experience, she chose a complex poetry form—terzanelle—to distract from feeling lost and searching for possibilities.

"*A House for Mom* as a Wave of Grieving" by Leilya A. Pitre tells a story of how the author is processing the loss of her mother. The road to healing is still far from complete, but the ability to write a poem and share it in a community is heartwarming and encouraging. Leilya writes her poem in free verse.

"Unfinished Symphony: Discovering a Door to My Emotions" by Denise Krebs. The author shares a self-discovery experience that allowed her to write about her alcoholic father by combining music and poetry. Denise writes her poem in free verse.

"Trenches and Summits: The Private Lives of Teachers" by Kim Johnson. This chapter spotlights the need for support when teachers must often maintain boundaries of privacy in their own personal lives. Finding a community of writers is one way that teachers can connect with others to find and give support. Kim's poem included in this chapter is written in rhyming couplets.

"In and Out and Back Again: The Journey into Therapy" by Susan Ahlbrand. This chapter is about the author's struggles with panic disorder; she discovered support through a community of teacher-poets who became her sanctuary. Susan's poem is written in free verse.

"Walking Through Grief with Poetry" by Margaret Simon. This chapter emphasizes the importance of a community where writing poetry, sharing, and extending HEALING are embraced and welcomed. Margaret writes her poems to cope with the loss of her father in free verse.

"Pursed Lips and Pink Tutus: Perks and Pitfalls of Parenting While Teaching English" by Wendy Everard. The chapter explores challenges of being a mother and teaching English, a subject that demands so much time on writing, providing feedback, and supporting students' emotional wellbeing. Both of Wendy's poems are written in rhymed couplets.

CHAPTER 2

Ten Reasons to Continue
Jennifer Guyor Jowett

I write to heal myself.

By 8:05 am, I have generally fielded questions about upcoming events and assignments, responded to concerns and worries of students, listened as they described their evening before—their fatigue from a softball game, their inability to fall asleep, their very valid anxiety about school shootings—and rethought how I might start class based on the vibe of the kids after reassuring them that today will be a good day (despite what goes on in the world)… the list goes on.

All of this happens before the very first word of the very first hour.

As a teacher with a journey of more than thirty years behind me, I should be accustomed to the challenges middle schoolers bring. They were not my first choice. I had planned to teach high school or college, following in my parents' footsteps, but the education department continued to place me in middle school during all of my observations and student teaching experiences. Like many, I hold few fond memories from my own awkward and painful middle years. No one was more surprised than I when I grew to love the energy and enthusiasm of this age and decided to pursue middle school education. I have taught in private schools in Michigan ever since.

Yet, with each passing year, I find myself becoming more of an emotional support to students as they struggle to make sense of a turned over world and less of a me supporter, and my reserves are swamped.

It is easy to lose sight of hope while drowning.

And teachers are drowning. We know it. The world knows it. We have signaled the SOS. Sent up the red flare. We are just short of burning the world down. (If it doesn't burn up on us first, but that's another worry for another day—I struggle to focus on climate change when students are falling apart around me).

Everything happens in a moment's time, and everyone needs something in that same moment: questions arise about assignments due despite posts to google classrooms and individual emails acknowledging what we covered, students arrive from absences without any idea of what happened while they were gone (I love telling them that we've solved all the world's problems during their absence), one needs to use the bathroom, another has a letter for the office, someone needs to talk to a friend, deliver a book to another teacher, find their lost water bottle, hoodie, pencil, chromebook... which doesn't give teachers much of a chance to rise to the surface.

It's become necessary to set the world on pause.

Go ahead. Push the button. A quick touch. It will be just fine. In fact, it can bring you healing. (Reader, I'm inviting you into the pause with me for the next few pages. Grab a notebook or your favorite writing device.)

There is an old-English term *haelen* which means wholeness, and it is at the center of healing. It is a restoration. A touch that cures. A return to wellbeing. Since the 1980's, there has been a sharp uptick in the use of the verb *heal*. As a society, we are in need. And we are seeking healing.

In January of 2022, fellow teacher-writer, co-presenter, LA County Teacher of the Year, and friend Stacey Joy asked us to consider lists when we came together at Ethical ELA, our online writing site. She had read Kwame Alexander's "Ten Reasons Why Fathers Cry at Night," a poem without the "poem-y structure" that later became a book, and was drawn to the format as someone who makes lists often—playlists, pros and cons for big decisions, countdowns to breaks. She encouraged us to give thought as to why someone might smile, laugh, or cry, or turn a playlist or shopping list into a poem. This type of writing allows writers to reflect upon the minutiae of life, to live within the moments that make a life what it is.

Her poem, "Ten Reasons to Have Hope in 2022", expressed not only the fatigue I felt as a teacher but also the peace found in the word hope.

Ten Reasons to Have Hope in 2022 by Stacey Joy

Because 2020 was like braiding water
    And 2021 lasted 365 days too long
Because effectively teaching remotely is remotely impossible
    And teaching in a mask is worse than a hot flash
Because too many lives were lost
    And not enough love was found

Because we learned to try new things
   Like baking bread and hosting virtual parties
Because normal held hate and harm
   And new normals never need naming

Oh, how that braiding water spoke to me — the impossibilities of all we've done and are trying to do summed up so perfectly in one image.

Words reach out across expanses and grab hold. They take off. They carry us with them. And Stacey's words held on with ferocity.

Often, when I'm overwhelmed, I pour my worries onto paper. It's a way of purging a bit of the burden. And what better way to let those worries flow than with a list. Stacey's prompt offered a chance to list in a creative way, a new way, and it got me thinking about hope. Along with the power of beginning.

Stacey spoke as a fellow teacher who, even on the other side of the country, knew the in and out of what teaching had become. She wrote as a fellow writer who recognized what we needed to read. She shared as a fellow human whose words would be read and felt and witnessed. As teachers, as writers, as humans, we can't just press pause randomly. We have to press pause in a space where we know we can breathe, feel seen, and allow ourselves to return to life fully. Our five-day monthly online open writing space with Ethical ELA is just the place for that pause.

For me, those five days are a respite within the whirlwind of work. The days begin in early morning before my usual alarm sounds, before I slip from bed, before I've fully collected my thoughts on what the work will be in the day ahead. Allowing myself to have thirty minutes or an hour (if I can snatch it) to dwell in the wonder of a prompt, the challenge of a new piece, the joy of reading what fellow writers craft, and the uplift of seeing how others respond to my words allows me to pause and be, just for a few moments, whomever I need to be to continue forward. Here is the piece I crafted that day:

Ten Reasons to Continue by Jennifer Guyor Jowett

Because one word is a pioneer
And others will follow.
Because in an expanse of grass, sprayed into uniformity, dandelions

sprout
And fields of wildflowers still exist.
Because in a world of artificial light, we can still see stars
And myriad more are hidden in black depths.
Because faith and science can live simultaneously in the
same space
And so can we.
Because Rosa Parks and Lydia Taft and Sacagawea and
Marie Curie
    and Junko Tabei
And you. And me.

Hidden in those lines were worries about climate (sprayed into uniformity) and finding voice (one word is a pioneer), worries about our ability to get along in an increasingly polarized country (faith and science) and discrimination (living simultaneously in the same space), and worries about being seen (awe exists even if we have to search beyond the artificial) and having strength (that list of fierce women). I held these worries. My students do as well.

In writing "Ten Reasons to Continue," I hoped to remind myself that, despite all the chaos and worry, there was a reason to be, to keep going, to take that step forward. Others had done it before me. And they'd done it facing a lot more adversity. If the Rosa Parkses and Lydia Tafts of the past had blazed their paths through racism and voter suppression, then I could certainly keep my head above water in a classroom.

Writing allows me to pioneer my own path forward to healing, allows my words to sprout, both in me and in fields and star-filled depths.

But more importantly, this poem allowed me to focus on becoming whole. It's not just a you. Or a me. It's an us. Moving forward. Together.

It can be risky to put your writing into the world, knowing others are going to read and react. Knowing the space is not just for me but for us and that the writing is a shared venture allows the words to breathe into their digital space. It's another pause. One that welcomes others to feel seen in the words we share.

Part of the healing of writing within community is in the responding. Knowing that your words land and uplift others mends the holes marring life's fabric. The community of responders within Ethical ELA handle each other's words with care. We are fierce women, mostly, who appreciate the words of one another because of the pause we find ourselves gentling into through reciprocity. Our hosts offer poetry prompts generously and we give back in words. We become present in them. We mark our pause together through them. We are seen in our togetherness within them. Fellow writer Fran, an educator from rural North Carolina, sees the risk when she responds:

> Jennifer - you had me with "one word is a pioneer/and others will follow" - speaking to the power of just beginning, taking that first step in faith (I see it applying to writing as well as to speaking words of encouragement to others). Your list of women, the perfect embodiment. I absolutely love the sense of "seeing beyond" in your poem – beyond uniformity, beyond the artificial or superficial, to profound mysteries hidden in depths. All reasons to continue, indeed. Incredibly powerful.

And Susie from Missouri finds the healing in hope:

> Gosh, Jennifer — You have so much depth in this poem... you really are a marvelous poet. "one word is a pioneer" — Oh beautiful! The "artificial light" against the power of "stars"... indeed! And calling upon us to think AND instead of OR in "faith and science"...think of how that could change the world! The hope brought to the last line...well, girlie, this is a great January start of a new year. Thank you so much for the hope here! Love this and you, Susie

While I've never met Fran or Susie in person, I know them through their writing and that makes the comments all the more meaningful. Because of the writing and responding we've done together, I recognize that they respond authentically. This back and forth between teachers/writers/poets creates relationships.

When we share our poems, we acknowledge the generosity of the host by commenting on her mentor poem. Stacey reciprocates:

Thank you, Jennifer, for this spirit-filling and hope-inspiring gift! I fell in love with so many lines I dare not copy/paste the whole thing!? I will savor: stars, black depths, wildflowers still exist, faith and science, Rosa and Sacagawea! Brilliant!

When teachers/writers/poets see words offering encouragement, we recognize we can begin together. This community consists of writers who serve one another. We hear each other in our words. We see one another in our imagery. In the offering of poems, the readers reciprocate with encouragement and support. This is the gift of writing together.

I was not the only one who contemplated stars from Stacey's prompt. Linda Mitchell wrote "Ten Reasons for Star Gazing," and what an incredible way to share our expansiveness.

Ten Reasons for Star Gazing by Linda Mitchell

Because curiosity is not overrated.
    We don't actually know everything.
Because we make sense of constellations with story,
    our first language.
Because you and I have not yet run out of wishes.
Because stars do not judge gazers.
    All are welcome to adore.
Because every one of our atoms began in an exploded star.
    We are made of star stuff.
Because we still navigate our way across oceans and skies
    We still use stars to get to Never-never land.
Because they are there even in day.
    The sun is also a star.
Because we yearn to touch what's out of reach.
Because it is the one place our piece of puzzle
    interlocks with the piece next to ours in the universe.

Finding that we share commonalities within our words brings an interconnectedness. And interconnectedness creates a whole. And that heals.

This found poem I wrote using lines borrowed or slightly altered from fellow writers showcases this wholeness.

{poem-ing} by Jennifer Guyor Jowett

There is space between the stanzas,
a spilling of words.
Often, when I yearn to hear myself,
I wander between them,
draw breath from their souls.
I carry their glimmer in my hands.

(Lines borrowed/slightly altered from Linda Mitchell, Jamie Langley, Maureen Ingram, Susan Ahlbrand, Tammi Belko, Emily Yamasaki)

We find ourselves in the words of others. We see our connectedness. The words of fellow writers take hold of me, reminding me in beautiful imagery what we have together. Our words reach out and gather us in. We carry their glimmer.

Your Turn

We conclude each chapter with an invitation for you to write. There's no better place to start than with educator Stacey Joy who exudes love in all that she does and continually brings the joy suggested in her name to fellow writers. Recognized for this same love and joy, Stacey was named L.A. County Teacher of the Year in 2013 and has over 38 years of elementary classroom experience. She continues to shine with her 5th graders and is also a UCLA Writing Project fellow.

Short Prompt

If you are ready to write, here is a short prompt to get you started: Take some time for healing today and use Stacey's prompt as your inspiration. Create a list poem by considering why someone might cry at night, laugh, forget, remember or insert your own idea. Or use an already existing list (to-do's, playlists, to-be-read's) and jump in. Any form will do.

Go to your journal or device. Extend your healing by writing a poem there. If you are feeling so overwhelmed that you're not sure how to begin, remember that one word is a pioneer and others will follow. And lists suit this concept perfectly.

Full Prompt

If you'd like a little more support, the full prompt is included below. For now, open your notebook or device and follow along with educator Stacey Joy's inspiration: For the Love of Lists.[1]

> **Inspiration:** Kwame Alexander's poem "Ten Reasons Why Fathers Cry at Night" is a powerful mentor text to inspire list poems without too much poem-y structure. I find myself counting all the time. I'm the "Countdown Lady" at school who posts the number of days remaining until our next day off. I often find myself listing reasons for or against something when I need to make a big decision. I have multiple music Playlists for various moods and purposes. Today's poem can be a list-poem of any number and topic. I suggest you not confine or force yourself to write ten items. Just go with the flow.
>
> **Process:** In the spirit of Kwame Alexander's poem, try starting with a list of reasons why someone might:
> - Cry at night
> - Smile or laugh
> - Forget

- Remember
- Or visit a playlist, a shopping list, a to-do list, or a to-be-read list and turn it into a poem.

Jennifer's Suggestions for the Classroom

Finally, while this chapter is for you, fellow teacher, we'd love for you to invite students to write. If you want to try a version of this prompt with your students, here are a few things to keep in mind:

- Have students make lists. Any kinds of lists. Words on paper become fodder for poems.
- After reading the prompt and mentor poem, share examples, including your own. It's helpful for students to see their teacher's writing in the creation of community. And it's helpful for the teacher to know what challenges might arise when writing.
- Beginning with the same opening line as the mentor poem can give students a place to start. They might begin the first line with Because…and the next with And…while continuing to emulate the shared poems.
- Provide a sustained quiet writing time for students to forge their thoughts onto paper.

You might further strengthen community by offering students a chance to share their words and respond to one another, either in writing, verbally in pairs, or as a class with an Open Mic. It's helpful to establish a safe space before responding. Mention this is a time to celebrate what other writers have done well. Encourage students to notice language that moves them or a phrase they were drawn to and identify it in their responses. I like to start with the emotion the poem stirs up in me (usually something I love). These noticings reflect and create our healing.

Link

[1] https://www.ethicalela.com/for-the-love-of-lists/

CHAPTER 3

No Small Thing: A Convergence of Parenting, Teaching, & Poetry

Tammi Belko

Raising children is hard. Providing space for them to grow, tackle life's obstacles, and discover themselves is harder. Much harder. I was learning that parenting lesson on a cold January day in 2022 in Northeast Ohio. For some, it might seem like a small thing, my fourteen-year-old daughter embarking on her first school trip with 150 bandmates. For some, it might seem like a small thing, stepping on a charter bus and driving away. For me, for her, for both of us, it was no small thing. It was no small thing for her to travel over 1,000 miles, across six states, from Ohio to Florida. This was a child prone to motion sickness and claustrophobia, and she would spend fifteen hours on a bus. It was no small thing for a child who avoided slumber parties, preferring her own bed and her own room to share a hotel room for four days with four classmates. Little did I know, it would be no small thing when a rock of ice would hit the bus windshield, shattering it and causing the bus to be sidelined in a gas station parking lot for nearly another full day (Thankfully, no one was hurt). It would be no small thing when my daughter would text in the middle of the night from Disney World that she was miserable, on sensory overload, and wanted to come home. Nope, no small thing. But life is full of these seemingly small moments that shape us profoundly. Small things that are not not small at all.

As a mother of two adult children, I had navigated the teen years before. The academic stress, the college decisions, the drama, and even some teen rebellion, but this — this moment of letting go with my youngest child — was an emotional tsunami. Logically, I knew that my daughter would grow from this experience. I also knew this short trip was necessary for me to practice letting go and allow my youngest child to spread her wings. Logically, as a middle school teacher who had taken my students on numerous overnight trips in my fifteen years of teaching, I understood these trips were extensions of learning, and that even the most anxious students always seemed to come out of their shells and thrive in experiential and collaborative learning environments. But emotions are funny.

Emotions don't follow rules. They have a way of subverting logic and overwhelming you when you least expect it.

So on that frigid day in January, when I needed to unpack my overwhelming emotions and mom-worries, I turned to the Ethical ELA community, to my teacher-poet friends, to poetry, seeking succor. I had discovered Ethical ELA two years prior in April 2020, in the midst of the pandemic. At that time, I was locked down, trying to teach online and, like most of the world, grappling with intense emotions and feelings of fear and isolation. I was looking for an emotional outlet through writing.

Although I no longer remember the exact keywords I used, I do remember typing in various iterations of poetry, poetry prompts, online groups, teachers, etc. until I struck gold. Normally, I don't leap, but this time that's exactly what I did. I didn't hesitate in writing and posting my poetry because it was what my soul craved at that moment. Upon reading my first prompt and the posted poetry from other educators, I immediately felt connected to the teacher poets from across the country who were navigating the same uncharted landscape of teaching, who were struggling with the same crippling uncertainties of unknowing. Some may think it odd that I was willing to write poetry with strangers, across a digital ether, but everything about the experience of writing, reading and responding to poetry — the poetic quintessence — of other teachers, just felt right.

Two years later, after I had written and responded to countless poems, the prompt, Paint Chip Poetry, was exactly the balm my soul needed on that day. District Literacy Specialist for Pike County Schools, Kim Johnson of Williamson, Georgia, provided this prompt, which encouraged us to discover inspiration by exploring paint chip colors. The task was pretty straightforward: "find your own colorful words for free from paint stores or on websites" Kim explains, "…and have fun arranging the descriptive colors into lines of poetry!"

Some poetry prompts require rumination. I might read the prompt in the morning and think about it during the school day. I might spend a bit more time reading the poetry of other teacher poets for more inspiration. Sometimes I take a walk or listen to music for inspiration, typing words and ideas into notes on my phone. Sometimes, I find myself struggling. However, Kim's paint chip poetry prompt resonated deeply with me. Writing poetry has always been a way for me to express my emotions, offering catharsis and reflection. On that day, the colors transformed into vivid poetic emotions. The muted winter sky. The snug camping-rolled colored blankets and stuffed animals. The bulging backpacks. All those images swirled in my mind as colors. So, I tucked in with a cup of coffee (I always need coffee) and my laptop. I had taken the day off from school, so there was plenty of time for color palette exploration and lots of coffee.

This is what I wrote and posted (paint chip colors in bold) on that fossil gray morning when I was feeling all shades of moody blue:

(Untitled) by Tammi Belko

No longer **Snowbound,**
I drop her off in the **Rosedust** morning.
She bounces out, with her **Needlepoint Navy**
backpack bulging.

I want to ask her if she needs help
pulling the suitcase,
balancing the **Dutch Tile Blue** fleece
and **Acanthus** pillow

I want her to say "yes" but I know the answer is
"No."
All the other kids are piling out of
cars and vans,
similarly weighted down,
like **Library Pewter.**

No adults get out of their cars.
No adults lend a hand.
So I don't ask.
We don't ask
Because we all know the answer.

I stay inside the **Twilight Gray** car.
I'm feeling a **Mellow Mauve** rush of lonely.

Is this what an empty nest will feel like
when the final chick flies?

She pauses at the car window,
Rembrandt Ruby smiles tells me she is ready
"Thanks, Mom," she says.
I am not ready
"I love you. Have fun!" I reply.

And she is off on her school band trip,
Just the beginning of her many adventures
like a **Drift of Mist.**

In the writing of this poem, I hoped to capture my daughter's departure as a photo. A snapshot of our life at that moment. Can you see it? I also wanted to convey a flurry of nervous excitement through my verb choices "she bounces out, with her Needlepoint Navy backpack bulging." This I juxtaposed with the bittersweet emotions of "I am not ready." I used dialogue to create an authentic narrative. Our lives are stories, and this moment was a story, so I chose to write this poem as a narrative in free verse.

Despite my worries, my daughter donned a "Rembrandt Ruby smile." I responded, accordingly, with "Have fun!" and like a "Drift of Mist," she was on her adventure. These moments of letting go are moments all parents experience. In writing about this moment, I was reflecting and naming my feelings, allowing myself to feel the grief of this ending to her childhood while also allowing myself to feel joy at a new beginning.

Publishing this poem digitally allowed for further validation of my feelings as our community of teacher poets is filled with parents and grandparents who have experienced many similar parenting milestones. I hoped my parenting story would resonate with other parent educators. While we come together in this space as educators who love poetry, we also come here as people who have experienced pain and loss, love and joy. We come here as people living the human condition, and this community reminds me I am not alone.

Teacher Poets Responded to my Words
Mo from Illinois wrote:

> What a touching story, Tammi. I love that you were able to work so many colors into your poem. I love Rosedust and Library Pewter.

As a poet and writer, it is my hope that readers will be touched by my words in some way and Mo's comment helped me feel that I had connected with my audience. Rachelle from Iowa wrote:

> Beautiful story told with paint chips, Tammi. Thank you for allowing us all to share in this moment with you. I love the pause and vulnerability in the line "I am not ready"

Rachelle recognized the sentiment I was trying to convey and aptly named it "vulnerability." This helped me feel heard. Cara from Oregon wrote:

> I love this. Today my youngest son got his driver's license. No longer is he dependent on me to transport him about. All of those little things that tear them just a little farther away are both celebrations and wounds. Your poem captured that balance really well.

Cara shared her "celebrations and wounds" when she commented on her son getting his driver's license, and I felt understood and less alone in my feelings. Denise from California wrote:

> Tammi, lovely telling of the story of this goodbye for five days using these rich colors. My favorite lines are these: I stay inside the Twilight Gray car./I'm feeling a Mellow Mauve rush of lonely. They are so melancholy and show the loneliness you were feeling. "Like a drift of mist" Wow.

Denise recognized the melancholy I was experiencing by identifying specific lines. This recognition of my words helped me to feel heard and signified that my word and color choices conveyed my intended tone.

Sharing my story of motherhood and parenting helped me work through my anxiety, and using colors to express those emotions felt like the perfect symbolic form of expression. In writing my poem and in reading the responses to my poetry, my soul was nourished. Knowing that others understood and could relate to my melancholy that day lifted some of my sadness. Responses in which others shared similar experiences helped me feel less alone.

Reading and responding to the poetry of other teacher poets was also cathartic. It allowed me to disentangle from my own musings, stop obsessing, and step into other perspectives and glimpse a picture of "Cleopatra's gown lit by the black flame/a phantom mist swirls at her feet" shared by Alexis. I also experienced the drive home from Pittsburgh with Heather and delighted in the snow "falling like a/phantom mist/through the/midnight hour/piling up on the/obsidian/pavement." My soul was nourished by beautiful poetry on that day, and it was no small thing.

Classroom Convergence

It is always interesting to see how others interpret and are inspired by the prompts presented, and this led me to consider how I could utilize this prompt in my classroom to connect with my students. So, shortly after the monthly Open Write concluded, I introduced Paint Chip Poetry to my 6th grade gifted ELA students. We had been writing poetry together throughout the year on Poetry Fridays. Generally, my gifted students loved poetry Fridays. They loved experimenting with poetry forms and the challenge of trying something new. They enjoyed the opportunities to exercise creativity, too. Often, I allowed time for my students to include artwork, graphics or pictures with their poetry, but it was mid-January in northeast Ohio, and we were all experiencing Winter Blahs.

I felt the Paint Chip poetry prompt would be a great way to energize my students while encouraging experimentation with word and color choices to convey ideas in writing. I introduced the lesson with my own paint chip poem about my daughter's trip. Being 6th graders, my students were generally interested in knowing about my family and me, and I enjoyed sharing my stories. So I indulged them with some more details about my daughter's trip and answered their questions about the ice rock that hit the window.

This moment provided a valuable opportunity for personal connection with my students, allowing them to see me not just as a teacher but as a parent and a person with my own worries and experiences. I offered a glimpse into my life, inviting them to reciprocate by sharing their own stories through their poems—a convergence of our life experiences. After our conversation, I instructed my students to recall an important event or milestone in their lives and write briefly about that moment. Next, they wrote or outlined their narrative snapshots and explored color palettes, selecting colors that represented their feelings.

Through this poetry exercise, my students grew. They grew as writers, exploring new words and methods of using descriptions, and we bonded as a community by learning about each other through sharing. Through Paint Chip Poetry, I discovered that Nora vacationed in the **Ionian Tide** under a **Forsythia Sunset** and that Scarlett had a baking catastrophe spilling **Snow White** flour all over the floor. I discovered Kylie plays soccer on a **Leapfrog** colored field and Ellie feels at home running through the **Gecko Green** woods. Sure, I could have extended this lesson to explore how poets and writers utilize colors as symbols of life, death, hope, love...

That might be a lesson for another day, but at that moment, during that lesson, my objective was simply to connect with my students. The following year, I would use paint chip poetry in the first few weeks of the school year to get to know my students. This prompt would also work really well during the fall as a seasonal descriptive poetry writing activity.

Building classroom connections and safe learning environments can lead to emotional and physical healing as well. In "Healing Through the Written Word," therapist and poet Karen Cangialosi advocates the efficacy of writing as a tool for healing. Cangialosi notes, "Writing helps us to form connections with what is going on inside us and with others" and suggests that the act of writing provides "the power to take control of how those emotions and events affect our lives."

Furthermore, building trust is essential in fostering a sense of safety. In *Maslow Before Bloom*, Dr. Bryan Pearlman encourages educators to consider the foundational rungs of Maslow's Hierarchy of Needs and posits, "If the human side of things are addressed, true learning can occur at a high level." Conversely, when we are not attending to the needs of our students, learning will suffer. In writing and sharing my poetry with my students, I opened a window into my life. As a middle school teacher, I believe that forging these connections is imperative. Optimal learning can not be sustained without building trust.

Through sharing my own Paint Chip Poem about my daughter's trip and my melancholy on that day, I shared "what was going on inside." I demonstrated the process of assigning words to emotions and allowed myself to be vulnerable, to be human. Through this writing activity, I strengthened connections with my students, creating a climate where my students would feel comfortable using writing to process emotions by putting words to their feelings. Since that lesson, I have continued to utilize poetry weekly with my middle school students and the connections and trust continues to grow. Sharing my poetry with students allows my students to see that I am not just their teacher. I am a mother, a daughter, a sister and a wife. Likewise, I see various facets of my students. I see them as dancers and singers and soccer players.

When we write with our students, we not only forge connections but also model the writing process. Through the frequent practice of writing poetry together, my students now see themselves as writers and poets. They aren't surprised or intimidated when we decide to go outside on a beautiful day to write poetry or when I ask them to write poetry in response to music or art. This lack of intimidation stems from poetry becoming a natural component of our classroom community, reflecting a convergence of our experiences and shared humanity.

Whether it is expressing the joy of galloping through the woods, lamenting over an argument with a friend, or discovering one's identity, poetry provides healing and inspiration. Every poem is worth sharing, and through poetry, I have built trust and strengthened my classroom community. It is no small thing.

Your Turn

Kim Johnson brings the experience of author (*Father, Forgive Me: Confessions of a Southern Baptist Preacher's Kid*) and poet to our writing. She is a contributor to 2 poetry anthologies, *Rhyme and Rhythm: Poems for Student Athletes* and *Bridge the Distance: An Oral History of Covid-19 in Poems*. Kim is also a District Literacy Specialist in Georgia.

Short Prompt
If you are ready to write, here is a short prompt to get you started: Gather some paint chip words from a website or a paint department and have fun arranging the descriptive colors into lines of poetry!

Full Prompt
If you'd like a little more support, the full prompt can be found on Ethical ELA at . I am including it here for your reference, but I've also included the prompt below. For now, open your notebook or device and follow along with Kim Johnson and Paint Chip Poetry:

> **Inspiration:** A stroll through a paint section can be just the right inspiration for poetry! You can purchase a set of Paint Chip Poetry cards from Amazon here, but you can also find your own colorful words for free at paint stores or on websites such as Sherwin Williams[2] or Glidden.[3] Just click on the color chips to discover vibrant color words (deep onyx, copper pot, heartfelt, hot cocoa, dirt road…)
>
> **Process:** Gather some paint chip words from a website or a paint department and have fun arranging the descriptive colors into lines of poetry!

Tammi's Suggestions for the Classroom
If you want to try a version of this prompt with your students, here are a few things to keep in mind: Provide necessary scaffolding based upon the age and abilities of your students. For younger students, discuss how certain colors convey certain emotions.

Student Steps:
- Brainstorm an event or important moment (snap shot) in your life.
- Outline, bullet point or free write your snapshot.
- Name the emotions you felt at that time (sad, excited, angry, worried, etc)

- Explore color palettes

Further extensions:
- Create a classroom collage or art mural to accompany poems
- Carve out time for a poetry reading or poetry gallery walk where students can share poetry.
- Use lines from student poems to create advertisements. For example: Needlepoint Navy backpacks will put a bounce in your step or Dutch Tile Blue Fleece is like sleeping on a cloud.

References

Cangialosi K. (2002). Healing through the written word. *The Permanente Journal*, 6(3), 68–70.

Pearlman, B. (2020). *Maslow before Bloom : basic human needs before academics*. Independently Published.

Links

[1] https://www.ethicalela.com/paint-chip-poetry/

[2] https://www.sherwin-williams.com

[3] https://www.glidden.com

Poetic Reflection by Fran McCrackin

Which of my poems do I remember best? Which linger, perhaps as unfinished, or as a partial exploration, or perhaps because they feel more worthy? Those that have some element of pain.

I remember being so afraid for my daughter, and writing a poem about her traveling alone in rusty, painted buses in a dangerous country; my gringa daughter, the local riders, and the chickens accompanied by armed guerrillas. I remember being so worried when her sister went past her due date and delicious anticipation turned into something much more complicated. I remember exploring my stale feelings about my marriage, as my husband and I became refreshed to each other by a walk in the wilderness alongside fresh bear scat, singing badly together to warn the mama and baby bear of our intrusion into their world. And I remember my reluctance to finally set down in poetry my guilt at making an unkind statement about my dying mother to the visiting hospice nurse, as my mother lay comatose but perhaps hearing.

Writing such poems can give us–well, relief isn't the word. What is this thing, that writing about something difficult provides? A little distance, a little glow cast about it, a view from a different vantage point.

Here is a poem that I wrote after walking back from vigil beside my daughter's hospital bed in a foreign country, during Covid 19 quarantine…

After the Accident
(Havana, Cuba 2020)

As I walk home to our room at Lisette's and see
The unmarred true blue of this sky
I think how my daughter would love
Seeing this, and the early evening sun
Sliding warm on the plastered buildings

As I feel the hot shower
And move my washcloth down my belly
I think how my daughter would love
Feeling this, to stand, water coursing over her
Smoothly, not interrupted by
Metal framework hammered into pelvis

As I rinse the shampoo

Out of my hair
I think how my daughter would love
Sudsing up her auburn waves,
Except her hair isn't auburn-
Watch the rusty water take the blood down the drain

And this:

Prayer

I don't know how to pray, but when
My daughter was hurt I
Breathed for her, felt my lungs
Expand and I pressed her
Feet, to warm them with my warmth and I
Adored the circle of old ladies in Honduras
Who I was told were praying for her and I
Imagined fairies winding strong golden wire
Around and around and around
To knit her pelvis back
Together, and I wonder,
Is this prayer?

Facing pain and sending it out to be shared. Is this how poetry can heal?

Fran McCrackin is a recently retired public school teacher in Washington D.C.

CHAPTER 4

When We Lose a Student
Barbara Edler

Dealing with the sudden loss of a loved one can be especially difficult. Healing during this time is essential. Too often teachers not only have to deal with their own grief, but they also are faced with helping their students cope with a loss. When we lose a student, the repercussions can be devastating. Unfortunately, society expects educators to be able to move on past these moments and continue through the days, following the expected routines as though nothing has happened.

Everyone experiences loss. My mother became bed-ridden when I was in second grade. One day my mother was well and the next she could not talk, walk, or feed herself. She was mentally alert, but this complete reversal in my life made me aware at a young age that life can be unexpectedly cruel. Losing a student is like that. One day you have a person in your life who adds a particular dimension to your classroom and then suddenly they are gone. Their absence is permanent. They are not skipping class or being irresponsible and their absence is especially felt by their close friends and peers who may have known the student throughout most of their life.

Throughout the years, I have lost several students, most often because of an automobile accident, perhaps because high school students are just learning to drive or because they have not learned how to deal with weather conditions or believe they are invincible. I have also lost students to disease and suicide. No matter the reason for the death, the loss of someone young seems especially cruel.

I remember several years ago losing a student right before graduation ceremonies. Students were having a party out in the country and not far from where I lived, a small residential area that is situated along the river. Consequently, many people enjoy driving down the river road we live by, a road that has several sharp turns and offers a handful of gravel roads that lead to creeks and a rock quarry young people enjoy exploring.

I will never forget that day. Walking into the high school building, a school of about 700 students in a small blue-collar community, I immediately felt something was off. In the office, I asked what was going on. When I discovered a student from my own classroom had passed, a student for privacy sake, I will call Joe, I was immediately overwhelmed with sadness. More than anything, I wanted to leave, go home and cry, but that would not be acceptable. I needed to be here with my students, not run and flee. I remember trying to control my tears, turning my back from my students while crying as I stared out the windows, waiting for the first bell to ring.

I heard a student ask someone else, "What's wrong with her?"

"Some kid died," was the reply.

My student, Joe, had been called to the office the day before from my last period class. I remember some kids teasing, "Oh, you're in trouble now." Although their tones were clearly playful, it now seemed like a premonition of the impending tragedy. The one thing that stood out to me was that Joe had a hole in his jeans. I wanted to say something about the hole, but thought it was better to leave it alone, afraid I might sound like some kind of pervert as the hole was rather large and on the student's thigh.

When my classes met the day after the accident, I let the students discuss the loss rather than pretend it never happened. Many of these students were friends of Joe. Students were especially upset because they believed Joe was not responsible for the accident. The road he and a friend had been traveling has a sharp turn at the bottom of a long hill. The car did not make the turn, went into the ditch, and Joe went through the windshield, smashing his head against a tree. What further complicated the situation was that my students believed the female passenger was the one actually driving the car. However, she denied those accusations. She escaped virtually unscathed and rumors flew that the only thing she was concerned about was some marijuana that was inside the totalled vehicle.

The day after the accident, I wanted to provide an opportunity for my students to process their grief and have a space where they could feel supported by their peers. More importantly, I wanted them to not feel forced to "move on" as though everything in life was perfectly normal.

My students took turns standing in front of their peers sharing their grief, anger, and disbelief. I can still see their faces as they processed their emotions. Of course, not everyone shared or was expected to say something, it was simply an open time to share. I believe my students benefited from this time to express their feelings, and it helped me as well, to grieve and better understand my students' conflicting emotions.

This type of space is exactly what I experienced when I first joined Ethical ELA during the VerseLove month in April 2020. This was a particularly difficult time in my life. I was grappling with my decision to retire from the school I had taught at for thirty years, as well as all of the new restrictions and fears of the pandemic. I was also still grieving the loss of my middle son who passed in November of 2018. I was fortunate to find myself with a group of peers who were willing to witness my anger, disbelief, and trauma through the poetry I shared. Although many were complete strangers, I felt supported by this diverse community, and I believed this month of writing poetry helped me to heal from much of the pain I had been holding back. Writing poetry was cathartic for me, and I felt fortunate to be able to traverse all the anger, guilt, and grief I had been bottling up in order to do my job and to take care of my family for the last sixteen months of my life.

On September 21, 2021 Allison Berryhill was the host for the day's Open Write. Allison is also a teacher in a rural Iowa school district. At this point I had admired Allison from afar because I recognized her active leadership for our state association, the Iowa Council of Teachers of English. Allison was also the reason I began writing with the Ethical ELA group during the 2020 VerseLove month. Allison's prompt was titled "A Poem to a Student." She shared the mentor poem "The Student" by poet Dorianne Laux, which describes a student's voice and the difficulty of speaking. Allison shared her own mentor text about her creative writing student, Austin.

Poem for Austin (student in Creative Writing)
Nov. 2018 by Allison Berryhill

Count syllables (3)
Astronomy (4)
He drums out each beat
Then counts it once more.

He picks up his pen
And he gives it a shot
His words are his rocket
He's their astronaut.

The lines that he writes
Are electric, bizarre
They flash through the sky
Like his own shooting star.

So Austin, keep writing
Put black upon white.
The universe needs you
Keep writing tonight.

Allison's poem depicts her student's powerful language which she describes as "electric" and "bizarre." In the final stanza she speaks directly to Austin encouraging him to keep writing. Something I hoped my own students would continue to do after they left my own classroom. Both mentor poems focus on the importance of words and are both rich in powerful imagery, making it easy for the reader to hear, see, and feel the emotions the poets express.

In Allison's opening comments she said, "I recently wrote a sonnet about meeting a past student in the grocery store and forgetting her name. Like many of you, I have taught thousands of students over the years, and I cannot hold them all firmly in my memory while making the necessary space for my current (needy!) students. But we also have students or student-moments that have left indelible memory marks. Today I invite you to write a poem about a student, past or present."

"Indelible memory marks" — wow, yes, those words inspired me that morning to remember past students who had left an indelible impression. At that time I had taught for forty years so I had a lot of memories of all the students who made me laugh and cry, and the ones I had lost. Eventually, I thought of my student Joe who tragically died right before the end of the school year, a time when students want to celebrate their accomplishments and embrace their favorite school memories. Joe was fun and vivacious, but often reckless. Because I had so many sharp "memory marks" from this tragic loss, I wrote about Joe and the memory I had about him from the afternoon before the tragic accident.

JT by Barbara Edler

I will always remember
The last day I saw you
Your brown eyes laughing
Unworried about being called to the office

In trouble again, I'm sure

Your jeans had such a huge whole in the leg
I was worried you might start revealing
a bit too much

That hole and those jeans
reminded me of my own senior year
when battery acid kept eating away
a perfectly fine pair of blue jeans;
the looks I received

I will always remember
That moment
like a still life photo
You walking out my door
a gaping hole in your jeans
but I didn't say a word

That night
I never heard the sirens
or the party at Bridge Out
less than a mile from
my front door

You never knew how to stay
out of trouble
nor the danger of a steep hill
with a sharp curve

I was able to write this poem fairly quickly, but I was nervous about what to include and what not to include. First of all, I wanted to protect those involved, and I may not have posted this poem at all had I believed someone from my local community would read it. After drafting the poem, I went back through it a few times looking for ways to sharpen it and keep it focused on my specific final memory. The belief that another student was responsible for the accident was an area I did not want to include as I felt this was too difficult to traverse; instead, I wanted to indicate how Joe died and that was because the car was most likely traveling too fast to handle the sharp curve at the bottom of the hill.

The sharp curve is also a metaphor for other challenges one might face in life and not handle well. The Bridge Out reference is the name of a place locals will recognize; it is also the place where my son lost his life. Bridge Out has an emotional connection for me that many readers will not understand. Knowing this does not matter to me as I can control the narrative. Having the agency to make these decisions is in itself healing. When I read this poem, I feel both losses: the loss of a student, and the loss of a son.

Although my poem only skims the surface of this painful loss, I felt it was important to capture the final image I had of Joe. I appreciated having the opportunity to process this event by writing this poem because of its impact on not only myself, but also my students. Their grief and anger is also indelible, but I genuinely wanted to focus on my own memory of my student, and perhaps attempting to capture my students' emotions was too difficult for me to write. Many people may not wish to share something this personal. Revealing highly emotional events can be frightening, but they can also be cathartic.

Sharing this poem with other poets was also comforting. I believed many would understand my loss. Whether they have been teaching for a few years or for numerous years, they will most likely have also experienced losing a student or a classmate. A loss is a loss. I was grateful to receive supportive remarks from several individuals such as Glenda Funk who said:

> Barb, Your poem has me longing to rescue so many students. It's students who live on the edge, whose choices make me cringe, I worry about and think about often. That's a powerful shift between "word" and "that night." I'm thinking about the contrast between whole and hole in the poem. The tone is so personal, and life is so full of steep hills and sharp curves.

Powerful poem. This memory will stay in my heart a long time.

Glenda's comments helped me to feel validated with what I was sharing about losing Joe. When others can share a connection with your poem, you've succeeded as a poet. I think, "Yes, someone understands. I'm not alone."

Margaret Young Ingram connected to my poem, too, by sharing:

Ah, Barb, this is so poignant. I am so sad. Beautifully written. I had to read this several more times — we have all had students like this. I am truly struck by the simple beauty of "Your brown eyes laughing."

Allison Berryhill, the poet host, also reflected on not only the style of my poem, but also her emotions. She said,

You introduced me to JT with such vivid and telling details (eyes/trouble/jeans). And then you stopped time in your poem. You put JT on hold as you revisited your own holey-jeans memory. As a reader, I FELT the diversion was giving me space to breathe before returning to what you had foreshadowed: the last day I saw you. That pacing was powerful. My heart is swollen tonight as I read about so many precious students.

The beauty of sharing poetry with others who truly listen/read is the ability to not only hear what others have to say about your poem, but also the opportunity to read other teacher's responses to the same prompt. I am always impressed by the amazing poems others write. Other teachers also wrote about the students who touched their lives in deep and meaningful ways. Mo Daley's poem is one she shared about her student Andre who couldn't read. Her poem is a response to mine and other poems here:

Andre by Mo Daley

Andre was twelve and couldn't read
He could come in, put his head on the desk,
Swear at me on occasion
Argue constantly, refuse to do anything,
But he couldn't read

When I asked Grandma why he was always so tired
She sucked in her breath and shared his story —
Andre didn't sleep
He was on medication for the nightmares
He could only fall asleep in her bed
"You see," she offered, "My daughter was killed
In a drive-by meant for his father.
Andre's dad was in the car and watched her die."
It was all I could do not to cry, but she persisted.
"Andre's dad took revenge on the shooter
And is serving time for his crime.
I'm doing the best I can.
I'm sorry he falls asleep in class."
I wanted to hug her. Hug him.
My heart broke a little bit for that seven-year-old who lost both
        parents

I couldn't give up on him
I wouldn't give up on him
I think we eventually wore each other down
And found a way to coexist
But the day he heard my daughter-in-law didn't finish *The Crossover*
Was one I won't forget.
"Get out your camera, Mrs. Daley. We gotta make a video."
Looking at the camera in disbelief, he proselytized,
"AMY! Listen to me. *The Crossover* is the best book I ever read.
It's got everything- basketball, family drama, love, rhymes —
You gotta give it another chance and finish it.
I give it five stars."

I don't exactly know how or when it happened,
But Andre became a reader
A reader who encouraged others to read
And he became my favorite person, too

Teachers also wrote in different ways about their students. Handling difficult situations is also present in a teacher's life. We know our students have issues, we know they are not always coming to school, and that they face numerous challenges. We seek to find a way to connect with them, to build a relationship, and a better understanding of how to help them along the way. Christine Ann Roy's powerful poem "When Shame Came to Visit" depicts an emotionally-charged moment with a student and its outcome.

Christine said, "My poem is inspired by the deeply rooted honor/shame culture that my students and I have grown up in."

When Shame Came to Visit by Christine Ann Roy

He walked into class, huffing
and puffing.

Anger.

I stopped mid-sentence
and greeted Yousif,
"Hi! It's great that you could join us!"

I ignored his anger.
He ignored my positivity.

"So, let's continue class…"

Ali shouted from the back,
"HA! He got caught, Miss! He
got caught…"

I looked at Ali.
Anger.

before I could stop
him from sharing more…

Yousif got up,
and launched himself
in Ali's direction.

Chaos.
Anger.
...

Control.
Anger.
...

Silence.
Anger.

The bell rang,
and I waited in quiet anger
for my class to empty itself.

"Yousif. Hold on."

Yousif looked at me.

Shame.

We sat together in the front of
the class,
and he wept.

Deep Shame.

I sat with him.
I understood.

Compassion.

I reminded him, "You are not bad, Yousif.
Getting in trouble doesn't define you.
It does not change how I see you. You are
still important to me."

Belonging.

He looked at me.
Gratitude.

Students are often the ones who inspire us to keep teaching. We realize how much they need to be loved and protected. Their lives leave an imprint as Kim Johnson's following poem illustrates.

The Best Reason by Kim Johnson

you are the one
whose picture I keep pinned
above my desk
for days that I wonder
why I do this

you were my best reason
for teaching
1999: new student
bruised arms, far too thin
you stood
in my classroom doorway
with your grandmother
holding her hand

after she left school
you had a complete meltdown
began breaking pencils
in triads with your bare hands

so many broken pencils
scattered across the floor

your speech was slurred
you had tell-tale tics
I wondered
about your story
learned your grandmother
was your angel
a savior who stepped
in and saved your life
because daddy was gone and
mama had beaten your ears

so severely with shoes
that you could barely hear

when I spoke
you tilted your head
at a sideways angle
to put your one able ear
in position to listen

you took most of your lunch
to your backpack
to share with your siblings
because
there wasn't much
with six of you

I knew you were sharing
even hungry yourself
I started slipping in extras
for you to find later

you were a child
ahead of your years
knew things your peers did not
were the smartest student
in the class
Principal's Honor Roll
the kid in Coke bottle glasses
who couldn't hear
whose smile brought tears

and still does
when I look at that picture
of you and your grandma
smiling in the cafeteria
on Math Night

you are the best reason
that I kept teaching

Each of these poems celebrate individuals and indelible memory marks. They share love, grief, acceptance, and anger.

Writing about students is an incredibly moving opportunity for both the writer and the reader, and I believe it's imperative to take the time to process grief and the sudden loss of a student or loved one.

Recently, our community lost another student at the same place Joe lost his life. Finally, nearly forty years later, the county has erected several caution signs to indicate the sharp turn on River Road. A memorial cross can also be easily seen by passersby. Markers like these remind us of loved ones lost just as our poems remember students we've lost. Students who have left indelible marks. In conclusion, whether you have lost a student or a loved one, I believe writing can be a powerful tool to use to help one heal because it provides an opportunity to share the grief and the memories we have of our missing loved one. I hope this chapter inspires you to write and share your own experiences.

Your Turn

The love of both writing and teaching is evident in Allison Berryhill's work. She lives in Iowa where she advises the journalism program, teaches English, and hosts a weekly Creative Writing club at Atlantic High School. She is active with the Iowa Council of Teachers of English, the Iowa High School Press Association, and the Iowa Poetry Association where she serves as teacher liaison.

Short Prompt

If you are ready to write, here is a short prompt to get you started: Make a list of past students who you most remember for various reasons or, for students, make a list of teachers or coaches. Use Allison's poem as a mentor text to describe the person first and then move into how or why they've made their mark on your heart or mind or memory.

Full Prompt

If you'd like a little more support, the full prompt is reprinted below. For now, open your notebook or device and follow along with educator Allison Berryhill's inspiration: Sonnets: Don't Run Away.[1]

> **Inspiration:**
> Hannah.
> James.
> Kenny.
> May.
>
> Allison Berryhill wrote a sonnet about meeting a past student in the grocery store and forgetting her name. Like many teachers, she has taught thousands of students over the years and cannot hold them all firmly in memory while making the necessary space for current students. But we also have students or student-moments that have left indelible memory marks. Today, we invite you to write a poem about a student, past or present (or for students trying this prompt, consider a teacher or coach. We recommend reading Dorianne Laux's "The Student" as a mentor text, too, which you can find on Poetry Foundation.
>
> **Process:** You may also choose to write about students/teaching/school in a larger sense. When I taught Creative Writing workshop-style three years ago, I gave myself the task of writing a poem to/for each of my students. This is one.

Poem for Austin (student in Creative Writing) Nov. 2018

Count syllables (3)
Astronomy (4)
He drums out each beat
Then counts it once more.
He picks up his pen
And he gives it a shot
His words are his rocket
He's their astronaut.
The lines that he writes
Are electric, bizarre
They flash through the sky
Like his own shooting star.
So Austin, keep writing
Put black upon white.
The universe needs you
Keep writing tonight.

Barbara's Suggestions for the Classroom
If you want to try a version of this prompt with your students, here are a few things to keep in mind:

- Think about potential memories, consider creating a visual of the event. Sketch out your ideas or create a list. Often as you begin to recreate a memory through a visual sketch, you will begin to remember more about the color, tastes, sounds, and feelings you experienced during the particular moment.
- Consider the voice you want to use in the poem. Do you want to show the conversation that occurred during the memory or capture what you thought to yourself? How do you want the readers to hear you? Consider your tone. Do you want to show your emotions, be light-hearted or sarcastic?
- Play with the details you want the readers to visualize? Notice the emotions this memory evokes. How can you capture this experience? Perhaps you do not want to be completely honest. Feel free to stretch the truth or eliminate details you do not feel comfortable sharing with others.
- Think about potential forms you might use to shape your poem such as a haiku sonnet, pantoum, or trimeric. Of course, free verse is always a way to let your thoughts, images, and voice flow.

Links
[1] https://www.ethicalela.com/sonnets-dont-run-away/

CHAPTER 5

Piano Lessons, Terzanelles, & Changing Schools
Sarah J. Donovan

For the past few years, I really thought I wrote a pantoum—not a terzanelle. In fact, I was so convinced "Piano Lessons" was a pantoum that even to this day—years later—when I feel the need for the comfort of a form in my poem, I turn to the pantoum (or rather the pantoum maker website, to be precise). So I misremembered what this formative poem was called, and perhaps that is part of healing. I wrote this at a time that I was quite literally lost and disconnected from everything and everyone I knew. We carry memories in ways we do, in the form we name it, in the form that will contain it, and we don't need anyone to forgive us for doing so. But just to be clear, this chapter is about a terzanelle poem that may have saved my life.

On November 12, 2019, retired St. Louis educator Susie Morice suggested we "take a shot in response to visual art." She invited us to "look long and hard at the piece of art, make a list of colors and what those colors might mean to you." She suggested we "have a conversation with the piece" and listen to what it says back to you." And in the form, she said "the mentor poem is a terzanelle. Free verse is just dandy as well!"

In that November of 2019, I had just moved from a suburb of Chicago where I was born and taught junior high for 15 years to Stillwater, Oklahoma to begin a career in teacher education. Just days before Susie's prompt, I had driven to a small 4-day school in Morrison to observe a student teacher. This was my second drive along unfamiliar roads and just days before Thanksgiving when I was missing home and wondering why I hadn't made plans to return to Chicago for the holiday.

I was all out of sorts with doubt and grief. Writing a free verse poem felt overwhelming for me, so I studied Susie's terzanelle: It has 19 lines. Five 3-line stanzas are followed by a sixth stanza which is a quatrain finish. The rhyming/repeating pattern was noted next to her poem a1/b1/a2; b2/c1/b1; c2/d1/c1; d2/e1/d1; e2/f1/e1; f2/f1/a1/a2.

Looking at that line pattern now, I wonder why I didn't run away from it, why I tried this complex poem at all at a time when I was desperately missing my junior high students but, more importantly, my Self — of who I was when I was a classroom teacher, who I was in Chicago. I think this puzzle of a poem was a distraction from my longing, an invitation to word-work, browse RhymeZone, play with Thesaurus for options. The form embodied possibilities.

For my art work, I decided on a sign I saw at the edge of a long driveway leading to a farmhouse on that unfamiliar Oklahoma road. The sign said "Piano Lessons." And I thought about the piano teacher in that house waiting for their students after school or on weekends. Maybe their student was a neighboring farmer who came by early in the morning. Maybe their student was a factory worker stopping by after a shift. The sign made me wonder — again about anything but myself. My imaginings aligned me to another teacher, too. That was a comfort. Then I remembered the wave of blackbirds that danced with the power lines, that seemed to be following me to Morrison. Had this wave been in Illinois, too, but I wasn't looking?

Here is what I wrote when I posted this poem:

> Okay, so I gave this nearly an hour working with the lines, rhyme, and meter of the terzanelle. It is my first and hopefully not my last. I think I get how it works now, and think it has potential, but for now, let it be enough. Much gratitude for any sense you can make of my drive in the country today. I was observing a student-teacher at a small school that meets just 4 days a week to give students a day to work on their farms.

And here is my poem:

(Untitled) by Sarah Donovan

"Piano lessons"–sign scribbled on the side of the road.
Asphalt unlevel, carrion remains scattered between lines,
as I wonder who is sitting on the bench with music to bestow.

The wind whistles through our cracked shield like a vine
winding its way into the car, chilling the wheel and dash.
Asphalt unlevel, carrion remains scattered between lines

as fallen leaves drift with blackbirds, tattered blankets of ash

looking for a place to rest among the acres of grain
winding its way into the car, chilling the wheel and dash

with empty searching and silent wishes for what remains
of the moon and what the sun may bring to the day
looking for a place to rest among the acres of grain

to watch the cars go by, staying safely away.
In the shadows of the barns long-forgotten, we wish
of the moon and what the sun may bring to the day

"Piano lessons"–sign scribbled on the side of the road
in the shadows of the barns long-forgotten
as I wonder who is sitting on the bench with music to bestow.

Teacher poets responded to my words.

> Glenda from Idaho: I love the way your poem turns an orderly sign and a typical Oklahoma town into a work of art. There's a dreamlike quality to the poem, too, in phrases such as "I wonder." You make the form work fluidly, and your poem is comforting.

> Kim from Georgia: The mood of this piece is so calm and relaxing, like a rural countryside in the fall, where no one is rushed to do anything and the beauty is there from the landscape to the sounds of piano keys. I want to be in that realm.

> Mo from Illinois: I feel like I was in the car with you. Your use of repetition makes the poem feel soothing to me

> Susie from Missouri: Oh, Sarah, you took this to a whole new level, and it really works. The unique repetitions (maybe that's an oxymoron) move our focus into a deeper look at this place on an Oklahoma road. The tone is downright unsettling, as what might seem melancholy or even a bit bleak becomes rich with a sensation of lives being played out between highway lines in the road and wind and "fallen leaves drift[ing]." The "empty searching and silent wishes for what remains/of the moon/and what the sun may bring to the day" are potent lines in that they chill us

just like that wind that makes its way "like a vine." We say roads wander off into nowhere, yet there are real lives in that nowhere…lives that might take piano lessons or give piano lessons. I like that disruption of image. I love "shadows of the barns long-forgotten." The rhyming gives it an added sense of the rhythm in a car rambling down an OK road. This is a really neat poem. Way to go, Sarah! Thanks for working with this one! Susie

Gayle from Maryland: Sarah, thank you. There is a sense of peace in the picture you paint for us here. (And that pattern was a bear to work with! I enjoyed the challenge!)

Allison from Iowa: Sarah, after spending my own hour knotted in the terzanelle rhyme scheme, I am especially wowed by how you remembered to bring imagery and detail to this lovely poem. The wind whistling through the cracked shield like a vine was maybe my favorite line…but also that "Piano Lessons" sign, and who's sitting on the bench. Lovely.

Teachers from all corners of the country witnessed this poem, my seeing the sign, my puzzling the form. In reading other posts, I was comforted to hear others had been doing a sort of productive struggle with this one. Perhaps more importantly, I was invited to witness the art and words other teachers drew on to make sense of their lives this November day. The perspective-taking that comes from reading poems offered to a similar prompt was so fortifying for me.

Stacey from California wrote:

Okkkk, I admit this was hard and frustrating and I stayed up 30 minutes past my bedtime because I refused to quit. With that said, I need more practice with this tricky poetic form. But please don't assign it again too soon. LOL. I might ditch class. Thanks so much for stretching me and showing me that I can try new forms to develop a new kind of flow. My picture is hanging on my bedroom wall. I call it Queen Mother and Child. A few lines I was grateful to read, grateful to Stacey for puzzling out were these: "Walking miles in a sun too wild/Backs straight with elegant grace/But years have passed since they've smiled.

In an odd way, I was sitting beside Stacey in her bedroom gazing at this mother and child picture in her home. In sharing this poem with others, Stacey allowed me to witness her process and the words she gathered; she offered a glimpse into her home, the place she rests and lives beyond the school day.

In Gayle's poem, she wrote about "this carved griffin" that is "plopped at the bottom of our staircase" and "worse for wear — three children, multiple cats, and an exposed perch have been rough on this creature." Gayle tells us that she "took some liberties with the pattern and added an extra stanza." Like me, she seemed to be saying "good enough" for now: "I fell from grace, apparently disinvited/From my perch of arrogance/Sold at auction, my hope unrequited" and then Gayle introduces me to her son in this phrase "My left wing, once held in reverence/Was broken by the resident/Boy-child, his clumsy turn/Left me useless, a legend spurned." And I just loved this turn in the poem.

Again, now, as I write these words, I am sitting among friends in their places and poetic forms. I have moved, changed jobs, and found poetry in a new-to-me state. And yet, my belonging, my sense of home defies physical space as I write with poets from all corners of being a teacher.

Your Turn

You are in good hands with Susie Morice, writer and editor. She is a consultant with Santa Fe Center for Transformational School Leadership and the Institute for School Partnership at Washington University in St. Louis. Susie is also a Teacher-Consultant with The Gateway Writing Project, a former public school classroom teacher for 30 years, and a poet, who is the winner of Member-at-Large Best Poem, 2014 – Missouri State Poetry Society contest.

Short Prompt
If you are ready to write, here is a short prompt to get you started: Go to Google Art and see what speaks to you. Talk to the artist in your poetry. Ask questions, wonder. If you want, try the Terzanelle to see

how the form comforts or frustrates as you write. There is poetry in the experience of trying.

Full Prompt

Now go to your device or paper journal that you have dedicated for this healing journey and write. The full prompt is reprinted below, so for now, follow along with Susie Morice: Terzanelle[1] (You can go to the link now to see other mentor poems, or save the link for later.)

> **Inspiration:** A Piece of Artwork. While you might not be able to zip off to the nearest art museum (if you can, do!), zero in on a piece of artwork – a painting, a sculpture, a ceramic piece… here at the St. Louis Art Museum (or your city museum), you might even be moved by a mummy, as we have some doozie Egyptian mummy pieces! You can use an art book or get online and call up a piece that rocks your socks for one reason or another. We're going to take a try in response to visual art.
>
> **Process:** As you look hard and long at the piece of art, make a list of colors and what those colors might mean to you.
> - Have a conversation with the piece. Talk out loud to it. What does it say back to you?
> - Notice how light plays into and onto the piece. Does it generate any of its own light, and if so, where does that come from? Is there a sense of action with the piece?
> - Place your piece of art – while we might view it in a museum or in an art book, somehow I just can't wrap my head around the idea that the artist created this piece to sit in a museum or to end up on a coffee table – Place your piece of art in an apt environment – let it live there.
> - Play with the life of the art piece and words that help it speak to us.
> - OR imagine the artist creating this piece – let us see the artist toiling over this piece, or bringing it into life.
> - Send a jpeg of the art piece to Sarah Donovan so she can upload it with your poem. She will try to get the artwork onto our blog pages.
> - Only if you feel like it, play with rhyming. The mentor poem is a terzanelle. Free verse is just dandy as well!

Sarah's Suggestions for the Classroom

We have written a lot about the role of relationships in healing, so we encourage you to try pair-sharing with your students, but it is really helpful if you have lots of firsthand experience sharing your own poetry with teachers so that you can empathize with your students. Read another teacher's poem and respond. Here's one thing I like to do when responding to others or something specific to notice.

- I always try to use their name as a greeting so that they know I know their name.
- I also begin with something that I love – a word, a phrase.
- And then I think about what I learned about this person, what they are sharing with me. This can be their way of thinking, but it is typically a glimpse into a fissure or fraction of their life that they are asking me to see. I let them know I can and do see and that I will carry that gift with me.

Finally, reflect on the healing in the act of writing a poem, healing in sharing or being seen by others; in what ways are you healing a verb?

Links

[1] https://www.ethicalela.com/november-3-5-day-writing-challenge

CHAPTER 6

"A House for Mom" as a Wave of Grieving
Leilya A. Pitre

As I think about Mom, my eyes are drawn to one of her final photographs. This touching image captures her bidding me farewell outside our childhood home in Crimea, Ukraine, as I depart for the United States after a short visit. At seventy-seven, she stands amidst the lush backdrop of green grapevines, dressed in her signature golden floral dress complemented by a delicate light-purple headscarf. Despite the vibrancy of her attire and a brave smile on her face, I sense infinite sadness and fear hidden behind her cheerful appearance. Throughout her life, Mom bore the weight of worry with remarkable courage — her wavering smile reflects her enduring strength. While I, too, can manage a smile now, the journey to this emerging level of inner peace and acceptance seemed intolerable just a few short years ago.

Grieving comes in waves, as I heard from a friend many years ago. I knew that before; I just never fully realized it until it became a part of my life. Understanding grief as a process, with sudden coming and going, intensifying and weakening at times helps me process what happened and how I react in response to it. This recursive process explains my mood swings and ability to cry at one moment and laugh just minutes later. It may also justify a desire to talk to someone about Mom and share my grief.

Writing is another way for me to heal though as it allows putting this tough-to-articulate ache into words. So, when another wave of grief comes, I write. It helps me process traumatic memories, makes sense of them, and serves as a coping mechanism (Harber & Pennebaker, 1992). According to research, writing therapy has been known and studied by medical professionals, and "otherwise described in the literature as 'expressive (emotional) disclosure,' 'expressive writing,' or 'written disclosure therapy,' may have the potential to heal mentally and physically" (Mugerwa & Holden, 2012, p. 661). Writing poetry seems even more beneficial since scholars consider poetry as a powerful therapy tool and define poetry therapy as the "intentional use of poetry for healing and personal growth" (McArdle & Byrt, 2001, p. 521). Furthermore, Soter (2016) claims that poetry affords voice to "whatever is too large, too incomprehensible to express in any other way" (p. 2). Indeed, poetry allows me to use fewer words and leave blank spaces for things and feelings I'm not able to name yet, but I think and process them already.

Waves of grieving come unexpectedly, and any little thing can trigger such a moment. I may be watching a sunset with my husband, walking in the park with a friend, telling a story to my grandchildren, reading a book, or responding to a poetry prompt on the Ethical ELA blog. When Darius Phelps, a doctoral student at Teachers College of Columbia University, invited us to explore recovery through Kyle Liang's poetry collection *How to Build a House* (2018) in April of 2023, I knew another wave of grieving was imminent.

As I read the prompt, my thoughts began to work their way through my personal connections to it. What caught my attention right away was the fact that Phelps was a graduate student. From a photo on the website, I saw a youthful, smiling man and wondered why such a young person would think about loss and grief, or rather I wished young people like Darius hadn't had to think about loss and grief. My mind quickly zoomed in on a memory of my graduate experience, and it hit me. I lost my Mom after the first semester of entering the program. Unlike Darius, I was older, but the age didn't matter. A long flight over the Atlantic Ocean with two layovers—Atlanta, GA, and Frankfurt-on-Maine, Germany—to Kyiv, Ukraine, followed by a fourteen-hour train ride to Simferopol, Crimea, and a week by Mom's bedside did not prepare me to say goodbye.

Here I was, twelve years later, helplessly searching for words to "burn a house" for Mom. To me, the prompt tasked me with an unimaginable step—it asked me to finally accept and come to terms with the most devastating loss in my life. Was I ready? No! I did want to face the challenge, and at least give it a try. I wrote, scratched the words, lines, stanzas; I cried, reread what's written, scratched, and then wrote again.

Crafting My Poem and Response from Teacher Friends

Through a couple of hours I struggled with the poem. I reflected on Mom's life and openly grieved for the first time after her passing. When I finished writing the poem, I introduced it with this comment:

Thank you for hosting today, Darius, and for such a prompt that threw me back right in my Mom's arms. Your poem has so many great phrases. I was struck at the beginning with the lines: "Each brick laid with intent// I'll make sure this time, he can't come in." It makes me think about the intrusion that ended tragically.

Below is a poem I posted that day.

A House for Mom by Leilya A. Pitre

Mom, I think I am ready (maybe?)
after twelve years
to burn a house
in the sky
for you to rest peacefully.

It will be crispy clean,
inviting, and beautiful.
It will have a garden
with your favorite flowers and grape vines,
just the way you like it.

I will throw soft carpet runners
on the hallway floors,
dusted with damp cloth,
to keep your feet warm,
just like you did it for us.

I will wash your shoes
after a rainy day outside
and won't let your hands get cold
in that freezing water,
just like you did it for us.

I will make you
a fresh cup of coffee,
serving it with candy and pastries,
just the way you did it
for your dear guests.

And when my time comes,
I hope my children will see me off your way.

We will catch up and share stories,
I will tell you about your grandchildren,
and their children, and how much we missed you.

My poem was born in tears. First, I didn't know what to include
and what to leave out of it. I remembered what Mom loved and
used to do for us, her eight children. These daily things that had
kept her busy from dawn to dusk were not noticeable, and, surely,
not appreciated enough at the time. "This is what moms do," or
"Mom will figure it out," a child me used to think. Many images
from my childhood flashed before my eyes: Mom smiling, sewing
our outfits, making our beds, cleaning the house, working in the
garden, and kneading the dough. Whatever she was doing was
accompanied with a song; she had such a beautiful voice and sang
in three languages—Crimean Tatar, Ukrainian, and Russian.
Despite a huge family, the house was always neat, cozy, and
decorated with an elegant taste on a minimal budget we could
afford. Scrolling through memories that day, I tried not to focus on
the hardships; Mom had always been so skillful at hiding them from
us.

Nursing a poem that day, I first wrote out my thoughts in prose
(most of my poems I write in the notebook first) and mentioned
things that would make a good house for my Mom based on what I
thought would make her comfortable and happy. I knew it had to
be clean with "soft carpet runners;" it should have a garden with
flowers and grape vines around it. I included the most memorable
acts of her selfless kindness and care: washing our shoes, keeping
hands warm, making guests feel welcomed and appreciated. Then
I thought about my own grandchildren and what stories I told them
about my Mom. All these thoughts went into the poem. I left out
Mom's singing because it was too painful to describe her voice—so
dear and beautiful. You may have noticed that I doodled, circled,
underlined, and scratched out words as I recorded my thoughts.
You can see my thoughts in Figure 1.

I prefer narrative poetry, so most of my poems are written in a
way people tell stories. "A House for Mom" is structured
narratively too. Each stanza is a complete sentence with a
conventional punctuation; the line breaks ensure smooth cadence—
"breath as an intake and a flow," a lesson I learned from Mary
Oliver (1998, p. 3). Keeping each stanza to five lines serves as a pace

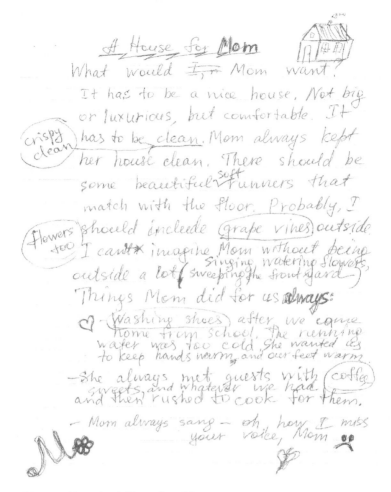

Figure 1. Notes for A House for a Mom

checker and creates a somewhat uniformed pattern throughout the poem.

Posting the poem, I thought that next time when I would go home to Crimea and visit Mom's final resting place, I could read her my poem; I could talk to her and tell how painful it was to write it. If only I could go soon; the Russian invasion cut off my road home for now, and losing Mom had become even more difficult to process. I often feel misplaced now: I lost both of my parents, my Homeland is invaded, and I am unable to go and see my siblings, relatives, and friends to share memories and grieve together.

A silver lining in my situation came from an opportunity to post the poem on Ethical ELA for teacher poets and colleagues. It was a safe place where sharing the most vulnerable moments was welcomed, embraced, and encouraged. While I often consider my poems not good or eloquent enough, I know my poet friends will be gentle, compassionate, and understanding. Since the prompt didn't require a specific poetic form or structure, the responses to my poem were directly to the content.

In the first comment, Mo from Illinois wrote:

Leilya, your mom sounds like a wonderful woman. The image of those carpet runners made me smile. I get what you mean about maybe being ready to write this poem. My poem yesterday was about my mom, who passed away more than thirty years ago, and it was still hard.

Mo's comment deeply resonated with me, especially the final part, where Mo admitted that even after thirty years, "it was still hard" to write about her mom. I immediately went into the previous day of poetry writing to find Mo's poem and reread it. I felt that I was not alone in my grief; others knew it too well, Mo knew it too well, and we could share with each other. I gratefully appreciated the emotional support in a few words that helped me connect with Mo at that moment.

Another comment came from Barb, who lives in Iowa: "Oh, Leilya, I love how you end your poem... I can feel how much you miss your mother and how much you appreciated all she did for you. Truly moving and loving poem!" She liked the poem's ending where I think about my children and share stories with my grandchildren. Barb noted that she could feel that I missed my mother and appreciated things Mom did for me. So maybe I found some words to show my longing and love, and maybe I am ready to heal while treasuring all of the memories about Mom.

The next comment was delivered by Allison, also from Iowa:

I am so glad you came to the page with this poem. Your opening stanza is somber, but your "crispy clean" phrase tilts us into your happy memories of your mom. I loved "I will wash your shoes..." It reminded me of the many small ways parents show love — often unrecognized. Lovely.

Generous and welcoming, Allison praised me for crafting the poem. She noticed my intent to capture "happy memories" despite the "somber" opening. Her comment made me think that those "small ways parents show love — often unrecognized" later become the most valuable memories because they show us love and care without any pretense. In Allison's words, I found encouragement both for writing the poem and sharing those personal moments about my Mom.

Finally, Stacey Joy from California, who by the way always channels love and joy herself, kindly noted:

Leilya, this poem is filled with loving care for your mom and it shows us how nurturing your mom was… All of your poem speaks to the love you shared. This stanza warms my soul…washing shoes, keeping hands warm.

I am certain you'll have the same done for you because you're such an incredible human.

This comment itself was filled with love and care. If my words were "warming" Stacey's heart, I seemed to be able to bring out Mom's nurturing nature. I always wanted to be at least half or a person my Mom was, so I particularly appreciated Stacey's final remark.

Reading the comments and knowing that others find my words relevant warmed my heart. All of those kind notes were written with care, consideration, and respect; they provided me with a much needed uplifting and relief. For me, sharing and receiving feedback was an extension of processing and healing. More than that, it was building connections with people who also experienced loss and are open to support and embrace me in the gloomiest moments — such a reciprocal response to each other's pain and vulnerability.

Healing Together

Before and after posting my piece, I read the poems posted by the others as well as the comments to them. In one of such comments, I found the phrase that makes this community's "writing of healing" so valuable. Allison from Iowa, who commented on my poem, responded to Mo's poem saying, "Your poem invited me into your experience while also reflecting mine." She recognizes herself in Mo's experiences. This is why writing and sharing poems are incredibly beneficial, particularly when people are struggling with losses in their lives.

Just like the teacher poets witness my grief and search for solace, I "saw" theirs and was endlessly grateful for such a nurturing community. I was also humbled by the opportunity to witness their vulnerabilities. I was particularly stricken by Ann's poem in which she grieves "brothers and sisters" dealing with "all the cruelty in our world." She offers to "water the earth / with our tears / so all / that is green and good / will grow," thus proposing how we can make the world better by being kinder and more concerned about each other. This metaphorical growth is a way to find the light in times of darkness and hurt.

In another poem, "Father and Son," Bryan reflects on his relationships with father. From the first stanza, I find myself afflicted by the lines: "I miss the nights / we'd stare at flames, "and I remember my father who also crossed over fifteen years ago. However, our evenings filled with conversations, sometimes even heated debates, flash back to me with Bryan's heartfelt opening. Further, witnessing how father and son quietly "sit in royal hoodies, grow closer to each other by burning things, "frustrations," and even "regrets," and "[s]imply / setting our silence / on fire" creates almost an ideal mediation exercise. At the same time, the poem becomes an ode to love and loss, to good times and fond memories. I thank Bryan for allowing me to bring back my memories while reading his poem.

The poem I found the most relatable that day came from Wendy Everard from New York, probably, because she was also "burning a house" for her mother:

I Will Burn You a Kitchen by Wendy Everard

Mother, do not worry
For I will burn you a house in the sky.
One where you seize control of your happiness
Without letting emotion take control of you.
I will burn you a kitchen
Where you treat yourself
Where I treat you
To what that you refuse to feed yourself
I will build you a bedroom
That will simply house rest
And not worry, regret, and despair
Of life
I will build you a room for living
In which you can put your feet up
And enjoy life's parade of theatrics
Taking your mind off of everyday drama
I would burn you a house in the sky
Burn your cares, your worries to cinders

Torch the past
If only you would let me.

Responding to Wendy's poem, I wrote:
Wendy, your poem is beautiful, and touching,
and gentle, and so caring. I love every word, but
the final stanza will stay with me: I would burn
you a house in the sky/   Burn your cares,
your worries to cinders/   Torch the past/
If only you would let me. Thank you for your
words today!

I was genuinely touched by Wendy's poem. It seemed to me that she found the words I could use to talk about my Mom. In five short stanzas, she was able to tell us about her mother, the things her mother might need, and things Wendy was ready to do if she were ever permitted. In another comment to that poem, Sarah from Oklahoma pointed out a powerful line that could be an anthem: "One where you seize control of your happiness." Indeed, if only our mothers were able or allowed themselves to take charge over their happiness or accept our help. The poem and the comments made me wonder more about the lives of our mothers and their roles.

Each poem written for that prompt told a story. Most of those stories—of mothers, fathers, siblings, friends, pets, and places—were overflowing with sadness and pain. Switching the role from a writer to a reader afforded us to acknowledge the feelings, to connect, and to offer words of sympathy and support to each other. That kind of poetic exchange helped me glide over when a new grief wave whirl caught me off guard. I understand now that I will never be able "to get over it," to stop grieving and being sad, but I am learning how to deal with it, how to smile and tell stories that Mom would tell me, how to sing songs she used to sing, and how to be happy even when I cry. I can look at Mom's other photographs now and tell my grandchildren about their Grandmother Zore, who lived a beautiful, long life in Crimea, Ukraine.

Your Turn

Darius Phelps offers a broad background to writers. He is an adjunct professor at CUNY Queens, Hunter College, Teachers College, and intern at Brooklyn Poets. An educator, poet, spoken word artist, and activist, Darius writes poems about grief, liberation, emancipation, reflection through the lens of a teacher of color and experiencing Black boy joy. His poems have appeared in the NY *English Record*, NCTE *English Journal*, *Pearl Press* Magazine, and ëëN Magazine's *The 2023 Valentine Issue*. Recently, he was featured on WCBS and highlighted the importance of Black male educators in the classroom.

To conclude the chapter, I would like to extend an invitation to you, dear reader, to write with us. Below, I suggest a short and a full prompt for crafting a poem on this topic, as well as some suggestions in case you want to bring the similar activity in your classroom or share with colleagues and friends.

Short Prompt

Try to work through this prompt on your own. Carve a few minutes for self-care today. Using Darius's prompt suggestion, think about someone or something to whom or what you will address in the poem. What would you include in the house you burn for them? What do you think they need, want, or might expect from you? Could this person be you? Then, what do you need or want to have in the sky?

You may begin writing in your journal right away to continue your healing. If it feels that you are not ready yet for a poem, you may just jot down some of your thoughts, write a narrative paragraph about your experience, or record these thoughts on your phone. You may always come to it later — you've already made the first step.

Full Prompt

If you need some additional support, I am including the full prompt here for your convenience. For now, open your notebook or device and follow along with Darius Phelps' inspiration: House in the Sky.[1]

> **Inspiration:** With the turn of each page of *How to Build A House*, Kyle lays down a brick of new foundation cemented in honesty, excavation, and emancipation. Emulating poetry as architecture, with his work, his tone, his voice, and willingness to bear his soul, Kyle doesn't just build a house in the sky by being vulnerable, he lays the foundation for a better world. One

where marginalized voices, specifically where fellow young men of color, are free to unapologetically be themselves, on their respective journeys towards liberation. I was inspired to share his poem as a mentor text and hope it resonates with fellow readers as well.

Process: In old Chinese tradition, families would burn houses filled with furniture because it was believed that it would then be waiting for them in the afterlife. Kyle wrote this poem and dedicated it to his father, his unconditional love for him, wanting him to have the best in his afterlife.

For today's poem, think of a person or object as the direct address and include what they or it needs most, which is what the speaker of the poem will burn for them. Another approach is for the speaker to be the person or object writing to you as the subject. What do you need? What is waiting for you?

After you read the poems in this chapter and write your own, think if you would like others to witness your experience. I invite you to join the community of poets on EthicalELA.com. It doesn't have to be for a particular prompt. You will find multiple opportunities to write and read poetry in that space. Allowing others to read and respond to your poems may help you heal and embrace your recovery as it is always better together. Another great way to share experiences is by reading and responding to other teachers' poems. There may be one, two, or more poems that touch your heart or revive some memories for you. When I respond to teacher poets, I usually make one, two, or all three of the following things:

- thank them personally for allowing me into their world by sharing the poem;
- notice the line(s) that resonate with me and help me realize that I am not alone in my pain and struggles;
- comment on the form, word choices, sound devices, or any other poetic craftsmanship that deserves praise and makes the poem even more precious to me.

This poetic exercise, as any other writing, may be concluded by writing a reflection about the poem composing, sharing, and responding to others. Does it help? If so, in what way does it help? How do your and other poets' words help you process loss, pain, or struggles? Do you have any other tools to cope and grieve? These questions may extend the reciprocal exchange among those who participate in writing and equip us with additional support mechanisms.

> **Leilya's Suggestions for the Classroom**
> - Word the prompt appropriately for your students' age;
> - Suggest a form(s) that may work for such a prompt;
>   Include a mentor poem. The more students read, the better they write. It helps expand their vocabulary as well.
> - Spend a few minutes modeling how to approach the poetry composing. Show them your writing process. Notice that you also may struggle with phrasing or finding the most fitting word.
> - Provide students with a choice suggesting an alternative prompt; allow students to reject your prompt completely and write something they choose to create on their own.
>
> Extending this writing activity to your students may result in developing closer connections with your students, their lives, and experiences. It might be that little nudge they need to open up, discover a way of sharing their inner emotional state, and find a path to healing with poetry in a safe space of their classroom.

References

Liang, K. (2018). *How to build a house.* Swan Scythe Press.

Harber, K. D. & Pennebaker, J. W. (1992). Overcoming traumatic memories. In: Christianson SA (Ed.). *The handbook of emotion and memory: Research and theory* (pp. 359-387). Lawrence Erlbaum Associates, 359–387.

McArdle & Byrt (2001). Fiction, poetry, and mental health: Expressive and therapeutic uses of literature. *Journal of Psychiatric and Mental Health Nursing, 8,* 517-524. doi:10.1046/j.1351-0126.2001.00428.x

Mugerwa, S., & Holden, J. D. (2012). Writing therapy: A new tool for general practice? The *British Journal of General Practice, 62* (605), 661-663.

Oliver, M. (1998). *Rules for the dance. A Handbook for writing and reading metrical verse.* Houghton Mifflin Company.

Soter, A. O. (2016). Reading and writing poetically for wellbeing: Language as a field of energy in practice. *Journal of Poetry Therapy: The Interdisciplinary Journal of Practice, Theory, Research and Education, 29*(3), 161–174.

Links
[1] https://www.ethicalela.com/house-in-the-sky/

Poetic Reflection by Glenda Funk

Poetry as *Withness*

In March 2018 I wrote a poem about my father's impending blindness. "Descending Sight" remains one of my most important poems. It showed me I can write poetry, even as a teacher nearing retirement. "Descending Sight" also provided a way for me to write about a defining moment in my childhood without pedestrian or pedantic language. Writing the poem placed me in my father's presence as both witness and participant decades after his death.

Reading and writing poetry embody acts of presence. As readers, we are present in experiencing the lived reality of a poem, which doesn't mean all poems chronicle specific events. Each poem, however, expresses ideas a writer frames as truth. As poets, we channel our lived reality into verse.

Poems invite readers to consider what the poem is doing, i.e., to name the ideas inherent in the poem. Poems ask readers to consider how the poem illuminates its ideas, i.e., what language (read: diction) does a poet use? What poetry-like things (read: figurative language, etc.) does the poem employ to express ideas?

Often we teachers get fixated on the formal structure of and devices in a poem. We emphasize these instead of being *with* the poem the way a visitor to the Louvre, for example, is *with* a painting.

Project a painting onto the screen. Edward Hopper's "Nighthawks," Picasso's "Guernica," and Grant Wood's "American Gothic" work well for this. Invite students to a "gallery walk." Ask them to take notes on what they notice: color, shapes, people, shadows, etc. Consider having learners sketch the art as a way to notice. Next, lead the class in a discussion about what they noticed. Now discuss ideas the art embodies. For example, "Nighthawks" speaks to the isolation and loneliness of individuals.

In a museum we are *with* art and enjoy it unencumbered by academic analysis. This is the metaphor I'd like to consider when experiencing poetry. As a visitor to a museum responds to a work of art, so too can teachers and learners respond to poetry.

During my career I often read a poem only once before sharing it with students. This meant that we experienced the poem together as though seeing an art installation for the first time. With our students we can be *with* the poem without formal analysis.

Thinking about poetry as *withness* places reader and writer close to or connected with the speaker or subject. Poetry offers ways to be *with* those whose experiences differ from our own. When I invite learners to read Lucille Clifton's poem "jasper texas 1998," their reading positions them *with* the speaker identified in the opening line: "i am a man's head."

Equally important, writing poetry provides ways to share our individual experiences as I did in my poem "Descending Sight." The poetic muse calls our experiences to be *with* the page and *with* our readers when we put pen to paper, or in my case, tap out a poem in an iPhone note.

Descending Sight

Descending the stairs
I peer through blue frames,
round the corner and
notice my father
posed at the diningroom table.

His shoulders rounded,
his face inches from the amplified bible,
a magnifying glass in his left hand
poised between verses and cloudy eyes —
he drinks the words.

I watch the fingers of
my father's right hand
glide across Isaiah's book —
prophecies, predictions, visions:
a promised sign, release from darkness.

My father doesn't see me.
Soon he won't see the glass, the
bible, the table.
Darkness veils the light.
Impending blindness amplifies
descending sight.

Glenda Funk has a MA in English Literature and taught English and speech communication for 38 years. She serves on NCTE's Children's Poetry Awards Committee, loves travel, is a dog and cat mom, and dotes on her two-year-old grandson Ezra. Glenda's poetry is featured in Teacher Poets Writing to Bridge the Distance: An Oral History of Covid-19 in Poems, *and* Rhyme & Rhythm: Poems for Student Athletes.

Link
[1] https://www.poetryfoundation.org/poems/49491/jasper-texas-1998

CHAPTER 7

Unfinished Symphony:
Discovering a Door to My Emotions
Denise Krebs

I was the sixth child growing up in a bustling home full of children, with a doting mother and a distant father who worked hard to make sure his seven kids did not appear to be going hungry. I was one of the little ones, too young to understand the complexities of our family life. I just felt lucky to have so many big people around all the time.

My older siblings were always there for me in ways my parents couldn't be—painting my nails, teaching me to read, taking us to the beach. The small house swelled at the seams, and as my siblings married, the younger ones played musical bedrooms, filling in the gaps. My brother and sisters had children of their own, making me a very young and very happy aunt. We remained close, even when the miles between us grew.

After college, in my mid twenties, I became a new wife, a new teacher, and a few years later, an expectant mother. I was a bundle of emotions and fears. While I was pregnant with my first child, I talked to my sister about a suspicion I had about our family. One day, I bluntly asked her, "Was Dad an alcoholic?" She happened to be a recovering alcoholic herself and had done a lot of recovery work. Her affirmative answer turned into a months-long conversation through letters and books sent in the mail from California to Iowa. After reading many letters and literature from her, I decided to see a therapist to help me further along on my own recovery journey.

"What is something you want to do that you never thought you could?" the therapist asked at one point early in our sessions.

"I want to write a letter to the editor," I said. This was before social media and online publishing. I wasn't used to expressing my own opinions, so I thought this would be a good indicator that I was able to risk speaking up and out.

As a child, I had learned early on that I didn't really have permission to feel and speak my mind. We were to be calm and not make waves, to make our small world a safer place with a volatile father in the home. This attitude of keeping things calm has followed me into adulthood. As a child, I didn't know the details of what was happening in my family, much less was I able to understand the why. But after discussing it with my sister and my therapist, I realized it was my history and I could accept it and use even this to improve my own life and relationships. I also realized I would likely pass some of my fears on to my children because codependency was clearly a part of my life.

My hope was that I could lose some of my lingering issues before it affected my children. In my parenting, could I help make my fears less a part of them? Though I eventually did write that letter to the editor, *not* affecting my children was a big ask, quite impossible really. However, I have raised two independent and successful daughters, both with their own issues that came from living life with me and their father, but life has been good.

One of the good things I have chosen for this life was to have a career in education. I have taught school in a wide variety of places—a small Catholic school in a tiny farming community in Iowa, a bilingual Arabic-English school in Bahrain, a private school in California, and public schools in Arizona and Iowa, as well as teaching education courses as an adjunct professor in Iowa. Though I moved from place to place teaching and interacting in new communities, the family wounds were carried along to pop up and ask for attention as needed.

As a teacher, I had always written poetry with my students and provided models for them, but I had never realized that poetry might have value for my own processing of grief and pain, or that I could experience healing in community with other teachers. It wasn't until I began to write poetry in the Ethical ELA community, that I realized poetry is not just something to model for students, to keep within the classroom walls, as I had done for most of my career. I learned that I could process difficult issues in poems, with others as a community of witnesses. The first prompt that helped me do this came from Stacey Joy, a National Board Certified Teacher, from Los Angeles. She shared, "Music is the source of beauty, memories, and emotions. When I was experiencing a dark and depressing period of my life, I turned to poetry and music for healing..." Then Stacey invited us to spend time with music, listening and thinking about musical terms, reading lyrics and more. That was the easy part. Then she said, "Dig deep in your soul to find something on which to focus your poem."

"Dig deep in my soul?" What? This was early in my time with a new group of writers. It was only Day 5 of a month-long poetry writing journey together. Since I had already experienced this group as a safe place, I took a chance and proceeded. I spent some time listening to music, reading lyrics, and researching musical terms, which actually facilitated the digging deep to find something to focus on. First, I'll share the poem, then I will share the process I used to draft it. The poem I wrote that day in April 2020:

dad by Denise Krebs

sometimes symphonies
remain unfinished
a long long time ago
he was 43 years old
the devil's only friend

the day the music died
he was singing
bye bye
too many kids to feed
too many emotions to weed
bye bye cigarettes
bye bye vodka

before they married,
his widowed bride
was blind to
all the minor keys
in which he played
his childhood
a telling overture of the whole
rhythm and blues opera
what would an
abusive alcoholic's
magnum opus
be anyway
maybe it was the
seven kids lost in space
trying not to misstep
bad news on the doorstep

they turned out nice
not into vice
stayed out of jail
tried not to fail
cute at all costs
not too many lost
to dysfunction with alcohol

one,
when promoted to CHP captain,
asked mom, as she
watched him on the stage, his
hands clenched in fists of rage,
do you think dad would be proud yet?

Did you notice all the musical terminology I (over)used? *Symphony, minor keys, overture, rhythm and blues, opera, magnum opus?* Wow. I am unfamiliar with most of the musical terms in the world, as I'm far from being a musician. However, I believe Stacey's prompt helped free me to write this poem. Researching musical terms and contemplating which song lyrics to pick kept my mind busy, while my heart and soul were then able to become open to a topic that I had not yet written about.

Typically I'm much more of a thinker than a feeler, but like for so many others, music is a door into my emotions. Occasionally, I hear a song and weep or laugh with a memory it inspires. Music was part of vivid experiences at my wedding, the birth of my children, the death of a loved one. In addition, music helps shape a myriad of small moments, like if I heard "Silly Love Songs" by Wings now, I would be transported to my senior year of high school, when my two best friends and I drove around one evening with a coupon book getting free small pizzas because we had gas in the car and a loud radio, but no other money.

"Bye, Bye Miss American Pie," still one of my favorite songs, is the one I quoted in my poem "dad." For some reason, hearing it always brings me back to eighth grade and reading *Flowers for Algernon.* When I considered which song to use for lyric inspiration, this one by Don McLean was a natural choice.

In preparing to write my poem, I wrote down a list of musical terms I had discovered and another list with lines from "Bye, Bye

Miss American Pie," which quickly began reminding me of early family dynamics.

I took the lists, and began writing a poem. I didn't follow any form, I just wrote one or two short snippets of lyrics I had collected, worked in some musical terms interspersed with my own short lines making it look like a poem. It flowed easily and I posted it as my first draft.

I so appreciate this prompt that led me to self-discovery. This was certainly not a model poem for my students; I took time to write for myself that day. Thanks to Stacey's prompt, I realized I was ready to process my own wound. As she had said, "When I was experiencing a dark and depressing period of my life, I turned to poetry and music for healing..." Wow, I love that invitation. Why was I almost retired from a lifetime of teaching with my two children already grown to discover this healing use of poetry? Stacey's prompt helped me take a new step by writing about my alcoholic father and doing so in a public (yet safe) space. Unlike learning to write a public letter to the editor decades earlier, this time I was inspired to write from my soul, from my very self. It was the first time I shared my heart in public, and it felt good and a step forward in my recovery for me to write and publish this poem called "dad."

In Community

Writing with an audience willing to read and comment on my poetry has further helped me on the journey of sharing openly. I posted my poem in the morning, and within minutes a person had left a comment. Throughout the day, as people came to the site, several more comments came, each made me feel seen and heard, respected and encouraged. Kim wrote:

> Denise, your perspective on this "unfinished symphony" is nothing short of mature perception with the ability to see things from others' vantage points. Your courage to go into some dark places and share with readers helps us see that it's not all about the hand life deals to us, but all about how we play it and respond to it. Thank you for sharing this!

Kim helped me to see that maybe I did have a bit of empathy

for my father, seeing from his "vantage point." It made me reread my own poem, thinking about the perspective of others in a way that I hadn't before when I wrote it and shared it. In addition, I felt affirmed in how I was playing the hand I was dealt.

Susie wrote, in part:

> ...so fitting as we share the hope that a parent would finally "be proud"...fitting as we wade through dysfunction born of alcohol. I particularly liked that you saw this as an "unfinished symphony"...that alone is our storied lives...none of us are finished playing it out...at least not today. Stay healthy. Stay strong.

Susie's comment helped me know it was a truth that we are all in "unfinished symphonies" of life. It is not just those who die young and sick who are unfinished, but as Susie says, it is *our storied lives* We will never be fully developed on this side of the grave. However, we can have hope to finish playing it out with gusto, this very day. Her comment (and others also) made me feel I was writing in a safe place, where I was understood. I was not alone.

I love that after taking the risk to publish this poem, I got to step back and take a whole new role in this community. I immediately was able to start reading other poets' work. It was a chance to get out of my own head and thoughts and be touched by others. The process of writing and sharing, but also being a witness to others, affirms the power of poetry as a means of mending. Looking into others through their poetry is a healthy way to give and receive. The day I wrote this poem, I read poetry about finding solace in returning to ukulele playing, a lighthearted song about searching for the next roll of TP, and a poem about a dying mother in hospice care.

In another poem called "Searching for a Minuet," Margaret shared this in her second stanza:

We are collectors of our story
searching for legacy
hoping for tomorrow
to take us out of today

Margaret's words helped me realize that perhaps I am also a

"collector" of stories. It made me want to keep digging deep for poems to surface, to search for my own legacy.

In the month of April 2020, there was another comfort that came from being in this writing community. Each day poems were posted about living through the initial lockdown of the Covid-19 pandemic. Jamie wrote about her daughter who had been sidelined in Mexico City due to the coronavirus quarantine. Here is a portion of her musical poem that day.

> come on home
> come on home
> no you don't want to
> be alone
> just come on home
> left me weeping thinking of Rachel

During the lockdown period, reading Jamie's and others poems helped me remember I wasn't alone in this. We were all sheltering in place with the roving germs, lingering questions about how the Covid virus was spread, and the distressing rise in daily death counts.

Writing poetry has brought significant restoration to my soul. I'm thinking back now on the poetry writing as primarily classroom models that I did for most of my career. They were real poems, authentic on some level, yes. However, writing as part of a poetry community — learning to understand and love others through their authentic voices, responding to their work with my reading, appreciation, and comments, and being understood by them through their responses — has perhaps been the most significant part of the healing process for me.

For me, after years of processing the death and alcoholism of my father on my own, I was at a place where I needed the healing and growth that came from this poetry prompt. We hold memories and pain for years and have it come out in bits along the way. Writing and even being in conversation with others about our writing can facilitate growth. We need to take care of ourselves as we write because we won't always be ready to process the pain. Sometimes there is anger and fear and denial, and we will choose not to share. That's okay, but when we are ready, I have learned there are other readers who will be there to help us carry the load.

Ongoing Relationships

Fast forward to April 2024, and I experienced this community in a new way. My sister Judi died suddenly in her sleep on April 28. I started out life with six siblings, and now I'm down to three. It was heartbreaking when I lost my first brother, then more pain when my oldest sister died. Then Judi. As they continue to die, the pain for each multiplies.

I had been writing with this poetry sharing community for four years by this time, and we were just finishing up a month of daily writing with each other. The prompt for April 29 was "First Time for Everything" with Fran Haley:

> ...brainstorm 'first times' in your own life. Jot them down...Give yourself a few moments with the memories. Go with the one that pulls the strongest. This is the poem that wants to be born today. You can bring it to life in any form you like.

In the morning, before my younger brother came over and gave me the news of Judi's death, I had gotten started on the prompt. I had just jotted down a list of "first times," then waited to see which one might be pulling the strongest. This is when I got the news. I forgot about the poem. After a few hours of making phone calls to other family members, I also decided I wanted to share my sad news with my "poetry family," so I came back and shared this:

Firsts I Considered Writing About Today by Denise Krebs

~~my first sister-in-law, who died last month~~
~~or all the 'firsts' from this week alone:~~
~~the first time I started an official bird watching life list~~
~~the first time our cabin bedroom got a closet~~
~~the first time I ripped out sticky vinyl tiles~~
~~the first time I got myself stuck on the so sticky floor~~
~~or the first anything else I wrote on my list of "first times"~~
~~this morning before I got word that~~
my third sibling died yesterday

It was all I could muster. I couldn't write about any of my firsts, so I used the previous day's prompt again, which was shared by Glenda Funk. The prompt was to compose a strikethrough poem — where you write some lines for the purpose of revising or editing out some of them. I just wrote the ideas that had been percolating through my head earlier that morning and then struck them all out. I didn't respond to any other poems that day. I couldn't, but I wanted these friends to witness my loss. I wanted to tell them, for I knew they cared about me. Four years after sharing my poem about my dad, I was reminded of the healing that comes through writing poetry, and in an even more compelling way, the value of writing and sharing poetry within a long lasting community. Here is a found poem, which is a kind of poem created and reframed using other source material, this time using lines from the comments others left for me on my poem that day:

Siblings — those who have known us always--
I am sorry to see your heartbreaking news.
Be tender with yourself
as you walk your aching heart.
Thank you for your every precious word.
Find comfort in poetry☐
How you honor us by sharing
your grief–
gut-punch of grief–
through poetry.
Sending love and light
Cathartic for you to slash over the firsts
To stop it all for this poem
to name your grief
to name yesterday
Don't ever forget,
we are here,
Your poetry family

Your Turn

This inspiration comes from Stacey Joy. Stacey is National Board Certified Teacher, Google Certified Educator, L.A. County and LAUSD Teacher of the Year with 38 years of elementary classroom teaching experience. She currently teaches 5th grade at Baldwin Hills Pilot & Gifted Magnet School. Stacey has served as a partner and guiding teacher for graduate students in the U.C.L.A. Teacher Education Program. Teaching her Joyteam students the power of knowledge, self-advocacy and justice are the core of her practice. Stacey is a poet at heart with one self-published book and several poems published in Savant Poetry Anthologies. Stacey is mom to her grown son, daughter, and a Himalayan cat.

Short Prompt
Consider songs and lyrics that inspire you. Write down some favorite lines.
Write in your journal about a topic that comes to the surface. Intersperse lyrics throughout.

Full Prompt
I am including the full below, so open your notebook or device and follow along with educator Stacey Joy's inspiration about music and feelings.[1]

> **Inspiration:** Music is the source of beauty, memories, and emotions. When I was experiencing a dark and depressing period of my life, I turned to poetry and music for healing. Find something in music or lyrics that brings you peace and healing to write a musical poem today. This could be done with students when they're experiencing stressful times (like now).

> **Process:** Spend some time listening to music or reading lyrics. Write as you listen or write after you've read some lyrics. Find some music terms that resonate with your spirit. Dig deep in your soul to find something on which to focus your poem. It could be an emotion that needs to be shared, a pain that needs to heal, a love that you need to express. Then write and find ways to include musical terms to make it a harmonious symphony of words.
> These links have an extensive list of music terms: ClassicFM[2] and Classical Music.[3]

Stacey's Poem

Riffs and Runs by Stacey L. Joy

Floating in the middle of the ocean
Surrounded by its rhythmic reverie
Chaotic syncopations of my life
Fade away on foamy bubbles
Crying for the cadence
Of love imagining its loss
Like lyrical letters written
In sinking sand beneath my feet
My staccato heart beats
To find a safe space
Between riffs and runs
and a wispy lullaby
Oh harmonious calore
Harp song to my pain
Be my orchestral poem
A requiem for my soul

Denise's Suggestions for the Classroom
Students, as you know, come to us each in a different place emotionally and developmentally. Some will love the invitation to "Dig deep in your soul to find something on which to focus your poem" while others may hide from that idea. Wherever your students are and whatever they choose to write about, please accept it as a legitimate expression of what they chose to focus on today in their musical poems. Can you imagine the heartbreak if someone told you you didn't dig very deep in a poem you wrote?

- Help students be in community to read and respond to each other's poems in a safe place.
- Provide sentence starters as needed to help them write positive comments for their peers:
  - I can relate to _____ because _____.
  - Your words "_____" really moved me because_____.
- In addition, please always give your students the option to reject the prompt altogether and write what they need to.

Links
[1] https://www.ethicalela.com/5of30verselove/
[2] https://www.classicfm.com/discover-music/musical-terms/
[3] https://www.classical-music.com/features/musical-terms/musical-terms-dictionary

CHAPTER 8

Trenches and Summits: The Private Lives of Teachers

Kim Johnson

One week before the school year ended, I was having lunch with two friends, discussing our plans for summer and what we'd done over Memorial Day weekend. Life was good in that hour, and we laughed and dreamed of the slower-paced days ahead. Two hours later, I was taking inventory of manipulatives in the Pre-K Literacy Lab when one of them called saying she was on her way to the hospital. Her husband was being transported by helicopter from his work to the Intensive Care Unit as paramedics fought to save his life. The urgency of this medical emergency prompted the other friend and me to leave work early to be with her. We arrived as she exited the ICU in shock after just finding out he was on full life support, and the prognosis was not good. As the three of us sat together silently in the seriousness of those moments at the table by the vending machine, closed off from a room full of her husband's work family and awaiting her children to arrive, she confided in us as she faced the darkest hours of her life.

I don't want a meal train, and I don't want anything on social media. I want to have private time with my children to grieve.

In those moments, we felt her heartbeat and understood that she needed her own grieving time to gather the strength she'd need for the days ahead. Even though neither of us had ever faced the reality of losing a spouse, we'd certainly had our own crisis situations that helped us understand the desperate need to be alone to have time to process the reality of the moment, to attempt to make sense of the surreal.

Privacy and Secrecy

I reflected, in those moments after leaving the hospital, about the private lives of teachers and the ways we navigate our challenges behind the veils of reality in a public spotlight. Memory took me back to my own most recent extended crisis six years ago to the day I'd seen a social media post. I'd breathed a sigh of relief as I'd read and reread the Facebook post shared by a close friend of my daughter's — Lisa, a 27-year-old recovering drug addict who, in just three words - *We do recover* - and a picture of herself with a sincere smile sporting all new white teeth to replace her real ones the methamphetamines stole, offered a glimmer of hope to all those struggling with addiction and their loved ones. Beside her was her 8 year old daughter, and in her arms her 3 month old daughter, back together as a family once again after her time in a drug rehabilitation facility. Missing was the baby's father, who had recently died of a drug overdose.

Even as the sense of relief swept over me because my own daughter, too, had completed a lengthy recovery and had miraculously survived a heroin addiction to tell her story, I felt the familiar heat of the need for secrecy. What teacher in the public eye could celebrate a daughter's graduation from a year-long recovery program without fearing the judgment and scorn of those who may threaten to cast stones? Whether we need privacy or keep secrecy, we all face struggles during which we need time alone followed by understanding and support of others.

Crisis sometimes seem to have the domino effect for those in the sandwich years between aging parents and adult children when the problems avalanche into our lives from all sides. The years leading up to that day in November 2019 when I'd seen my daughter's friend's post had been a proverbial train wreck, fueled by the prolonged illness and death of my mother, who had encouraged me through the years to earn a doctoral degree in education and who died only ten months shy of cheering me across that marathon finish line. My work demands and living five hours away in addition to navigating the strong currents of that degree program had left little time for me to be a part of Mom's final year of life. My guilt, coupled with unrelenting grief, was overwhelming.

Mom's Parkinson's Disease with Lewy Body Dementia had knocked the world off its axis and left our family spinning in orbit. As a full-time teacher seeking a graduate degree, sandwiched between the waning health of my mother and an adult daughter who was trapped in an abusive relationship and drug use, there was far too little oxygen left in my own mask to be able to help anyone. Work and student deadlines, death timelines, and drug and relationship worries hole-punched me, leaving no room for other children, grandchildren, or my husband. I felt like a dinghy lost at sea trying to stay afloat in the treacherous waves, pummeled first one way and then jerked another. We'd all found ways of coping, but healing was an entirely different matter in the ripples of the ever-present grief that remained after our tidal wave of loss.

Enter Poetry

As a preacher's kid growing up on an island in coastal Georgia in the 1970s, I'd tested most of my bad-behavior limits as a child who stole chalk from the Sunday School class to play school in the backyard. The one solid grounding force that kept me in check was an obsession with poetry that all started with a knock on the door. When the World Book Encyclopedia salesman came calling at 208 Martin Street on St. Simons Island, my parents bought the full 1974 set and the bonus set of Childcraft volumes 1 through 15, beige with the colorful rainbow of numbers on the spines. I never made it to Volume 2 because *Volume 1: Poems and Rhymes* mesmerized me so much that I spent hours on the floor of my closet with the flashlight reading, rereading, fixating on the rhymes and rhythms of language. *Overheard on a Salt Marsh* by Harold Munro was the poem I read at least a dozen times a day over the span of a few years. I felt a connection between the nymph and the goblin in that setting on an island cradled on its west side by the Marshes of Glynn.

When a childhood friend and I started writing poems back and forth to each other in elementary school, I knew then that I wanted to be a teacher so that I could live in the world of reading and writing. So much depended on reading Childcraft Volume 1 on my closet floor under the flashlight, beside the fluffed pillows. A seed of interest bloomed and grew throughout my life from those early days, and a cast of colorful poets paraded through the years as I moved through the stages of life. This was the passion that led me to become a teacher, moving from preschool to elementary, from middle to high school, from school Literacy Coach to District Literacy Specialist for my school system in rural Georgia. After thirty years in education, I look back through the telescope over all the years of life with wonder about the magic of a single moment and its power to shape the future. Reading poetry was my magic, and I wished this same magic for children everywhere.

And poetry was the saving grace when life took unexpected turns all at once, leaving me feeling helpless and hopeless. So many mornings of pouring my tea alongside Mary Oliver and Billy Collins, Lucille Clifton and Robert Louis Stevenson, Sylvia Plath and Edna St. Vincent Millay. Roots of childhood poetry only strengthened in adulthood, and these were no imaginary friends I'd grown up knowing. I longed for the connection I'd felt with Missy, my friend with whom I'd written poems in school, but I thought it would seem strange to reach out on Facebook to ask if she'd like to return to our playground days of swapping poems at recess.

Enter Ethicalela.com

At the National Council of Teachers of English (NCTE) Convention, I attended a session led by Sarah J. Donovan, whose contact cards were on each chair. On the back of mine, she'd penned, "Thanks for coming! Free book!" I couldn't wait to see what I'd won, overjoyed to discover that she was giving away a copy of her autobiographical YA novel in verse entitled *Alone Together.* Equally appealing was an invitation to write with her poetry group during the month of VerseLove, a celebration of National Poetry Month, on her website www.ethicalela.com.[1] I eagerly joined, discovering the magic of writing poetry with others once again, just as I had done with Missy as a child. I didn't know it at the time, but the years ahead would bring powerful connections with poets I would come to meet in person at future NCTE gatherings, and alongside whom I would bear witness to life — its hopes, its joys, its laughter and scars. Our monthly gathering of writers have become family — all of whom have experienced trauma and are healing from deep wounds. Our poems bear witness to our journeys. Betrayal. Divorce. Death. Illness. Depression. Anxiety. Despair. Addiction. Loss. And more.

Poetry Prompts Healing

I opened the website and read the day's Open Write prompt from my favorite chair by the window in the living room, my computer opened on my oversized lap desk and my journal off to the right side, allowing me to scribble some notes. Sarah Donovan's prompt *Overcoming a Struggle* invited teacher poets to write rhyming couplets about a time that we'd prevailed in a struggle. She inspired us by leading us to reflect on our greatest struggle and to tell the story of how we overcame or were overcoming it and further urged us to consider how enduring the struggle changed us. She encouraged us to write in rhyming couplets, but reminded us, as always, to write as we felt led. Finally, she showed us with an example and mentor poem that a couplet is made up of two-line stanzas with the final word of each line rhyming. Here is Sarah's poem:

Public Speaking by Sarah Donovan

Most days it is a struggle to be
part of a world that is all about me.
This is not to say that I am not self-absorbed.
I am always worried, not worthy of being adored.
but for people to listen to what I have to say,
they need to know my words, face, and ways,
and, for me, that is a struggle.
I want students to have a voice
in what they read and write, a choice.
I want them to create –not fill in
worksheets that restrict, ideas dim.
I want them to collaborate without screens,
to look into one another's eyes and being.
The struggle is not in here but out there.
How do I help them everywhere?
For that, I have to go into real, virtual worlds,
show my face, use my voice, publish words
worried no one will care, or worse, will judge
what I say, how I speak and not budge.
To overcome, I think,
"It's not about me
but the literacy lives of teens."
Then, speaking out gets easier.

I closed my eyes and considered the mountain of possibilities for this poem. I grabbed a pen and jotted down on a fresh journal page all the struggles that came to mind as I had these conversations with myself. I brainstormed for two full minutes on the left side and left space to begin composing on the right, also writing words that came to mind as I thought through the struggles. Here is my list:

- Hit by a drunk driver waiting for my school bus in 1979 - still have nightmares about the car careening toward me.
- I went through a wicked awful divorce in 2005.
- I suffered a miscarriage in 1991.

- Grew up under the microscope as a preacher's kid in the Deep South.
- One of my daughters' addiction/recovery.

And these were just some of the topics from the many struggles I could have listed.

My Poem

Thinking of the universality of struggle and the growing problems of substance abuse led me to write about my daughter's struggle from a mother's perspective. As part of her work with Celebrate Recovery, my daughter shares her story of addiction and gave her permission for me to share the poem and where her addiction began. In the midst of my mother's illness, my daughter's pain of childbirth and euphoria of prescription painkillers eased both childbirth pains and the emotional pains of loss. When the painkillers grew too weak, she set out on a treacherous journey into harder drugs. A journey of the loss of custody of her child, an abusive relationship, homelessness, and jail. A journey of the will to live, of recovery, of doing the hard work of the soul, of getting back on her feet. She celebrated six years of sobriety in June 2024 — and I still treasure those words on her friend's Facebook post that glimmered in shimmers of hope: *We do recover.*

Trenches and Summits by Kim Johnson

A world of drugs – of heroin and meth
Led my firstborn child down a dark road of death
Her journey began with the birth of her son
Her sleepy glazed smiles fooled everyone
We saw a proud mother adoring her child
Not knowing she had painkillers stockpiled
Doctors whose orders seem helpful and kind
Can be the start of a helpless decline
Addiction abducted with needling claws
The kind that gives mothers a new prayerful cause
But as walls kept on crumbling and tearing her down
Her family kept praying that she would be found
And God heard our prayers – she landed in jail.
Her once healthy body was sallow and frail

I'm ready, she said. *I want to get well.*
We know, we assured her, *you've marched straight through*
hell.
And what's happened since then is a miracle still
An addict recovering and seeking God's will
She now works with others to steer and to guide
To help those who need one like her by their side
The thing about trenches so treacherous and bleak
Is that they become summits that others will seek.

Our poems share reassurance that no matter our situation, there is hope for healing. As a traumatic experience is being lived and the pain is being borne, poetry acts a witness and gives a vent to recount and share the lived trauma and otherwise private anguish with others (Akhtar, 2000). Rather than reaching for an evening glass of wine or a sleeping pill to stop my mind from spinning when I'm feeling down, I reach for a book of poetry, a journal and a pen. The simple acts of meditating, of thinking in rhyme and rhythm, of considering analogies and metaphors to my own dark places help me cope during times in life when no matter which way I look, sadness and despair permeate the landscape. Poetry not only brings peace to my mind and soul, but peaceful moments with Mary Oliver and humorous verses of Billy Collins and life-is-real moments with Lucille Clifton remind me that I'm not the only one who experiences troubling times.

My writing group, too, was a healing heap of people all in recovery from life's disappointment and despair. Each writer brought beautiful scars - powerful reminders that *we do recover* from heartaches. Testaments to the triumph of recovery from divorce. A chorus of voices singing the music of recovery from losses of loved ones — parents, spouses, children. Yes, we do recover from abusive relationships. We do recover from childhood trauma and physical injury. We do recover. We all do — from something. And from those darkest hours of life emerge the most powerful poems of all, offering hands to hold — hands of those who have been there.

When I look back today on the poem I wrote in response to Sarah's prompt about a struggle, I cringe a little, want to cry a few tears, and all at once want to fall on my knees in thanksgiving for the miracle of drug recovery for now not one daughter, but two daughters. I'm rarely a rhyming poet, but sometimes the need for rhyme helps me think in other ways — the attention to detail and word choice even more finite in rhyming poems for me, so when I read a poem I've crafted using rhyme, I realize that the engagement with structure and wording was another layer of engagement for me. As a poet, I tend to write poems of anger and sadness with rhythm and rhyme, but poems of epiphany or discovery or meditations on life are mostly non-rhyming. Sometimes, the holistic knowing of self and the ways I feel the need to write are barometers of what is happening in my life at the time—and sometimes, predictors that something troubling may be on the horizon. My subconscious senses a ripple and poetry rushes in to heal a forthcoming wound, like white blood cells coming to the rescue even before the blow.

This is why I continue to write daily. My obsession with reading poetry as a child bloomed into writing poetry as an adult. I didn't know it at the time, but the roots of reading poetry as a child fixated on the page would sustain me and ground me as I navigated the years ahead. I began, in those early days, to read between the lines—to look for the inexplicit messages, to look for the invisible ink that revealed itself to those who would join the quest with seeking eyes. I wanted this for all children, so as a teacher I made poetry a priority in my classes from primary school to high school. My second graders could recite "A Visit from St. Nicholas" by Clement C. Moore with all the hand movements and twinkling eyes. My high school students chuckled at the innuendo in Emily Dickinson's "A Narrow Fellow in the Grass" and felt the silence of the empty womb in "The Death of the Ball Turret Gunner" by Randall Jarrell.

Human nature wants to sweep problems under the rug. Human nature is the proverbial ostrich, burying its head in the sand to avoid the struggles and pains of life. Poetry, however, wants to confront a legion of demons and scorch them with a torch, then pick them up and thank them for the scars of experience. But poetry doesn't stop there. It wants to do an autopsy. Poetry wants to reveal what the mind and heart have first rejected, finally embraced— to share the journey so that others know what to do with the snags of life. Encouraging words of my family of fellow writers reinforce this importance of sharing the journey. In our stories, in our poetry, in our life experiences, we shine a light on hope and healing by revealing our struggles.

Powerful reminders of the collective power of healing began to emerge in response to my poem. Stacey Joy commented:

Kim, First of all I am grateful to read that your daughter is in recovery and helping others on the journey. It's healing to be able to share and better yet, to make pain become poetry.

I knew the sincerity of her words. She and I both write often of the impact of the loss of our mothers on our own lives and the gaping holes in our hearts.

Glenda Funk wrote:

My admiration for you and your bravery has grown ten-fold. Thank your daughter for being brave, too. Your poem is beautifully crafted, but it's the honesty and trust in us your readers that means most to me.

Her words reminded me of the power of relationships in a writing group. Somewhere in the courage to share the truth of our journey, trust was earned through honesty. Poets who bare truths and expose the pain along the way assure readers that they are not alone in whatever they may be experiencing—whether their children are caught in the grip of addiction, whether they have lost a loved one, or are dealing with illness. Whatever the heartache, hope is found in verse.

Glenda's words also shed light on the importance of taking the time for privacy or secrecy to do the hard work of the soul, but then to emerge from that darkness with not just our own light, but a light to share with others who find themselves where we've been. To come alongside another, offer a hand, and show the way through the trenches and tunnels so that others, too, may step into the light.

Your Turn

You will find that Sarah Donovan is the most giving of writers, educators, editors, and mentors, and her prompt will nurture you, just as your own writing will

Short Prompt
Pick up a pen and begin right where you are. Make a list of challenges you have faced, and jot down five or six of them in list form. Don't worry about secrecy or privacy — this is just for you. Next, circle one you wish to write about. Jot down some phrases and words, and come up with some simple rhyming words to form rhyming couplets. You can decide how many lines you'd like to write. For now, just begin. If it helps to set a timer, try this and give yourself 5 minutes before you continue reading. Poetry does not have to be a masterpiece to be healing. It only has to be offered from where we are standing in the moment. I'll go first.

Step Into the Light

We're all a bit scared to put thoughts down in ink
Frankly, we're tired. We don't want to think.

But when we join hands and step into the light,
We find that, together, we heal when we write!

Full Prompt
Inspiration: Sarah's prompt became an invitation for every reader to pause and write a poem, to swim in secret memories of pain, regret, embarrassment, despair, grief, anxiety, depression, fear, and even shame. Give yourself permission to write about these things, and to keep your poem in a safe place until it is ready to be offered to the world. Give yourself permission to never offer it to the world and to keep it only for yourself. Give yourself permission to try, to flop like a young gymnast whose first attempts at writing look a lot like a cartwheel landing in the bushes before ever becoming a roundoff-back-handspring on a floor mat. Try it, and feel the magic, even if you have never written a poem before. Sarah's prompt: Overcoming

Process: Find a pen or a pencil without an eraser (accept here and now that there are no mistakes worthy of an eraser). Take a blank piece of paper and read the prompt below, similar to

Sarah's original prompt. Reflect on your own greatest struggle, however you define it, and give the elephant in the room a peanut. Invite elephant conversation, the kind we all want to talk about but no one ever does. Close your eyes and think about what you and the elephant in the room would say to someone embarking on the same struggle, just before they stick their toe into the calm waters where the rushing rapids await them around the next bend. Whisper aloud your story of what they need to know—how you overcame or are overcoming what they will face. Consider how enduring the struggle has changed you. How did this change who you were, how you acted, and how you saw the world?

Try to write your poem in couplets today. A couplet is a poem made up of two-line stanzas with the final word of each line rhyming.

> To meet, to know, to love–and then to part,
> Is the sad tale of many a human heart.
> –Samuel Taylor Coleridge

- The two lines rhyme in this couplet, and both lines have a similar number of syllables.
- This is called meter, which gives the poem rhythm. RhymeZone.com[2] can help you with rhyming.

I recognize healing and recovering as a lifelong process that is girded in commitment, stamina, determination, mindset, habit, drive, forgiveness, grace, mercy, human weakness, and divine strength. Poetry is all of this, and more.

Kim's Suggestions for the Classroom

A conversation with a college art student who struggled to write comes to mind to remind me that the struggle is real. I'd given her the advice to listen to her thoughts in her head and to write them all down as a way to get started on her writing. I was her tenth grade English teacher, and she graduated college in May 2024. We have kept in touch through the years. When she came to visit and showed me her portfolio of art pieces, I remarked that I wished I could sketch and paint with her talent. I'll never forget the lesson she taught me in her response.

"It's easy," she urged me, "you just envision the picture in your head and draw what you see."

Then I understood— not every writer hears the little voice in their heads with enough detail to write it down, just as not every artist sees the picture with enough detail to draw it. The use of a voice recorder on a cell phone might help for writers who need a place to start; if they can speak their thoughts into the recorder, it will help them with what to write.

One strategy my student shared that had helped her with wordplay was having pun wars. We'd take a word—like farms or chickens, for example, and every time we could relate our classroom conversation to chickens, we'd make a pun. He had a fowl attitude, we'd say of a character, or she was eggstravagant in her tastes. Every few days we'd pick a new word and volley the puns to build vocabulary and build word banks while keeping the conversation lively and fun. This worked for her as a writing strategy—building a word bank to twist for poems.

- Show students how to use RhymeZone.com and other tools to find rhyming words.
- Write alongside students, tapping syllables and going through the think aloud process of writing.
- Invite students to share if they'd like, and teach students how to give positive feedback. (See the Complimenting Writers chart on page 29.)

References

Akhtar, S. (2000). Mental pain and the cultural ointment of poetry. *International Journal of Psychoanalysis, 81*, 229–243.

Munro, Harold. (1974). Overheard on a Salt Marsh. *Childcraft. Volume 1: Poems and Rhymes.* Chicago: Quarrie & Co.

Links

[1] http://www.ethicalela.com
[2] https://www.rhymezone.com/

CHAPTER 9

In and Out and Back Again: The Journey into Therapy
Susan Ahlbrand

You can't go back and change the beginning, but you
can start where you are and change the ending.
—C.S. Lewis

In 2018, I encountered some medical issues that threw my life into constant chaos. At one of our son's ball games, I started feeling "off." My heart started racing, my body was covered in cold sweat, my head was cloudy, and I could barely put together words. This type of scenario repeated itself numerous times at different times and different places. I would be rendered immobile with fleeing the scene being foremost in my mind.

Each time, I assumed I was having a medical event. I ended up in the ER a time or two with eventual outcomes being referrals to a cardiologist and a neurologist. As each test revealed nothing of concern, I would journey down the rabbit hole of naturopathic/functional medicine looking for reasons for my constant lack of equilibrium. Was it red dye? Too little protein? A recent root canal? The potential causes were many in our scary world. A naturopathic healer had me downing shots of a tincture he concocted multiple times a day. I went to yoga multiple times a week. I prayed like crazy and gobbled up every book and scripture on peace.

Nothing helped.

As a middle school teacher of 30 years, it was a massive challenge to get up and go to work and spend my days attempting to teach English language arts to a classroom full of eighth graders. For the entirety of my career to this point, I had been comfortable teaching in the small southern Indiana town where pretty much everyone knew everyone. During this stretch, however, I found the familiarity and interconnectedness of the community to be suffocating. I worried that the nurse at the cardiologist's office would pass judgment when things came back okay. I had her daughter in class, and I worried she would question my stability. For the first time ever, I longed for anonymity.

I dropped 30 pounds. I limited going places out of fear, but as a mother of four kids under 19, I didn't have much of a choice. I tremored my way through work and life responsibilities. I looked for exits constantly, and my head was filled with interior dialogue convincing myself to stay wherever I was. I stood in front of my classroom full of student desks arranged in pods of six having an out-of-body experience most days. I seemed to always be concocting a reason to leave the room and gather myself. The ninety minutes each group of students was with me seemed to drag on interminably. I continue to wonder what those students must have thought. I spent my evenings scrolling sources for answers. My life consisted of feeling completely off-kilter and digging through Google for answers.

At one point, I hit rock bottom: my husband of 25 years came home to find me in a fetal position on our bedroom floor with me imploring him to commit me to an insane asylum. While he knew that wasn't necessary and didn't do that, it was clear I was at a crossroads where I could no longer zombie my way through my days. I submitted to the medical world and met with a nurse practitioner in the local hospital's counseling center, leaving my "Voodoo healer" as my friends called it.

It was in entering the world of mental health care that I realized what a struggle it was for people to get help. When I finally submitted to calling for an appointment, I was told I could be seen in six weeks. I have found that once someone reaches out for help, they needed it a long time before they made the effort. Now that I was willing to get help, I couldn't believe I had to wait so long. As luck would have it, the office manager taking the call was a former student of mine unbeknownst to me at the time. She called me back an hour later and had created a place in the schedule for me. I could be seen the next day. Oh, I was reminded of the blessings of a small town, which helped stem my yearning for anonymity.

The next day, I sat in the office across from a compassionate woman and shared my journey. She asked questions and patiently waited for responses. Because I was in a Catholic hospital and due to my having shared that I was disappointed that I couldn't pray away the feelings I was experiencing, she even asked to pray with me. I was taken off guard but found great comfort in her manner. She put me at ease that I was not going crazy but that I was dealing with what was called "panic disorder." With the right medication and counseling, she promised that the outlook was encouraging.

Call me ignorant or in denial, but I didn't really even know or understand what anxiety was, much less panic disorder. With medical care, experimentation with the right meds (I was absolutely convinced I would not submit to being a pill taker after watching each of my parents rely on prescription pills throughout life), and a fabulous therapist, I started to emerge from the dark. It would have made sense for my therapist to be at the hospital's counseling center where the nurse practitioner was, but because our school corporation had an Employee Assistance Plan set up for five free visits with a therapist at a different facility, I ended up with a therapist there. It complicated things to have to schedule appointments at two different facilities. And, the number of appointments clogged up both my work schedule and personal schedule, so I was always feeling as if an explanation was in order. At first, I would simply tell people that I "had an appointment," being purposefully vague as to what kind. But after a few sessions, I realized that owning my experience was going to be part of emerging from the darkness. So, I returned to the "open book" me I was before the descent and openly told all "I have therapy."

The path out of the darkness was not quick or easy. The first anti-anxiety medication I was prescribed seemed to worsen my symptoms. Next came some trial and error with different meds, leaving me incredibly frustrated. Eventually, the nurse practitioner ordered genetic testing, which revealed the psychotropic medications that work with and against one's metabolism. After discovering that there were only three that worked for me, the potential pool was made much smaller, and we landed on a medication and dosage that lessened my panic episodes.

While continuing to piece my life back together, I came across a free read on Kindle Unlimited: the verse novel *Alone Together* by Sarah Donovan. As fate (or God if you so believe) tends to do, I was led to Sarah's website that drew me in because of its name: Ethical ELA. Once again, down the rabbit hole I went. Sarah's introductory narrative that mentioned a number of leaders in the field of reading and writing that I had learned about in both my undergraduate work at Indiana University and my graduate work at University of Southern Indiana pulled me in. Then, I clicked on a video of her talking about creating safe spaces for our students and I was hooked. I spent hours reading post after post that I knew would enhance my teaching, but it was when I fortuitously saw a post promoting Open Writes that my world was changed. Within that digital universe, I found a sanctuary and the third piece to my healing: a community of teachers who wrote poetry together.

All of this backstory has a point: in writing, especially poetry, I discovered healing in a way that no pill, no therapist, no prayer, and no yoga pose could. For five days a month, a different teacher crafted an inspiration for writing each day. Some steered us toward a new form; some to a specific topic. Regardless of the prompt, my brain and heart worked together and created. I found a conduit through which I could process and express everything I had experienced.

My life stabilized. After a few months with the right medication and many sessions with a fabulous therapist (who happened to be exactly what I needed even though on paper he was everything I didn't want . . . a middle-aged man with no children), I started to feel hope. I incorporated coping strategies that he provided as well as following some suggestions offered by both my priest and my massage therapist. I truly felt that I was being restored — rebuilt into a functioning human being.

I have always loved to write, but I found during these months and years that written expression was a key component to my recovery. I journaled some. But the real insight and processing came through the monthly poetry writing (and reading) I did on Ethical ELA. I found a community of teachers from all walks of life in all parts of the country who vulnerably shared their writing. In turn, they compassionately commented on other writer's poems. I felt seen and understood for the first time maybe ever. There were days that I felt the prompt was designed specifically for me as it allowed me to dig deeply into some of the traumatic events I had uncovered through therapy.

On February 15, 2021, Rex Muston posted a prompt titled "Out and Back." In a nutshell (the full prompt can be found at the end of the chapter), it presented us with the challenge of writing about a Road Trip, real or metaphorical, where we were deeply changed after going from point A to point B.

For these prompts, we are supposed to write our output in a short amount of time; I seldom do. I had adopted the habit of getting up earlier in the morning to allow time to read the prompt and begin writing. Our living room couch became the place where I sat with my laptop perched on my criss-cross-applesauce knees. I tried not to read the poems that had been posted already, in fear that they might influence me unduly or intimidate me too much.

With a cup of warm hazelnut coffee nested in my hands, I pondered various trips that had changed me. All of them shared trauma. I wasn't surprised. We had recently gone through an in-service training at school on trauma-informed care, which helped all of us to realize how challenging it was for students to learn when weighed down by deeply-rooted trauma.

It was in the brainstorming, the trying to decide which "road trip" to write about, that I realized that so much of my writing served to help me process and reflect, and ultimately, to heal. I felt like I had quite a few options for writing in response to Rex's awesome prompt, but I landed on the choice of writing about my first time walking into therapy. What began as a very private journey—due in part to the stigma associated with mental health concerns—was becoming an opportunity for advocacy for me. My beloved therapist, who had helped me uncover so much, had just passed away unexpectedly. I wanted and needed to capture the experience and to reflect on his influence on me. Here is the poem that I wrote as a result of Rex's prompt:

Leading Me out of the Dark by Susan Ahlbrand
in memory of Doug Hayworth

I trudge from my car
into the facility,
head down,
the weight of the world–
my world–
on my shoulders.
Seeing a therapist
was not something
I anticipated.

I see others . . .
derelicts,
nut cases,
court-mandated losers,
lunatics . . .
sitting in the waiting room.
I feel like a criminal

116

when I check in.
My face flushes with embarrassment,
maybe even shame.
Oh, the stigma.

I sit without making eye contact
or acknowledging the others.
I would typically tap my foot,
pick up a magazine,
engage with someone.
But, I am a zombie
eaten up with anxiety
nerve endings protruding
out of my skin
leading me to feel
Everything.
I can't even muster up
movement.

Helpless
Hopeless
Embarrassed
Shame-filled
Not wanting to live
But swearing I'm not suicidal.

A tall, lean man with gray hair approaches me
and asks if I'm Susan.
I wanted a woman with children
who could relate with my experiences.
I get a middle-aged childless man.
I would roll my eyes
if I had enough vigor to.

We stroll to his office,
him leading the way
with an amble of easy confidence
I didn't know was possible.
I follow like a scolded child,
wanting to make eye contact
with no one,

carrying my own weight
a huge task.

He escorts me to a chair
sitting across from him
the room a little more spartan
than I expected.
Some fiddle objects and play toys
line the shelf and counter,
diplomas and certificates of completion
patchwork the wall,
a large window with a wooded area
to my right,
a gadget looking like a mini-billboard
sits on a stand to my left.
He summons me to
electronically sign the paperwork,
he even less tech-savvy than I.
After a few pleasantries,
including talk of baseball, Catholicism, and Terre Haute,
he poses some
open-ended questions to me for an hour
and he listens.

Listens
with no judgment
yet no trace of pity
on his face.

He listens as I unburden
things I haven't been able to say
to others . . . friends, family, my priest.
No answers are provided,
No advice is given.
No attempts to solve me.
Through the unburdending,
I feel lighter.
A little.

He leads me back
to the lobby, telling me something on the way

about his wife.
He knew I needed that connection,
that similarity to my life.
The receptionist says (with the warmest smile),
"Are we scheduling another session, Doug?"
He looks at me, tilts his head a little, raises his left eyebrow
no words needed.
I look at the kind lady's face then drop my
eyes to her tattooed wrist and mumble, "Sure."
She responds with "I figured as much. This
guy gets them all back"
followed by a flirty chuckle.

As I walk out,
the judgment is gone,
replaced with an empathy
I knew I possessed in other ways
but never dreamed I would in this one.

I lift my eyes to look at the people in the chairs.
I smile slightly
knowing now that we are far more alike than
we are unalike.

I stroll to my car
A little less helpless
A little less hopeless
A little less embarrassed
A little less shame-filled
Wanting to live
and not wanting to die.

It was in writing this poem that I fully processed my entry into therapy and honored my therapist through recalling the experience. As I recalled and recorded the details, I became aware of the power of description. I encourage my students to use anaphora to help drive home the impact in repetition, so I was pleased that I incorporated some in my writing. Even today, I'm still struck by the word choice. There is a great distinction between "not wanting to live" and "wanting to die" and "suicidal." The denotation may be very similar, but, to me, the connotations were vastly different, and I hoped the use of those words in different places helped show that.

As much as it helped me to capture this experience, true affirmation and healing came from hearing the other teachers in the community. I heard from so many brilliant writers with such intuitive and compassionate responses. I felt strengthened and emboldened by their words. Barb wrote:

> Susan, wow, this is such a powerful poem. I love how you share this experience so clearly, especially about how you were feeling. I am so sorry you've lost your counselor. Thank you for pulling me into this place and experience so I could also meet Doug. He clearly made a difference not only in your life, but also in other's. Unburdening our pain, our suffering is so incredibly daunting, and I love how you showed the positive impact of being able to share your feelings because that experience made an important difference from how you felt to how you empathized with others. My truest and deepest thanks to you for sharing your experience through this incredible poem! Hugs and peace to you, Susan! Barb

Barb's genuine feedback confirmed my choice to put such a personal poem out in a public space. She was appreciative that I shared my experience! Maybe, just maybe, she needed to hear that others struggled similarly to her. Maureen commented:

> Susan, thank you for this beautiful, open poem. I am again reminded what a gift this community is, such safe and caring sharing. I wonder if you could ever share this poem with this therapist's family? He was truly doing great work, and your words might help them in their own healing from grief. You, too, are doing great work; this poem shows the tremendous work of taking care of ourselves in our darkest times—you are brave and strong! Thank you for sharing this.

Thanks to Maureen's prompting, I did indeed share it with Doug's wife. And I have since shared poems with others who I thought would benefit from my words. She helped me to see that our words can be gifts to others.

And Cara shared how reading my poem reminded her of her own healing:

> This is such a beautiful portrayal of the difficulties of seeking help—and why so many do not. Those who are "Helpless
> Hopeless
> Embarrassed
> Shame-filled
> Not wanting to live
> But swearing I'm not suicidal."
> Need to read this so they know they're not alone. Isn't that the beauty of poetry, after all? Showing bits of ourselves to offer connection to our readers? Thank you for your honesty, for making me remember my own demons and the warriors who helped me, and for the truth in your words.

Cara's words helped me to see the value in connection, in seeing others who feel like us. We are not alone! More and more, I began to recognize the community being developed through the reciprocity of sharing and commenting on these poems. For some reason, I felt much more willing to share things with these "strangers" than with people in my "real" life. I once wrote a poem in homage to our group and titled it "strangerfriends." I think there is something in the loose tethers that offers freedom.

With our online community, I always get as much, if not more, out of reading the other writers' poems. I sit in so much awe—sometimes downright envy—at what they create, but more so my empathy has grown tenfold. Instead of being intimidated, I decided to be inspired and each month, I strive to be as open and skilled as the other writers.

For this particular poem prompt, the other teachers in our group wrote about a variety of journeys, but one that stuck out to me so much was written by Gayle Sands, who had to take a sick day

121

on March 13, 2020. As most will recall, that was THE DAY that so many schools shut down, never to return (unknowingly, of course) for the rest of that year. It was also the year Gayle was retiring, so she missed out on the end of the year *and* the end of her career. Her poem brilliantly captured that situation, and I was left speechless and tearful by her ending:

(Untitled) by Gayle Sands

Months later,
I entered my stuffy room
and said a final farewell
to the walls
and the learning
and all that love.
Boxed up my soul
and hauled it home.

This is the way my world changed...
Not with a bang, but a whimper.

I was so touched by the image of boxing up her soul along with her belongings. And, as one who very much values the recognition and pomp and circumstance of endings, the "not with a bang, but a whimper" made me sob for her and the lack of closure and celebration she had in her career.

I am certain writing that poem and revisiting that situation almost a year later unearthed even more emotion for Gayle and the rest of us who read her words. Her poem prompted baby steps toward healing from the Covid shutdown for all of us.

In the two and a half years since I wrote to Rex's prompt, I have processed many, many emotions and life happenings through writing poems. The countless ways this online poetry community helped its members navigate Covid-19 and everything associated with it could be a volume all of its own. Many of the monthly prompts provided by the members of our community have led me down many paths into territory I needed to travel. I processed becoming an empty-nester, being the oldest teacher in my hallway, having unresolved family issues, dealing with the pitfalls and frustrations of education, uncovering the helplessness of dealing with students with a plethora of concerns, and appreciating the dynamics of lifelong friendship to name just a few.

In turn, I have made the same practice core to my classroom, offering regular writing time with some directed prompts to help the 8th graders I teach to capture and process the things that they feel. I even shared my poem about therapy with my students so they could see the danger in stereotypes and hopefully destigmatize therapy! That day, the words poured out of them as they captured trips out and back that had changed them. (To read more about how I incorporated this into my classroom and to read some student examples see Chapter 13 in Part II.)

We make countless trips each day, each month, each year. Most of our days consist of going out and back, out and back, out and back. Most are routine and leave little impact or need for reflection. Other seemingly benign journeys hold more impact than we know. Every month, the journey I embark on with my fellow Ethical ELA writers is one that offers me time for reflection, healing, and growth. I always come out on the other side a changed and improved writer, teacher, and person.

Your Turn

Rex Muston has taught language arts and coached a bit at Keokuk High School for 25+ years. During his undergraduate years at Iowa, he worked six summer seasons in Yellowstone, and a winter in Utah. He began teaching in Keokuk after receiving his MAT in Secondary English. He credits his asthmatic childhood, growing up in Iowa City, and his time out west as having the biggest impact on his continuing desire to communicate through poetry.

Short Prompt
Now, I invite you to open up your notebook or a Doc on your computer and write. Write about anything. Write about mental health. Write about stigmas. Write about your classroom culture. Or, write about journeys you have taken In and Out and Back Again. Anything goes.

Full Prompt
I am including the full prompt below so you can open your notebook or device and follow along with Rex Muston's inspiration: Out & Back (A Form).[1] (You can also go to the link for even more mentor poems.)

Inspiration: One of the first poems that really resonated with me was William Stafford's "Traveling through the Dark." I think there are so many instances, at least for me, where I am going somewhere purposeful, and then something happens that alters my perspective. Maybe it'd be considered a Road Trip form, or an Out and Back form. We are in a process going from point A to point B, and sometimes returning, when something asserts itself in a poetic sense. For me it has been weathered roadside memorials, a dead cat, the progression of road signs on a route, or the way the ice creates a glare on a rural stretch of Wisconsin highway in the darkness. It could be an out and back walk with the dogs on Sunday, or dropping off your son at the dorm.

Process: How are you different than when you started? How was the routine broken? What hyper specific thing jumped out for you to notice as a sensory trigger? How did figurative and literal sit side by side because of your changed way of looking at your journey? Could it be something as simple as walking slower, or the fact that your pupils were just dilated at the eye doctors? Do you tap into a memory of a past trip, and reprocess it? What do you see on your re-turning? Is it just seeing what is in the refrigerator, REALLY seeing what is in the refrigerator for the first time? Have fun with it, and come back to it when it has had time to fester/ferment/flower.

So much of the journey is…
The things I find when I re-turn…
I chart my forward momentum, I …
The voyage of my adolescence…
After Captain Nemo dropped me off…

Susan's Suggestions for the Classroom

Finally, while this chapter is for you, dear teacher, we'd love for you to invite students to write. If you want to try a version of this prompt with your students, here are a few things to keep in mind:

- Share the prompt and mentor poem. Allow time for processing and questions.
- Display and share a few sample poems, including your own output. It helps students to hear examples and to see you be vulnerable.
- Create a quiet environment for students to write so they can be still and listen to their thoughts.
- Encourage brainstorming. Model it. Help them see the value in writing down possible ideas and then choosing one that speaks

the most.

- Consider writing while they are . . . showing your work using a document camera so they can see your process . . . the "messiness" of drafting a poem. They need to know it's safe and encouraged to mark out, move ideas, doodle, etc. while drafting a poem.
- Consider revisiting the writing the next day to look at it with "fresh eyes" and make some revisions.
- Consider allowing for sharing time. Depending on your seating arrangement, pair and share may work, or an open mic style may as well.

Links
[1] https://www.ethicalela.com/out-back-a-form/

CHAPTER 10

Walking Through Grief with Poetry
Margaret Simon

> *Art isn't a goal to be checked from a list of goals, any more than art's value can ever be objectively codified like a kind of math; for me, at least, art is the result of my having allowed myself to stray from any marked path and to become lost. The poem is the evidence — like tracks, or footprints — of my quest into and across strange territory, the shape I've left almost as if unintentionally behind me.*
>
> — Carl Phillips

The Poem is Evidence

I came to poetry as a young teenager, revisiting the form for a brief time in college, but I did not come back to poetry until I was entering a masters program through the National Writing Project Teacher Institute almost 30 years ago. The poems I write now are my footprints in the sand, stained by tears of grief. In April of 2022, while Ethical ELA held its annual National Poetry Month daily VerseLove prompts, I was watching my father die. This was real life in-the-moment grief and teachers from across the country were there, guiding my pen to write about it, and supporting me with comments of authentic caring.

I got the call from my sister-in-law while I was teaching my first student of the day. My father had a stroke while having breakfast. I teach small groups of gifted students at two public schools, so I sent my student back to her regular class and left school to pack and drive 4 hours to my childhood city of Jackson, Mississippi. What I thought might be a few days turned into two weeks living with my mother in her independent living apartment. These few weeks in April coincided with spring break, so I was grateful I was not losing time with my students, and because I am itinerant, no substitute was called. I was able to turn off my teacher's brain and tune into my family.

My father's stroke was a shock to my world. Even at the age of 88, he was still reading about astrophysics and writing a short story.

I thought he had many more years left. I've known friends who've lost their parents, but it didn't prepare me for the deep grief I would feel when it happened to me. In addition to losing my father quickly, eleven days from his stroke, my siblings and I became more fully aware of the limitations of my mother living with Alzheimer's. Dad was her caretaker. After the stroke that left him without speech, I was visiting the ICU with Mom. He pointed to the clock which read 11:30, pointed to my mother, and pointed to his mouth telling me that it was time for my mother to have lunch. My mother had lost the ability to tell time, and until that moment, I didn't know it.

Loss of parents is profound at any age. As the oldest child, I felt a responsibility to keep my mother in her independent living home where she and my father had found a community. Along with my siblings, we decided to hire a service that would get my mother to meals daily.

Shifts such as these are life-altering. The experience shattered me. I turned to poetry. I had words. And I had an empathetic audience at Ethical ELA, so I wrote then and I continue to write through my grief.

Writing has become something more to me than what I do with students during writing workshop. If ever there was a time I could take a break, this would have been it, but I was drawn in by the prompts that helped me find a way to process the grief I was feeling. Grief can be isolating. I decided to keep an open notebook and share my thoughts with a community I had come to know as a safe place to share my writing.

On day 25 of VerseLove, just three days after my father's death, I responded to a prompt from Linda Mitchell to write a *Scientific Method* poem. She offered us 6 steps to writing using the scientific method:

1. *Make an observation*
2. *Ask a question*
3. *Form a hypothesis, or testable explanation*
4. *Make a prediction based on the hypothesis*
5. *Test the prediction*
6. *Iterate: use the results to make new hypotheses or predictions.*

The structure of the prompt offered a space for my grieving process. I took a line from Maggie Smith's poem "Good Bones": "You could make this place beautiful." I was back home in my own

127

kitchen observing and noting these observations, but at the same time feeling lost, holding a loss that I could not understand. Rather than state what was missing (my father), I decided to show it by looking at an empty chair.

Often when I don't know what to write, using another poet's line and using my own observations, I can find a way to write. The poem became like a pep talk to myself. I share poetry because I draw strength from others in a community of writers. I don't feel this sense of safety with just anyone. There needs to be norms in the group around encouragement and positive feedback. (See chapter 1.) In Ethical ELA's VerseLove space, I felt comfortable sharing.

A Place at the Table by Margaret Simon

You could make this place beautiful.
Can you place a flower in the vase and call it home?
Flowers, a white cat, a black dog, coffee brewing, what could be missing?
The empty seat at the table is cold, lonely.
I move over, sit in his chair, open the last book he was reading.
Time will fill the space at the table, even in the midst of absence.
There will be beauty again.

Fran Haley is a poet-teacher I have never met in real life, but we know each other through the sharing of poetic space on our blogs and in the Ethical ELA community. She knew of my loss and offered this comment:

> The question "can you call it home" after the loved one is gone... and to think of sitting in his chair, picking up the last book he was reading. Such a symbolic act of love, life, and legacy. Yes, there will be beauty again. Meanwhile, the ache... much comfort and peace to you and yours.

Fran spoke to specific places in the poem where she connected. She recognized that I needed to process through my voice and her comment honored me.

I thrive on this kind of feedback and students do, too. It's the seeing of the other person, that connection from your words to their heart. This kind of response takes practice and makes each person vulnerable. When we share our vulnerability with others by sharing our most fragile pieces of writing, we open ourselves to this kind of empathy. Empathy that can heal.

Grief doesn't go away, but as the year turned, my poems about my parents transformed. Poetry is transformational, if you let it. A

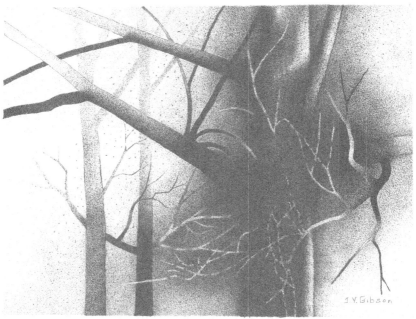

Figure 2. Trees by John Y. Gibson, Margaret's father.

mentor once told me the best poets are the ones who give themselves the most permission. Ethical ELA's prompts are handed to me with permission to be myself on the page.

The Shape He Left

My father was a pointillist artist. He made art with dots of pen and ink, dark and light. I am surrounded by his work and love feeling his presence in them, knowing that his hands touched every dot. When he had his stroke, he was sitting with a friend in the independent living facility who suffers from Parkinson's and depression. He took great pride in being a counselor to his friend. He talked about it often. He felt it was his way of giving back. (See Image 1.)

When Angie Braaten led the prompt for the June, 2023 Open Write on Ethical ELA, I was thinking (and still grieving) about my father, questioning if I could be like him. Angie's prompt was based on a poem by Chen Chen, "When I Grow Up I Want to Be a List of Further Possibilities": *Think about everything you want to be if you could be anything in the world.* Her poem brought to mind how much I want to live in my father's legacy, his art and his knowledge of how to counsel others.

When I Grow Up, I Want to Be a Painting
by Margaret Simon

> everyone stops to see,
> gathering strength or inspiration,
> a deep inhale of peace.
> Maybe a child will look
> at new possibilities – a future
> of clean air, open fields, enough
> food, enough, enough
> of all that he longs for.
> I want to be a place
> where people belong, a sanctuary
> of solace.
> When I grow up,
> I want to be like my father
> comforting a troubled victim of Parkinson's
> telling him everything will be OK.
> Am I OK?

I like how this prompt can act as a sentence starter. The title becomes the first line of the poem. I also like how repeating words can build strength inside a poem. "I want to be" is anaphora, a repeated phrase at the beginning of a line. Alliteration of s in "sanctuary of solace" is satisfying to read aloud. At the end I turn my father's reassurance to his friend toward myself. Am I OK? I'm not sure yet as I feel grieving has become a part of me and my writing.

Kim Johnson, an educator from Georgia, made a connection to my poem. She wrote:

I love all of your words, Margaret, but particularly that you want to be a place where people belong, a sanctuary of solace. My mother, too, died of Parkinson's with Lewy Body Dementia and the troubling look was always there behind the uncertain furrowed brow. The moments of reality were the real torment, I believe. Yes, I want to be there with you, too, comforting the troubled who are caught in the wicked grips of Parkinson's Disease. What a beautiful way to want to live as you grow — being a nurturing comforter, assuring all that they are OK even when you question your own OKness.

Your Turn

This prompt comes from educator Linda Mitchell, a librarian, mother, wife, animal lover, and poet. She writes a blog at A Word Edgewise.[1] When Linda is not in her school library, she is either collaging at her craft table or researching her latest project at the Library of Congress.

Short Prompt Begin with an observation. How does this observation open up a vulnerable place for you? I often have flowers on my kitchen table. Why do I do this? I once told someone I was rescuing the flowers from the supermarket. While this is fun to think about, I also find hope in flowers. And I want visitors to my table to feel that hope and comfort. What is a way you find hope? Sharing poems is like sharing a bouquet of flowers.

Full Prompt
The full prompt is included below if you'd like more support, so take your notebook or device and follow along with Linda Mitchell's inspiration: The Scientific Method.[2]

> **Inspiration:** The scientific method has five basic steps, plus one feedback step:
>
> 1. *Make an observation*
> 2. *Ask a question*
> 3. *Form a hypothesis, or testable explanation*
> 4. *Make a prediction based on the hypothesis*
> 5. *Test the prediction*
> 6. *Iterate: use the results to make new hypotheses or predictions.*
>
> This method is also a good formula for creating a poem. Here is

a model poem written by Kim Douillard who writes a blog *Thinking Through My Lens*[3] and often writes poems to photos she takes on the beaches of Southern California.

Cormorant by Kim Douillard

I see you sitting on the beach
alone, on the sand
are you lost? are you ill?

Most days you fly against the horizon
like a jet plane, pointed due north
wings in constant motion

Today you are still
feathers like midnight
eyes like stars
unperturbed by my approach

Is it avian flu?
Bird dementia?
Or just a relaxing day on the beach?

Relief pulsed through my veins
when I saw you later
floating in the surf
looking for a snack

before blasting back into the sky
continuing your coastal journey

Thanks for stopping by
and posing
for a portrait

Process: Using a photo or observation, begin writing about that observation. Then find a question in your mind about your observation. Continue writing until you feel satisfied with your words and phrases. Format into a free verse poem with line breaks and stanzas.

A poem can be a thread of yarn that weaves itself in and out of our lives. We can go away and we can come back. The invitation to write is always there. All you need to do is open to a clean page. Pain may come out, but so may joy, and most of all, hope.

Margaret's Suggestions for the Classroom

- Photos can make a wonderful jumping off place for writing with students. Have students make observations from the photo and add in their own perspectives. They could even write from the perspective of an object or character in the photo. I post a photo every Wednesday on my blog as a prompt for writing: *Reflections on the Teche*[4]

- Using a line from a mentor poem is a good way to begin if you need a jumping off place. I also ask students to collect words from a mentor poem and try to use them in their own poem.

- Consider using a timer for quiet writing time. I use an app on my phone called Insight Timer that provides ambient music. Students will usually honor the writing time if it is 10 minutes or less. After the timer stops, ask students if they need more time and give them time to come to a stopping place.

- Sharing is always optional. I try to build a safe space for sharing in my classroom by writing alongside my students and sharing my rough drafts. I also give little or no feedback. A simple "Thank you for sharing" is enough. If I find gems, I point them out "a lovely metaphor" or "that word choice helps me to see the scene in my mind."

Links
[1] https://awordedgewiselindamitchell.blogspot.com/
[2] https://www.ethicalela.com/scientific-method/
[3] https://thinkingthroughmylens.com/
[4] http://reflectionsontheteche.com

Poetic Reflections by Jennifer Cameron Paulsen

Tell It

Celebration

My husband Chuck and I struggled with infertility for five years before the blessing of a twin pregnancy arrived in June 2001. Thrilled at Lucie and Lillie's impending arrival, we made all the proper preparations — once we stopped freaking out about needing two of everything.

That June, I also took my first Iowa Writing Project (IWP) course. My writing often centered on our little miracles, and the entire group celebrated with me.

Suffering

It wasn't until I was strapped into the ambulance for Iowa City Hospitals two days after watching the 9/11 attack on CNN from my hospital bed, that I realized something must be seriously wrong. Six months along, Lucie and Lillie were in danger, but none of the doctors or nurses would look me in the eye. What did the ultrasound show?

The next morning, we could see them floating peacefully, tucked together, in the darkness of the ultrasound. No movement, no heartbeat.

We left the hospital on an impossibly sunny Saturday morning. Clear blue sky. Fresh waves of torment bolted through me as I sobbed all the way home. My husband retreated inward. The suffering was simply unspeakable. All we could do was hold each other. And respect each other's methods of grieving.

Haunted Lonesome Hours

While I could mostly keep it together during the day, I had never cried for so long and so often. Night after night, the pain dragged me to the kitchen table. I hunched over my navy steno notebook, scribbling through the haunted lonesome hours between two and five a.m., trying to pin the pain to the page:

FRAGMENT

Spiraling in this whirlpool
of burning bitter tears
cradling my empty-aching womb
I dissolve
in murky depths
vanishing
in the slipstream of shattering silence

Healing

My IWP journaling class was really the only safe space for me other than my home. Writing was truly a therapeutic act for me as well as an artistic one. Having a supportive audience for that writing, all of whom already knew the backstory and responded to my poetry with loving care, was the most healing medicine I could experience. They helped me save my own life.

Story

Twenty-three years ago I began this journey.

This is what I know:

Celebration
Suffering
Art
Love

We are all fragile beneath the surface.
All hearts of cracked glass.
Be gentle.

I also know:

Haunted lonesome hours
Healing
Story

All we can do is tell it.
Our way.

Teaching English and history for 30 years, Jenny Paulsen has been a poet since her 7th grade teacher said so.

CHAPTER 11

Pursed Lips and Pink Tutus: Perks and Pitfalls of Parents While Teaching English
Wendy Everard

Parenting while teaching is not an easy task, and parenting while teaching English can be especially hard. All teachers need time to plan and grade and do much of this on their own time, but factor in the time it takes to read and respond to piles of student essays, and it's clear that teachers with writing-heavy courses face a unique challenge.

Both of my kids were diagnosed with anxiety and depression at the onset of puberty, a predisposition to the conditions passed down to them from both sides of their family. Working with them through these difficult times while simultaneously teaching was the height of challenge. Writing was one of the most healing things that I did for myself, as a teacher and a mother, during these times.

Crafting poetry about my kids—their challenges and triumphs, their young years and older—kept me centered during these past few years of teaching. This year will be my 26th in the profession, and writing poetry regularly during my kids' pivotal teenage years and during the Covid-19 years and its aftermath in the classroom has been instrumental in giving me motivation to push forward through tough times.

My participation in a Summer Institute with the Seven Valleys National Writing Project during the summer of 2018 spurred me to revisit the poetry writing that I had loved during my young years and which had fallen by the wayside in more recent ones. But it was my participation in Ethical ELA that made poetry writing a regular and joyful habit. Kim Johnson's "Unphotographed" prompt during the November 2022 five-day Open Write, for example, inspired me to observe my daughter and tap into a lovely moment of peace and restfulness. Kim's prompt asked us to imagine an unphotographed moment, to draw on a moment from memory, and to use figurative language to breathe life into it in a poem.

Kim's prompt drew me to an image, in my mind's eye, of my sleeping daughter, Emily, and how peaceful nighttime found her— a respite from her angst-filled days at school. I sat with the prompt for a while to think on it, and my contribution, oddly, manifested in lilting rhymed couplets when I envisioned writing this poem; I kind of liked the juxtaposition of the playful rhythm with the somber subject matter:

Emily by Wendy Everard

Lips that purse like little "o"s
Comfy blankets covering toes

Blonde hair falling lightly over
Rippling o'er cozy cover

Eyes that seem at peace, at rest
She thinks bedtime is the best

I watched her like this when so small
Those years now so tough to recall

At sixteen she's the length of bed
I stare and think – "What's in her head?"

What's she wishing? What's she dreaming?
Fare for peace, or fare for screaming?

But

Her face does not a feel betray
A placid mask of overlay

In her arms, a baleful look
From cozy cat in cozy nook

Who wishes me to leave them be
And I retreat, soft, gingerly.

It was moments like these in my parenting, ones in which I was anxious for my girls, that led me to write poems reflecting on my fears and concerns for them. Reflecting on moments when my anxiety was heightened, I was able to work through my feelings, process them with careful attention in a poem, give voice to my feelings, and come away from the experience feeling some catharsis, having produced a piece of art to reflect on how I felt. Besides the therapeutic value of writing poems like these, engaging with other English teachers in the Ethical ELA community has proved invaluable in building my momentum as a writer in progress. The community that a group of writers offers can inspire teachers to reflect on and celebrate moments in their personal and academic lives in a unique way, sharing these moments with a supportive and nurturing writing community. Not only are we invited to post our work on Ethical ELA, but other writers respond to give us support, as seen in the following feedback:

> Wendy, what a sweet snapshot of Emily at 16. I see a series of poems, perhaps, in the same format about her at other ages... 'I watched her like this when so small' Precious!
> –Denise Krebs

> Wendy, mmmmmmm what a powerful scene sharing the angst of teen years and feelings parents can easily relate to. Beautifully captured! – Barb Edler

Denise's comment spurred me to follow up with another poem about my daughter, one that I wrote in response to Katrina Morrison's "Ekphrastic Poetry"[1] prompt, also from the November 2022 five-day Open Write. Katrina asked us to:

> Select a work of art. It might be a famous work only available to you online or on the pages of a coffee table book. It might be a local work of art or one hanging in your home. Perhaps, posted on your refrigerator is the work of a child or grandchild. Focus on the artwork. Find details you may have missed in prior viewings. Using whatever poetic format you choose, describe the work."

This time, I focused on a picture of Emily from her young years. Both Katrina's prompt and Denise's comment spurred memories of her and I dug out my favorite photo of her—such a juxtaposition of her lighthearted young years with the worries and anxiety that pressed upon her now! Focusing on the playfulness of the photo prompted me to approach this piece, again, with lilting rhymed couplets. As I mentioned before, sometimes when I approach poetry writing, I sit with the prompt for a bit until a fitting form reveals itself to me, be it free verse or a tighter meter or another form that seems to complement the occasion and subject matter. My contribution to the prompt was a reflection of a happier, lighter time in Em's life:

(Untitled) by Wendy Everard

Look! Here is a tiny dancer
Whirling, twirling peony prancer

Caught, there, in a moment's time
To inspire future rhyme

See what loving hands she clasps
Well eluding future's grasp

Cares and worries have to wait
As round the grounds she trips and prates

Dressed in pink once (now in grey)
She knows nothing of the day

That sadness grips this frilly form
Which small pink tutu once adorned.

No more of that, though – let's, for now
Encourage her to take a bow

To dream of friends and family – flowers –
Rainbow days and superpowers –

And shield from this cheery sprite
A grey and pond'rous second sight

And leave her to her day of peace
Where sun and good times never cease.

Again, commentary from my fellow writers on Ethical ELA proved as validating and motivating as the poetry writing was cathartic, and the community's responses illustrate the dialogic and supportive nature of our writing community:

> Oh, Wendy! Hooray! I'm so glad I came back to be able to love this second poem in your Emily series. So much to love here. It reminds me of Emily 16, in the switch at about the same place–the "But" in the first poem, and the "No more of that…" here. – Denise in California

> Wendy, I feel the NOW strongly in this poem – – celebrate the day, and let the future emerge. What a great message for all of us! – Kim in Georgia

> Wendy — There's so much joy and hope in this poem. The images were beautiful. – Tammi in Ohio

As I responded to other writers' poems, I was struck by the similarities in our subject matter, as well as the differences. Responding to other teacher-writers via Ethical ELA has the effect of exposing us to the worlds of other writers, while affirming our own themes and subjects, too. Gayle Sands' poem "I See You," a portrait of her grandfather as a young man, reminded me of my daughter, while it called attention to striking differences. The power in Gayle's final line ("Look at me. See who I am now.") provoked me to think about how a poem from Emily's perspective, written in the first person point of view, might sound, as Gayle took on the challenge of writing in her grandfather's voice. Writer Stacey Joy's poem "In Stillness" also resonated with me, as she wrote:

> We close our eyes
> kiss
> cry
> holding tears we fear will fall...

Stacey's poem called to mind my poems about Emily — particularly the one about Emily sleeping — but approached similar feelings with such a different form, structure, and tone. "Stacey," I wrote to her, "this evokes such a sense of peace — both your poem and the picture — and the pacing and structure help to do that." The sense of community that writing with a cohort of open and responsive writers has brought into my life has infused my teaching with more joy and my parenting with a heightened sense of reflection, sensitivity, and peace.

Teaching writing has been so much easier and more joyful as a result of engaging in poetry writing communities such as Ethical ELA and the National Writing Project. Not only do I participate (in both class and on Ethical ELA) as a writer, but I've passed the joy along to my students, and they have contributed to poetry prompts for Ethical ELA as well as contributing their writing to the site. We often use Ethical ELA in our English class to provide us with poetry prompts, and I couldn't be more pleased with the joy for writing that I see within my Creative Writing students. An email that I received at the end of the year from sophomore Maggie speaks to the joy that kids can derive from writing poetry regularly in the English classroom:

> Personally, I was thrown into this class as a last resort, and dreaded the first day- since I hated writing. But as the classes went on, and I wrote more and more, I developed a love for writing- poetry in particular. [This class was] an experience that I will cherish for the rest of my high school career. – Maggie, Grade 10

Sharing this passion with my own kids has also made us close, creating bonds of artistry between us. I share with my kids the poems that I write about them. They give me feedback and reaction (it certainly helps that both of them are involved in arts of their own and appreciate the creative instinct). Choosing to embrace the role of a teacher-writer has not only lent my teaching authenticity, as my students see me write alongside them, but has provided a healthy outlet for parental worry and frustration. It's given me a point of bonding with my kids as we travel through these tough and fraught years together. A few years ago, when my kids were quite young, I attended an in-service with a psychologist who urged us to remember—as parents *and* teachers—how important it is to try to preserve the relationships that we have with the kids in front of us, be it our own children or our students. He reminded us that, once our children are grown and flown, they don't *have* to be our friends — it's their choice. His advice stayed with me for a long time. It made me think about how much I wanted to be friends with my adult children and that I should always be playing a long game with regard to our relationship if I wanted to see that happen.

Poetry is one of the strategies that helped me to make this happen. When the kids and I hit a rough patch, when one of them grew uncommunicative, when we didn't understand each other, I could — among other strategies, of course — always sit back and use poetry writing to process what I was feeling or try to put myself in their shoes, attempting to empathize with how they were feeling or what they were enduring. It made me more reflective, more easily able to take a deep breath and process the situation, all while enabling me to value myself, at the same time, as a creative adult and carve out some time for myself to be an artist. Journaling has wonderful therapeutic benefits—any writing does—but poetry demands that the writer immerse themself in a particular and peculiar art form and, thus, has the unique advantage of being cathartic and empowering, simultaneously.

Your Turn

Kim Johnson is a truly giving writer, responder, and prompt creator. She lives in Williamson, Georgia, where she serves as District Literacy Specialist for Pike County Schools. She enjoys writing, reading, traveling, camping, and spending time with her husband and three rescue schnoodles – *Boo Radley* (TKAM), *Fitz* (F. Scott Fitzgerald), and *Ollie* (Mary Oliver).

Short Prompt
Try to work through this prompt on your own. Carve a few minutes for self-care today. Using Kim's prompt suggestion, think about a "moment etched in your memory for which there is no photograph." Use sensory details to capture this memory and, as Kim says, "bring us to your moment."

You may begin writing in your journal right away to continue your healing. If it feels that you are not ready yet for a poem, you may just jot down some of your thoughts, write a narrative paragraph about your experience, or record these thoughts on your phone. You may always come to it later – you've already made the first step.

Full Prompt
If you need some additional support, I am including the full prompt here for your convenience. Open your notebook or device and follow along with Kim Johnson's inspiration in Unphotographed.[2]

> ### Inspiration
> In his book *Lightning Paths: 75 Poetry Writing Exercises*, Kyle Vaughn's resources are rich and plentiful for exploring various forms of poetry. I began exploring Vaughn in more depth and discovered his website, where I discovered his exercise Unphotographed. I began thinking of all the ways I use photos to inspire poetry…..and Vaughn reshaped my thinking about all the photographs not taken.
>
> ### *Process*

To sharpen descriptive techniques and synesthesia in writing, consider a moment etched in your memory for which there is no photograph. Use sensory details to capture the photograph that doesn't yet exist—and breathe snapshot life into a picture of words. Write an unphotographed moment, from corner to corner, whether Polaroid, black and white, sepia, digital, 35 mm with or without filters......whatever the effect. Step into the frame. Take our hands. Bring us to your moment.

Unphotographed Grief by Kim Johnson

your furrowed brow
thumb and forefinger cradling your chin
your lips quivering like her hand ~ unstoppable
teary eyes fixed on your shoe
   on anything
      on nothing
you in your chair
   in the room
    where she drew
   her last breath

where her whispers linger
   screams
     laughs
      cries

where there are no words

to hide the thudding drumbeat
   of your broken heart

Wendy's Suggestions for the Classroom
Finally, while this chapter is for you, dear teacher, we'd love for you to invite students to write. If you want to try a version of this prompt with your students, here are a few things to keep in mind:
- word the prompt appropriately for your students' age;
- suggest a form(s) that may work for such a prompt;
- include a mentor poem. The more students read, the

better they write. It helps expand their vocabulary as well.

- encourage and allow students to talk to each about their memories and "unphotographed moments" to gain inspiration.
- spend a few minutes modeling how to approach the poetry composing. Show them your writing process. Notice that you also may struggle with phrasing or finding the most fitting word.
- provide students with a choice suggesting an alternative prompt
- allow students to reject your prompt completely and write something they choose to create on their own.

Extending this writing activity to your students may result in developing closer connections with your students, their lives, and experiences. It might be that little nudge they need to open up, discover a way of sharing their inner emotional state, and find a path to healing with poetry in a safe space of their classroom.

Links
[1] https://www.ethicalela.com/ekphrastic-poetry/

Part II

why we write poetry

with students

Part II: Students Writing

In Part II, we invite readers to witness how we have shared the experience of poetry writing with our students and invite readers to do the same with their own classes. Many teachers who write poetry and have engaged in teacher-poet communities have learned how to model writing poetry with their students and nurture a space of poetic thinking and being that has had some wellbeing outcomes. In these chapters, we detail how poetry has empowered students to become engaged writers, to express their feelings, and to experience healing alongside us.

In "Unburdening," Jennifer Guyor Jowett, a junior high teacher in a Catholic school in Michigan, shares a routine of writing poetry called The Daily Fifteen and the impact this has had on her students' writing. Readers will gather several forms and topics to try out in their classroom.

In "Helping Students Plant the Seeds," Susan Ahlbrand, a middle school teacher in Indiana, writes a story about Andie, a student navigating implications of a cyber-predator and mental health treatment in the early days of COVID-19, and how poetry became a thread connecting Andie to her teacher and classroom community in "Helping Students Plant the Seeds."

Leilya Pitre, a teacher educator in Louisiana, contributes "Inviting Students to Poetry: First Steps to Describe Feelings with an I Am Poem," which tells a story of her students making the first step toward recovery—finding words to name their experiences in the "I Am" poem format, a structure that offers visible support for students to nurture a poet identity

Margaret Simon, a middle grade teacher, shares a chapter "Write Along With Me: An Invitation Accepted" about writing alongside a student through shared grief. Margaret shares the poetic journey of one student who processed her grief, the loss of a beloved grandmother, through various forms and topics of poetry.

Wendy Everard, a high school creative writing teacher in New York, contributes a chapter,"'That Could Be a Poem!' Poetry and Student Engagement." This poem explores the ghazal form and the mosaic form and how two students engaged with poetry in Wendy's creative writing class.

In "Finding Home," Jennifer Guyor Jowett shares the story of one young writer. Misa, a new student from Palau, expressed her longing for home through poetry in their junior high class. Her writings, inspired by daily prompts and exploring her memories, vividly captured her emotional journey. Over the school year, her growth as a writer showcased her deep connection to her homeland and her evolving voice.

CHAPTER 12

Unburdening
Jennifer Guyor Jowett

> *It's not the volume of your voice that matters, it's the content.*
> — Abhijit Naskar, *Mucize Insan: When The World is Family*

We are on a healing journey, my students and I.

Amidst the details of vacations and adventures and friendship or family dilemmas, students pour out whatever weighs them down onto paper and into digital journals, and I respond.

The classroom is silent. It's our fifteen minutes of writing time, a non-negotiable, sustained quiet time to nurture thoughts into writing and allow students to find who they are as writers. This Daily Fifteen didn't start out silently. In fact, at the beginning of the year, students actively resisted by talking to one another, "looking" for a new page in their binder or for a pencil (does *anyone* have a pencil anymore?), or asking to go to the bathroom. But somewhere along the course of that first quarter, a shift occurred. Marked by questions as they entered the classroom (Are we going to write today? Can I sign up for open mic?), this whole class shift was gradual but evident. Though I'd witnessed this transformation in previous years, it always managed to surprise me.

Every fall, I wonder if this will be the year students wouldn't discover what writing could do for them, if they'd be the group to scoff at our work together, if they'd become so jaded and burdened by the time they reached middle school that writing would remain meaningless to them. But with purposefully chosen prompts, responsive comments meant to encourage, a nurturing in learning to read and to respond to one another, and lots of care, students have discovered the strength that comes from voice. And finding voice helps them not only to say what's on their minds but also to heal.

Students come to our classrooms with a *meh* attitude about writing. They've spent years working on the mechanics of our language. And years losing the strength of their voices. State requirements and the measure of tests can have that effect.

By giving them the time to write and offering choices through prompts, student voices gradually come alive. And students recognize this. Henry, a typical 7th grader who just wanted to get the daily writing done, reflected at the end of the year:

> I could see my writing slowly improve day after day because of our digital journal. The difference between my first piece of writing and one of my future pieces is crazy. I loved writing daily throughout the year. Which I find amazing because before this year I didn't even like writing.

There's great satisfaction in seeing a 7th grader come to enjoy writing, to recognize it as something beyond an assignment, and to realize the growth made over the course of nine months. This transformation is not always easy to see in the middle of the ups and downs of a school year, especially at the start when there's often student resistance. Despite having spent over three decades in a classroom, I'm still moved when students recognize the value of the written word, especially as they don't always share their appreciation.

Lila hesitated to use her voice aloud in the room. But her writing spoke volumes as to who she was. In her end of year reflection, she shared:

> Teachers have their own way of teaching, but my teacher teaches for the future. She teaches for the students, not for her paycheck. My teacher goes down to my level. She knows what is best and understands our world for how we see it. My teacher found me through my words and feelings.

My teacher found me through my words and feelings. That's what writing does. It allows writers to be found and heard and seen. Lila was a student who appeared conflicted throughout the year. Through writing and discussions, we realize that so many of our students deal with weighty stuff: friendship problems, parents divorcing, deaths of grandparents, worries over socio and political issues, and Lila was no exception.

But while she believes I found her, she really found herself—the writing gave her the chance to discover and explore those words and feelings. It gave her the chance to work toward healing. Having a writing routine is a way in for healing, it is a way of being, a way of engaging. Writing requires time looking—in word choices, structure, and message but also into yourself. It is productive. It's agentive. It is finding self.

After reading mentor prompts for inspiration and looking at craft moves to emulate, Lila wrote this piece based on C.G. Hanzlicek's "What I Want" poem:

What I Want by Lila

What I want is
to be normal.

To feel alive within me,
to not be scared.

Not only of my reflection,
but of my past.

I want to dig deeper,
but the horror of humiliation runs near.

I not only want or wish,
but I need to find myself.

It's necessary to cultivate relationships with students. I focus on making comments on students' writing that celebrate what they do well. It takes time, trust, and nurturing, but the writing grows into flourishing.

I can read a room.

Early on in my education career, a teacher-friend told me that when children are treated badly, they turn around and treat someone else the same way to get rid of the hurt. This act, as horrible as it might be, unburdens them. But there are other, better ways to unburden hurt, to find healing. Writing is one of them.

I can remember a time when I sat with my grandmother on our front porch, slowly sounding out the words to *Madeleine* while reading aloud to her for the first time. I would have been five. Her love of poetry, of celebrating words that sing and soften, her recitation of Dickinson and Frost, and the joy she showed at seeing my own poems, nurtured my love of the written word. She became and remains the most significant individual in my literary journey, even after her passing. My loss at her death was profound. It felt like a burden to carry it with me. I wrote of that loss in this untitled poem:

(Untitled) by Jennifer Guyor Jowett

my Grandmother who planted words like poets
scattering the rhymes
across Flanders Fields
up from the meadows
alongside buttercups
gilding Terabithian ravines
who swung the bat in favored lands
bringing joy to children
mightier than Casey
who skated upon bronze Brinker blades
through the canals of Belle Isle
sharing kindness like medals
who left Detroit for New York City
a WAVE holding back seas
who raised three children
after losing a husband
who lost her closest sister
who never failed to find the words
to gather the rosebuds
that smile today
has run the race
and set the sun

My students have heard me talk of her. They know she grew up in Detroit during the Depression and that she loved baseball so much that she'd spend her hard-earned pennies for seats in the bleachers at a Tigers game. Sharing stories makes us vulnerable just as sharing aloud our writing does. When students witness our vulnerability, it helps them to see our classroom as a safe space to share.

My recognition of the importance of routine writing for students came from my own consistent writing time with Ethical ELA, an online writing space for teacher-poets. I have noticed in the course of my writing within the Ethical ELA community that my grandmother continues to surface again and again in my words. With each new poem about her, I am working toward an unburdening of loss. I am moving into healing. I am *becoming* healed.

In writing to discover my own unburdening, I realized that the weighty loads carried by students appeared within their words as they wrote to unburden themselves.

They wrote of losses from friendships, of pets, within families, through social justice issues, from the stress of technology, of their burdens. As our daily writing turned into weeks of writing with self-selected pieces shared in a digital journal or open mic celebration, it became evident that some themes appear over and over. Friendship typically lands at the top of common themes.

Friendship is a struggle for middle schoolers, especially as 7th graders shift interests, and friendships sometimes follow. Sophia, a friendly, thoughtful, emerging writer wrote:

What I Want by Sophia

What I want isn't an object
Yet, something I wish to foresee.

What I want can't be bought
But it is priceless.

What I want is a best friend
One that will stick by my side.

Someone who will not believe rumors
And to know me for who I truly am.

What I want is a best friend,
Who can check up on me

And for them to truly see me
For me.

Sophia wasn't the only student writing about friendships. Thalynn was a deep thinker, dedicated to perfecting her writing. Her growth was exponential throughout the year. Thalynn's Location Poem, which I describe in Chapter 17, Finding Home, offered her own exploration of friendship.

Location Poem by Thalynn

I know rocks too well.

I know the sleek sheet formed on top
after a downpour, the one that
can be wiped, the one that
can't be formed again.

I know the heavy weight
Terrorizing its neighbors, bringing every
Thing down with it

I know rocks

I know the chill sent up my fingers and down
My back, touching the surface
The warm gray surface

I feel the pebbles under my feet
In my hands, and the dust
Coating everything in its path

I know rocks

I know sandstone
And writing on the sidewalk
And smashing the rock
Over and
Over and
Over until
Obliterated.

I know that rocks don't belong in
The grass, for the lawnmower will

Have issues.
Wasn't
My
Rock
There
First?

I know rocks

I feel the tension between the two of them.
I feel the pressure breaking
Them down.

I know that this poem isn't about rocks

The theme of friendship threaded its way through the school year, showing up in a variety of poetry forms. A diversity of prompts allows writers to have a choice while making writing as accessible as possible in as many ways as possible.

Students often enjoy the challenge of a new form. 100 One-syllable poems can be both easy and challenging simultaneously. The form asks for just one-syllable words, one hundred of them, which is welcoming but limiting too. It's helpful to push students to the challenge of the prompt but also allow for individual choices that serve their purpose and voice too. Maeve created this poem about friendship from a 100 One-syllable Word prompt.

100 One-syllable Word Poem by Maeve

Friends suck.
One day,
They are nice.
The next day,
they back stab the life out of you.
Friends will still suck in ten years.
Not one thing will switch.
It could if you want it to.
It would take lots of work.
I do not think it is worth it though.
But you might
And it is your choice.

The joy of a friend is great
But like I said,
They back stab the life out of you.
How do you know a friend is fake?
You don't.
You guess.
You leave them when you want.
Friends still suck.

For Maeve, the topic of friendship arose again and again. She began to observe changes in friendships, as often happens in middle school. Notice the same beginning line (What I want is a good friend) in two further poems—a What I Want and a Skinny—the first in December and the second in March.

What I Want by Maeve

What I want is
A good friend

To share what I want
What I want is

Someone I can talk to
When I need it

But what they want is
Something different

Than what I want
They want to get rid of a friend

Even though
That's the only friend they have

Skinny Poem by Maeve

What *I* want is a good friend
Happy
Caring
Funny

Truthful
Happy
Thoughtful
Trustworthy
Sincere
Happy
A good friend is what *I* want

Based on Ezra Pound's "In a Station at the Metro," the Skinny allows for the repetition of a line along with the reordering of the first and last lines as well as the added challenge of using few words to construct clear images. Maeve chose *happy* for her repeated line, which adds both to the commentary and her strength in writing honestly about the shifting world of middle grade students.

Because students are writing frequently, craft decisions develop naturally, especially as they begin to see and hear what works from our responses to each other. Any drafting they do is their choice. If a daily prompt isn't working for them, they have a week's worth of possibilities to choose from to share.

Lila found comfort in friends, one spot I knew uplifted her. She wrote about them in a Location poem:

Cabin to Cabin by Lila

The rain on the window,
splish, splat.
Me in the first cabin,
my friends in the last.

I run in the rain.
My ankles and shoes drenched,
squish, squash.
The thunder roaring its name,
so loud and so clear.

I get to the cabin,
safe and sound.
I look around with hope,
with no one around.
My body shivers as the thunder roars louder.

I cry with the clouds,
as my mind pounds with the thunder.
I feel the warm comforting arms,
as if it was,
my mother...

Students wrote for their own unburdening, whether they recognized it or not. The comfort felt here through friends suggests a healing, just as routine writing develops a comfort with words that allow writers to heal.

Your Turn

Allison Berryhill's experience with writing will help ease you into this prompt. Allison lives in Iowa where she advises the journalism program, teaches English, and hosts a weekly Creative Writing club at Atlantic High School. She is active with the Iowa Council of Teachers of English, the Iowa High School Press Association, and the Iowa Poetry association where she serves as teacher liaison.

Short Prompt
If you are ready to write, here is a short prompt to get you started: Think about what you really want. Create short two line stanzas. Consider building upon details of one memory or combining several different memories based upon one theme, if you wish.

Go to your journal or device. Explore your voice there. If you are feeling so overwhelmed that you are not sure how to begin, remember that writing daily is a form of self-care.

Full Prompt
If you'd like a little more support, the full prompt has been included below. So, open your notebook or device and follow along with educator Allison Berryhill's inspiration: What I Want Is

> **Inspiration:** I love this mentor poem by C. G. Hanzlicek: "What I Want Is." It is written in a series of two line stanzas; each couple answers what the poet wants:
>
> > Enough money
> > To have what I want
>
> The poem continues, taking the reader deeper into the poet's

---

imagination. I hope you'll read Hanzlicek's poem at least twice to wrap your head around his line breaks and use of enjambment.

Process: What do you want? Use Hanzlicek's poem as a model as you explore the longings in your heart. I encourage my students to use C. G. Hanzlicek's style as they "sign" their poems. (I become A. L. Berryhill). Begin with a declaration of a want, and allow your mind to explore the imagery related to your "want" with prepositional phrases: beneath that hill, in the pond, on the mud... Consider matching Hanzlicek's number of stanzas—or go rogue. You might conclude your poem by counting, as Hanzlicek does: Coyote 1, Coyote 2. I have used this poem as a model many times, and it never fails to elicit successful poems.

Jennifer's Suggestions for the Classroom
Finally, while this chapter is for you, dear teacher, we'd love for you to invite students to write. If you want to try a version of daily writing with your students, here are a few things to keep in mind:

- Daily writing allows students to develop and expect routine. I nudge students to return to their writing throughout the day, as their brain continues to sort through word choices, direction, and meaning even while actively working on something else.
- Both Open Write and VerseLove at the Ethical ELA site offer myriad poetry prompts, along with mentor poems, inspiration, and process. I'll walk through the process with students, nurturing their poet ears by noticings and craft techniques.
- Write and share your own poems with students. It allows them to see you as a writer in an authentic way and helps to forge connections. It allows you to see what spots they may struggle with while creating another authentic mentor poem.
- The importance of positive feedback cannot be emphasized enough. Your voice in their "ear" becomes their voice in their head. Celebrating what writers do well encourages them to build upon what works while noticing the positive in each other's words.

Link
[1] https://www.ethicalela.com/february-day-2-5-what-i-want-is/.

Poetic Reflection by Jessica Wiley

Poetry is Healing…and Hopeful

As a special education literacy inclusion teacher, I collaborate with the general education teachers so that our students can learn to independently engage with one another and explore content with their peers. I provide additional support and strategies to enhance students' learning experiences. I would like to describe three experiences that contributed to my poetry writing success.

During their 4th-grade poetry unit in December 2023, students at my school were exposed to a variety of poetry. I volunteered to facilitate three activities where students crafted poems based on mentor text. Some students expressed their disdain for poetry. I had a challenge on my hands.

For the first activity, students created poems modeled after "The Red Wheelbarrow" by William Carlos Williams. The students didn't quite understand the meaning of this poem, but once the significance of the wheelbarrow was discussed, they were able to grasp the concept. Although this was a shared writing experience, this was not their favorite activity. It wasn't mine either. However, we were able to say we endured something new, together.

In the second activity, students created their own "Love that _____" poem, based on the poem in the book of the same title, *Love that Dog* by Sharon Creech. Students were given partial text and sentence stems to support their language skills and promote effective communication in their writing. After reading the poem, I shared my final product to provide an additional mentor text for support. Once I'd shown students my poem, I worked with them in small groups to recommend text to insert into their poems. Some of the students had a great time making concrete phrases. Others were very humorous for 4th-grade learners.

The last activity was a prompt from hosting an Open Write on April 28, 2022, on Ethical ELA "By My Self-Love."[1] When I found out 4th grade was studying Eloise Greenfield's poem *By Myself*, I was excited! In 5th grade, my daughter had previously studied Greenfield's poem and created her own. I also had my poem to share during the lesson. I shared my plan with my son's teacher and she was more than happy for me to take over this task. I shared our poems, as well as a few carefully selected others from the blog. The process was difficult for some students as they struggled with figurative language. Once I was able to guide them in thinking abstractly, their work came to fruition. This activity was most memorable because after reading the mentor poems and the created masterpieces, I felt this was a true testament to our inner selves. Seeing their final products, students were able to demonstrate their creativity, their vulnerability, and their love for who they are as individuals.

I truly hope that these activities contributed to these now-rising 5th-grade students. Whether they failed or flourished, I hope they were able to at least say they took a risk. It is up to them to attempt it again, or shut the door and lock it away forever.

Jessica Wiley has been a special educator for 15 years in central/north central Arkansas, empowering learners through literacy instruction.

References

Creech, S. (2001). *Love that dog*. HarperCollins.

Greenfield, E. (1978). *Honey, I Love and other poems by eloise greenfield*. HarperCollins Publishers.

Williams, W. (1923).*The Red Wheelbarrow*. In C. MacGowan (Eds.), *The Collected Poems of William Carlos Williams, Volume I, 1909-1939*. New Directions Publishing Corporation.

Link
[1] https://www.ethicalela.com/by-my-self-love/

CHAPTER 13

Helping Students Plant the Seeds
Susan Ahlbrand

*Plant healing words in your heart's wounds. One
day, you will discover a garden full of love flowers.*
— Alexandra Vasiliu

The world is hurting, our children are hurting, our students are hurting. In my role as an 8th grade English language arts teacher, I have always approached my classroom as being much more than a space to learn standards. I have always wanted students to grow as people. When I saw this quote, I instantly knew that I wanted to use it to guide my work . . . using writing as the vehicle for healing. If my classroom could become a "garden full of love flowers," so could others, and, in turn, our world could become a better place.

As a mother of four teens with a full-time teaching position and a very busy husband, I began to struggle mightily with my mental health. After experiencing first-hand how much writing and reading poetry helped me to process various emotions and traumas (for more detail, see Chapter 9 in Part I), I decided to be much more intentional in offering my eighth-grade students a similar experience.

A veteran teacher of 34 years, I have taught the same subject and grade in the same school for my entire career. Jasper Middle School is the only public middle school in the small southwestern Indiana town of Jasper. The population hovers around 15,000 and our school enrollment sits at about 700. For generations, there was very little mobility in and out of the community, and many of my students are children of previous students. That has started to change in the past decade as migrant workers have flocked to our manufacturing town to fill employment needs with that shift bringing with it many challenges.

I have never been what I could call a very "traditional" teacher. I have always tried to keep up on trends and best practice, adjusting my instruction as I learn new things. The one thing I have held tightly onto, however, is a focus on reading and writing poetry. While I have always "covered" poetry in my 8th grade English language arts class, once I experienced the community of Ethical ELA, I was equipped with more strategies and content to use to take my students more deeply into poetry, to "uncover" poetry. For all of 2018, I took part in the Open Writes each month for five days and VerseLove's thirty days of poetry in April, which is National Poetry Month. I headed into the 2019-20 school year knowing that I wanted to incorporate a similar structure for writing, reading, and responding to poetry in my classroom.

As a bellringer on the daily Slide Deck displayed on the panel at the front of the room, I would provide prompts like the one shared by inclusive and diverse teacher writers in the Open Writes. We would write during class, and volunteers would share. They eagerly volunteered to display their poems on the panel and stepped up to read aloud as others read along. By November, we had built a great culture of writing, sharing, and responding to poetry.

Due to time constraints, I had to put limits on how many could share each day. Then, eventually, I used the poetry prompt bellringer only twice a week so that other strands of ELA could be the focus. I was surprised that the students actually asked for the poetry prompts to happen more frequently! Without a doubt, the days could be filled with nothing but poetry and we all would have been happy.

Then came March 13, 2020.

The day the schools shut down to flatten the curve of COVID-19 — not to return to normalcy for months, rather years.

In the heart of the COVID-19 shutdown and its wonky aftermath of all sorts of mixes of quarantine and instructional delivery, I really found that students embraced writing poetry. Their lives were off-kilter and uncertain, and poetry, with its no-rules-apply vibe offered a great way for them to express their thoughts and feelings.

Since we no longer shared physical space, I would share a prompt — sometimes a specific topic, other times a mentor text — on a Discussion Board on Canvas, our Learning Management System. I think it was being physically distanced that prompted the students to be more willing, even eager, to participate. They yearned for interaction, and digital interaction was better than nothing.

Since we had August through mid-March to build community, the online version was fairly seamless. Students wrote raw poems and shared them bravely. Fellow students commented with insight and compassion. Students would use tech tools such as Flipgrid to send videos of them reading their poems to their empty bedrooms. All from their homes scattered around our rural area, the connection was like nothing I had ever seen. My conviction that poetry was the best vehicle for getting middle schoolers engaged in English language arts was strengthened.

In the summer of 2020 (what I call The Covid Summer), Sarah Donovan, the creator of Ethical ELA, offered a novel study on verse novels via Zoom. Not only did that course provide me a much-needed professional community with connection during a time of which I had very little, it exposed me to a handful of verse novels to use in my 8th grade ELA classroom: *White Rose* (Wilson), *Other Words for Home* (Warga), *Redwood and Ponytail* (Holt), and *They Call Me Güero* (Bowles). I knew that a few of the books would be put into student hands as soon as school started back up in August.

I realized from this experience that the days of waiting for professional development to be provided by corporate leadership were behind me. I needed to be the one to seek what I wanted. And, still today, Ethical ELA consistently answers the call!

Returning to in-person school was awkward and surreal and uncertain and a bunch of other adjectives. In my 30-plus years of teaching, I had never experienced anything remotely (pun intended) like it. Desks six feet apart, masks required, the classroom a revolving door of students being sent home due to contact tracing. It was a time of remarkable instability in all ways, but especially emotionally for mercurial adolescents. I think being stuck at home for six months sent kids down all sorts of rabbit holes, and many of them did a lot of introspection and also were exposed to a lot of new thinking online.

Our classroom felt fragile. I had been here before . . . after 9/11, after a rash of student suicides, after school shootings. In the aftermath of these tragedies, literature, especially poetry, served as a healing agent. I anticipated that the same thing would happen here.

For the remainder of this chapter, while I could share many stories, I am going to focus on one specific student, Andie, as a powerful example of poetry's healing and transformative power. Andie's story is very complex and I will try to share the most relevant parts. As with most healing, there were many agents that helped Andie, and while writing poetry was one of them, mental health professionals were heavily involved. I engaged our school social worker early in the game. She and I have gotten very close over the years as concerns often reveal themselves through student writing. I learned early in my career not to tip-toe into waters I was not educated to, to always involve the social worker, and to document like crazy.

Shortly after school started Andie had shared a getting-to-know-you project in front of the class using our presentation panel. There was a rainbow on it, and Andie shyly, hesitantly said, "And there's a rainbow because, ya know" and walked off. She clearly wanted to own who she was but was still hesitant to do so with elaboration. I didn't know this young girl well, but everything about her — her dress, her hair, her presence — brought out my most compassionate side. A few days later, I handed her the young adult book *Redwood and Ponytail* by KA Holt, one of the verse novels I had read with Sarah Donovan.

The next day, I could tell Andie had heavy thoughts. I went over to ask her what was up and she started crying. We went to a private spot, and she shared that at lunch earlier in the day, some boys had walked by her and said, "Don't get too close to her . . . the gay might rub off." She was so upset. She shared that she advocated for herself in the moment in the cafeteria, but as she was reading the book, she was overcome with emotion that she knew she failed to relay when addressing those boys. In *Redwood and Ponytail*, two middle school girls fall in like. A cheerleader and volleyball player start cheering one another on — on the court and in life — discovering their feelings for each other and finding a way to be comfortable in their own skin. Andie and I talked for a while about the book and the harm the boys caused. I invited her to keep me posted. The subtle and even outward hate and bigotry toward those of different sexual orientation present in our little microcosm of society raised my radar about her wellness.

Our rapport was still in its infancy. During a passing period a few days later, she returned the book to my desk with a card under it. What she created and what she wrote took my breath away, and I just knew poetry was the portal. [Insert image when permission is signed.]

A week later, our class read the poem "Hanging Fire" by Audre Lorde. Here is the important refrain from Lorde's poem: "and momma's in the bedroom/with the door closed."

This relatable poem by the famous social justice warrior never fails to spur conversation within my classes. With its focus on the speaker's feeling of isolation while experiencing various sources of teen angst, the short verse always offers plenty to discuss. I provided them with a template to mimic the poem, expecting them to stay pretty true to Lorde's format. We really focused on the use of refrain at the end of each stanza to add power and to unify the ideas in the poem. In response, Andie wrote a poem and raised her hand to share it in class. This is what she wrote in a matter of minutes during class:

And I Don't Want It To by Andie

I never knew I could hurt this much
I never asked to be this way
And still nothing will change
Nothing CAN change
And I don't want it to

It's like a hook in the heart
A piece that keeps getting tugged
The fishing line won't ever cut slack
And still I'm told to stay silent
It's not a huge part of me anyways
My pulse is still beating, right?
So what's it to me a little pain
Can I just let it go already?
But nothing can let me go
And I don't want it to

They told me that my line will cut
That my hook would fall
That it's just a phase
And I believed them
I was still young, my heart would still grow
Maybe the hook would shrink into nothing at all
Maybe if I just ignored it, maybe it would fade away
But it is still here, my hook will never fade
And I don't want it to

She scared me at first
Her beauty was terrifying
Her smile was sweet and loving

She cared and played with me
Her laugh matching with mine
Her pearly cold hands so soft and pretty
Her brown freckles stars on her fair skin
Her hair twisting and turning and curling with my stomach
And still I was scared of her
Scared that the tugging would never stop
That the hurt would never go away
That the hurt would stop feeling good and turn into pain
But it never did go away
And I don't want it to

It didn't have to be this way
It wasn't like this before
When did it become insulting?
When did my hook seem so much heavier?
When did my heart seem so much heavier?
She is telling me the same
Pointing at all the signs
But she is scared too
I can see it in her eyes
That's what hurts the most
The forbidden word, the hidden secret
The skeleton in the closet
Well, who made the rules anyway?
Kind of silly if you ask me
So I lead her away to a safe secret place
And show my heart
Still beating, still bleeding
And she showed me hers
They never have stopped being in sync since
And I don't want them to

We tried to keep them safe, for a little bit at least
Still trying to figure out if it was really meant to be
But our single line kept getting snagged
Snagged by the untold judgment of others
Our tie fraying under the weight of disapproval
We still held on though
hoping they would stop
But they never did stop

And I don't want them to

His words
His words hurt me the most
The one in particular
Not in the way it hurt before
This time it tore me
He tore my heart
His words single handedly
Ripped
My
Soul
That word
His word a hook in my brain
A ugly crooked hook
I bleed
I bleed and bleed and bleed
It won't stop hurting
And he laughs
He laughs and laughs and laughs
While I lay there dying
Crying
Screaming for advice nobody can give
Looking for answers why
Why is my cut so deep?
Why is my hook still here?
Why does it hurt so much?
And yet I don't want it to leave

As much as it hurts I know that it's good
I know that I'm right
I know I am honest
Because that's the least I can do
Not lie
Not hide
And although they can try to pry
Try to rip out the hook in my heart
My shiny and perfect hook
I will not die
And still my lovers widow
Even when I'm alive

But despite the pain and the calas my soul has built
The barrier
The wall
That only true love can fill
I still let them look through my plexiglass eyes
See my soul for what it is
Let the silver turn into gold as the sun hits it
Let the wounds scab as the blood hits air
No matter how much it hurts
I won't appease to their beliefs
I won't change
Because I can't
And I would never want to
Even if I could
Because I am who I am
And the hook in my heart will never leave

It's a part of me
And despite the bad that can come from being me
I'm not sorry
And I never will be

It was raw. It was brave. It was beautiful. The class was completely captivated. A fluent writer, she went well beyond expectations of length, but she utilized the refrain expertly. When Andie finished sharing it, there was silence then a chorus of WOWs. One of the boys who had been so unkind to Andie in the cafeteria and who was typically very free with racist and homophobic comments, let's call him Sam, spontaneously chimed in. He quietly murmured, "Well, that sure is food for thought." She felt so emboldened in both her sexuality and as a writer. And, the other members of the class, in turn, seemed to realize the power of words. It was an awesome moment! It was only September and our class culture of writers using language for agency was forming.

Not every student was as fluent and expressive as Andie, and it took a few moments after she shared for others to muster their courage. Then, the hands continued to go up, tentatively at first then with growing confidence. Some students still relied on rhyme since they thought that's what poetry was, and some wrote short, pithy verses. But they all wrote and many shared and the positive feedback from peers emboldened them.

I continued to mimic Sarah's Open Write protocol of inspiration, mentor text, modeling my writing, inviting students to write, and then exchanging poems in my classroom routinely. Many students emerged with new understandings of poetry and their identity as poets with comments like "I thought I hated poetry" and "I didn't realize this was a poem since it didn't rhyme."

Around the holidays, it was shared that Andie was at a residential care facility after an attempted suicide. While she had certainly found her voice through poetry, her mental health was incredibly unstable and the world of online predators threatened her wellbeing. In an effort for her to keep up in school, she still had access to our assignments, and on December 16, she posted the following poem on our LMS in response to a prompt that asked the students to incorporate the power of three into a poem:

Three Black Birds by Andie

Three black birds
Staring back at me
They move with the white clouds
Against the blue sky
While I sit perched at a window
A cage
I want to fly with them too
Fly with the black birds
Alongside white clouds
Against a blue sky
So I will
Three black birds
One heart

She was in residence at a mental health facility yet her mind — and her heart — went to poetry. The imagery, the metaphor, the effective use of repetition all worked together to express her emotional state in a way prose simply could not.

When school resumed in January, she was able to return to school, clearly still quite fragile and clouded with meds that were an attempt to stabilize her. Because of the timing of her stay, students seemed to be unaware that she had been away.

In mid-January, I tweaked the very prompt that I shared in Chapter 9 about taking a journey out and back and writing about the differences and presented it to my 8th graders, quite uncertain of what I would get. I perceived some kids living seemingly charmed lives, some living innocent and maybe naive lives with optimism for our world. But through their poems, I came to realize more students than I thought were navigating challenges with unprocessed trauma and mental health diagnoses. The range and depth of the created poems definitely varied. Some were light, some were funny, some were thought-provoking, and some took my breath away. They wrote the poems they needed to write.

And Andie wrote and bravely shared with the class . . .

Dear Past Patient by Andie

Dear Past Patient.
You were the first to say hi.
We met the same night I thought I was gonna die.
I was so tired
And so sad
But you said hi.
Past patient.
That's what I'll remember you as.
We told our stories to one another
As a list so matter of fact.
Because we have told these stories so many times
We don't remember how else to recite them otherwise.
We ate
We colored
We sang
In an oasis of doctors and therapists
You were my everything.
I prepared for the day I would have to go away.
I knew we couldn't last forever
And we shouldn't.
In a place like that, it's meant to be that way.
We locked toes
We butted heads
We made trouble with staff
You braided my hair
We were different.
But our connection was alike.
I had a home to go to

While you were still looking for one that's new.
I was cool and level headed
While you were still silly and tempered.
You were always the first to get out of bed
While I still was under the covers wishing I would stop breathing.
But still we linked arms
Like nothing there mattered
But everything did.
Everything always mattered.
It was never meant to be forever
And it shouldn't be.
Our attachment was temporary
And our treatment was necessary
So as much as I love you, past patient
It was my time to go.
And I don't regret hugging goodbye
Or saying hi back.

The content of that poem and her vulnerability to share it allowed her to step back into the class that she did so much to shape just months before. Compassion bubbled to the surface of Sam's skin and it was displayed through a knowing head slant. But tantamount was the healing that Andie, through this poetry, experienced. The maturity and self-awareness she shows in the lines "Our attachment was temporary/And our treatment was necessary/So as much as I love you, past patient/It was my time to go./And I don't regret hugging goodbye/Or saying hi back."

And she realized that writing was fundamental to her healing, telling me, "Writing was my connection at Touchpoint. It kept me alive." What a powerful testament to the power of writing.

Things stabilized for Andie for a while, and she continued to impress the class with her writing. One day while Zooming into class due to being quarantined, she sent me a chat and asked if I could project her for the class to see and hear. She had written a poem after a mini-lesson on anaphora: the purposeful and effective use of repetition at the start of successive phrases, clauses, sentences or lines of poetry. Of course, I said yes, and her beautiful face filled the screen of the large panel in the room, and she read this poem:

Take Me With You by Andie

Take me with you.
Take me away to a happy place
Any place but here.
Take me with you.
Take my soul
Take my body
Take my mind
Take my heart
And ring them dry.
Salt my tears
And lick them from my eyes
So they don't have to hide.
Bottle my blood
And the soot from my lungs.
Scrape my liver
Fresh from disease
And replace my heart
With one that beats with ease.
Take me with you.
Take my old parts and make them new.
Take my scars
Take my memories
Take my ovaries
Take my tongue
Take my teeth
And make them fresh again.
Give me heels
Give me lashes
Give me new eyebrows
Give me boys
Give me girls
Give me abs
Give me a new body
Because god forbid I live a normal life
At least let me be suicidal but look pretty at the same time.
Let me be sad but look happy.
Let me cry but smile pretty.
Let me breathe but eat nothing.
Let me die but feel alive.
Take me with you.

Because god forbid I trust a soul
At least let me die with faces at my sides.
Take me with you.
And then forget me.

Even from her bedroom across town, she shared her very personal poetry with the class. Her fellow students continued to celebrate her work and show compassion for her experiences. It wasn't long until other hands thrust into the air eager to share their poems after Andie bravely shared hers. Our class was almost like a Poetry Cafe with people sharing and snapping and crying, tears of release, maybe relief.

While I wish that Andie's story and poetry as a healing agent ended there, Andie needed more mental health support. Due to a spike in COVID-19 in our area, she was relegated to an at-home "residential therapy" with Zoom sessions, but her mom was a daycare provider, and Andie was often in her bedroom alone. I was so worried about her.

I think this is a part of teaching nobody talks about. For some of our students, we are their touchstone. In trauma-responsive studies, we know that one healthy adult connection can make a big difference in a student's life. I am glad that Andie trusted me and found me to be that source of support, but I wasn't always sure how to best help her. About a week in, she sent an email to me saying, "Poetry and drawing are all that are keeping me alive" and attached the following poem:

I Think I'm Lying by Andie

I think I'm lying, and I don't know why.
Worst of all, I think I'm lying to myself.
I think I'm lying, because I'm scared.
Scared to go back if I tell the truth
Scared to disappoint if I go back
Scared if I go back I'll make it worse
Scared if I make it worse I'll never see light again.
And then life will really be over.
The surrealness would just feel numb.
I don't want to feel numb.
Not anymore.
But I lie to myself that I feel in the first place.

I think I'm lying, and I don't know why.
Worst of all, I'm lying to everyone else.
I think I'm lying, because I am fine.
I can handle the burden I put on myself.
I can carry the weight for everyone else.
So why should I cry for help?
Why should I ask for more?
Why should I want a break?
Why do I just want to sleep my problems away?
Why do I feel this way?
I think I'm lying.
But who am I lying to?

Another powerful poem with very effective use of repetition of the idea of lying to intrigue the readers and pull us to the end. This poem was a cry for help; I knew that I needed to engage our school social worker after Andie sent me this poem in order to make sure that she was safe. With continued intervention and appropriate medication, Andie was again able to return to school. Therapy continued to be a core part of her treatment, which included writing poetry. Her therapist encouraged Andie to share her poems with friends. Andie realized that this helped open up the lines of communication among them and helped their splintered friendship heal.

On the last day of school, Andie hugged me hard and through her tears said, "Thank you for being part of the puzzle that has kept me alive. Writing in your class and having my classmates recognize talent in me helped me like myself." There we stood, in the middle of the wide hallway blossoming with energetic students ready to spring loose, embracing and crying… both knowing that neither of us would ever be the same.

Writing is a salve that heals better than any pill or tincture or pose. Poetry — with its compact language, lack of strict conventions, and freedom of expression — offers wonderful opportunities for growth and healing because of the agency it offers in line breaks and the partial knowing shown in its white space.

In our class, when we write, the sharing starts immediately for some; for others it takes a while to be sure that it is a safe space. Only together can we cultivate safety. Of course, some never do share anything of depth but perhaps poetry serves them in other ways — maybe the healing is in the meter they create or the puns they craft. Or just in listening to others.

Vulnerability doesn't come naturally to people, especially teenagers. It takes time to develop a culture that allows for it. In my classroom, it typically begins with me. I share very personal, raw pieces of writing with them, and it usually doesn't take long before others feel safe enough to do the same. Often, the students who have dealt with the most trauma tend to struggle with conventional writing, so poetry is right up their alley. It feels safer when they realize it's not about a grade or meeting a standard or showcasing understanding of a convention. It's about expression and word play and using writing to peel back the layers of self.

It took a while, but I learned to be okay with not putting a grade on a piece of writing. Not everything is about assessment or standards; authentic writing, especially poetry, needs to feel safe and when students see red ink or a score, they can tend to shut down. That being said, I also found it very important to make sure I was indeed reading what they wrote and being genuine in my feedback. I wanted them to know that I saw them and heard them, but I also knew that there was a chance something had been written that might need to be turned over to our school social worker. I was always very transparent about my legal responsibility to do so.

Sure, there are some students who don't or won't do something if they don't feel there is a grade attached. They may not see the purpose in a school setting to do something if it isn't going to be part of their grade. But, the majority embrace that aspect and feel so much safer creating and sharing knowing that it's not about right and wrong. This year, on April 2, I got a surprising email from two freshmen girls who I had in class the previous year. They informed me that they got onto my Canvas classroom and downloaded this year's April Poem-a-Day spreadsheet and decided to read and write each day because they enjoyed it so much during my class. That confirmed the value of the changes that I had made in my classroom... including more poetry and encouraging sharing. As April wrapped up, they shared their thirty poems with me, eager for an audience beyond each other. One of the girls started an Instagram account for the sole purpose of putting her poems out there. She has hundreds of followers already.

In a world of humans lacking empathy, poetry — reading it, writing it, and sharing it — has the potential to open minds and hearts like few other things I have ever experienced in the classroom. Of the many instructional units and strategies I have tried over the years, poetry is something I will never let go of, no matter the standards or curriculum maps or pushback. Nothing will stop me from cultivating my own little "garden full of love flowers."

Your Turn

Susan Ahlbrand offers us an invitation to write along with her through the short and full prompt below, along with her suggestions for the classroom. She has a great love of poetry, which makes April her favorite month, since it's filled with daily poetry writing challenges. Susan teaches 8th graders in Indiana.

Short Prompt

Revisit "Hanging Fire" by Audre Lorde at PoetryFoundation.org. Think about the things that are stressors for you. Grab your notebook or device and share them in almost a rant as Lorde does. Use poetry writing to get some things off your chest. After getting your ideas down, try to structure it into stanzas, and, if possible, include a refrain to unify and add power.

Full Prompt

Inspiration: Take some time today to think about things in your life that you spend a lot of time thinking about that would help for you to write about and get off your chest. Use Audre Lorde's poem "Hanging Fire" as your inspiration (in class, this comes after a lot of discussion of and analyzing of the poem). We noted that the speaker in "Hanging Fire" blurts out 13 different details of her life that she thinks about, or she worries about, or that frustrate her. We also noted the idea repeated at the end of each stanza, "and momma's in the bedroom with the door closed," and how it adds power and unity—and many questions and theories.

Process: Think about your life. Things that worry you, excite you, frustrate you, entertain you, bother you, etc. Brainstorm them in a chart similar to the one below. You need to think of some idea, some happening, some situation or scenario that stays constant through the many "blurts" you include to use as a refrain. Try to be as specific as you can. Use sensory details. Use specific word choice. Use details pertinent to your life and being a teenager.

Go to your journal or device and work on healing something

---

you think about a lot by using "Hanging Fire" as a mentor. If you are feeling so overwhelmed that you're not sure how to begin, remember that it starts with one thought and others will follow. Include a refrain—some repeating lines like "momma's in the bedroom with the door closed"—that will help add power and meaning. Take the details that you included in the chart and your refrain and write them out in more of a poem form with line breaks and stanzas.

Susan's Suggestions for the Classroom
This prompt lends itself very well to use in a middle school classroom. Some ideas for including this in the classroom:

- I find that often budding poets like clear instructions such as the number of lines or stanzas or a rhyme scheme. However, some are more fluent or free writers and don't want to be penned in. I tend to accept any effort.
- I had small groups fold a sheet of paper to get 16 boxes. Then, I asked them to illustrate what was happening in each of the 16 moments in Lorde's poem. Doing so called for insight and understanding and led to fascinating outputs.
- I found a number of student-created videos on YouTube that interpreted this poem. We watched and analyzed. Then, an option was to create a video interpretation.
- Table pairs collaborated to create a One-Pager that represented character, theme, setting, imagery, sound devices, figurative language, and any other desired ideas. We spent a lot of time discussing and analyzing the poem. Then, the mimic idea was presented.
- Don't allow the quiet in the room to worry you. This writing often takes a lot of introspection and time. Let the quiet become comfortable for them and you!

References
Bowles, D. (2018). *They call me Güero: A border kid's Poems.* Cinco Puntos Press.

Holt, K.A. (2019). *Redwood and Ponytail.* Chronicle Books.

Lorde, A. (n.d.). Hanging fire. *Poetry Foundation.*

Warga, J. (2019). *Other words for home.* Balzer + Bray.

Wilson, K. (2019). *White Rose.* Versify.

Link
[1] https://www.poetryfoundation.org/poems/42580/hanging-fire

Inviting Students to Poetry: First Steps to Describe Feelings with an "I Am" Poem

Leilya A. Pitre

In the 2009-2010 academic year, I worked at the capital city public school in Louisiana. This was the first time in my teaching experience when I taught in the classroom, where I was the only one who looked different than my students. All of them came from the neighboring community of African American families — seemingly carefree, energetic, and boisterous 18 eighth graders. Being from Ukraine and teaching in the United States for only four years, I had to learn more about my students and learn it quickly.

The day we returned from a winter break, I chose to begin with a writing prompt that would ease us off to a narrative writing unit. Using journal prompts routinely had proved to be a helpful practice as students would shift the focus from the previous class or anything that had happened before the class. More than that, it allowed me to know my students better through writing as they would often share some personal information, such as hobbies, likes and dislikes, and their views on certain societal topics. In my practice, planning to write for about ten minutes and a follow-up discussion for five to seven minutes also proves to be a time-efficient procedure with a smooth transition to the lesson's main daily objectives.

I asked my eighth-graders about their winter holidays — what interesting things they experienced, and which experiences would stay with them. I expected them to brag about holiday celebrations, receiving gifts, visiting with friends and family, and going places. That day we wrote together for about ten minutes. I always write with my students as I firmly believe in the benefits of writing alongside students to foster a more engaging and empathetic classroom environment (Calkins, 1994; Rogers, 2002). It aids both teachers and students in improving writing skills (Murray, 2004), building a supportive community (Elbow, 2000; Pitre, 2019; Whitney & Lensmire, 2016) and understanding writing as a valuable, ongoing process (Gallagher, 2011). By sharing the struggles and triumphs of writing (Dean, 2010; Atwell, 2015), teachers reduce students' fear of failure and encourage a growth mindset. I observed the benefits brought by writing with students numerous times.

After the writing was complete, and I asked for volunteers, there were not many hands raised. I was surprised, yet not too alarmed. Most of the days, these kids were eager to share their opinion on various questions I asked in the prompts. Not that day though. One of the students told me about going "up North," seeing the snow for the first time, and being excited to actually play snowballs and make a snowman. It sounded exciting and adventurous; while winters were usually warm and pleasant in Louisiana, I missed snow and playing outside with my daughters, as we used to do in Ukraine. Another student mentioned it had been a boring break, and she would rather be in school. "School must not be so bad," I cheered in my mind.

I collected the notebooks to read and respond to the kids' writing at home and went on with my lesson. Reading papers later that night, I cried out loud. What they wrote in their entries was far from what I expected when I assigned the task. Throughout this chapter, I am going to use pseudonyms instead of students' real names to protect their privacy. Desiree told about her terminally ill father, who had just a few weeks left, and she spent most of her days sitting next to his bed and reading him stories to distract him (and herself) from pain and suffering. Jaylen's uncle was shot over the break, and instead of the traditional Christmas celebration at grandmother's house, the family gathered at a funeral home. Another entry, written by Brianna, was a horrifying story of her cousin who had "gotten in a fight with some gang members." He had been jailed a few days later for drug possession and distribution. There wasn't a single journal entry full of joy, careless hanging out with family and friends, teenage awe of adventures — anything of that nature. Thinking back, I am also somewhat grateful there hadn't been much sharing in class as I surely wasn't ready to respond to their writing that day.

While research on teacher training in social-emotional learning (SEL) as well as trauma-informed pedagogy has gained increasing attention in recent years due to the recognition of the significant impact that these factors can have on student wellbeing and academic success, at that time, I had not been trained to understand the developmental impact of trauma, recognize trauma-related behaviors, or respond in ways that do not exacerbate trauma symptoms" (Jennings & Greenberg, 2009). I was unprepared and overwhelmed by the trauma-related needs of my students (Borntrager, Davis, & McCullough, 2017); on one hand, it affected me personally causing secondary trauma, and, on the other hand, I felt an obligation toward those children and their needs.

Turning and tossing that night, I didn't know what to do. How could I deal with their grief? Should I report things they shared with me to a school counselor? Should I talk to them the next day? If so, what could I say not to make things worse? The students' stories affected me as a member of our shared classroom community (Duane & Venet, 2022). Again, I was not prepared to process the pain, struggles, and grieving that my fourteen-year-old students were facing, nor was I ready to respond (Dunn & Garcia, 2020). To clarify, I did not come from a carefree family, and I wasn't raised in a pink bubble, not knowing any hardships. My parents had to work several jobs to provide for us, eight children. I often didn't have the simple essentials and felt embarrassed in front of my classmates. My adulthood began with the loss of my first husband to a tragic work accident, and I, too, had to put in double effort to raise my two young daughters. However, there was so much love, kindness, and support surrounding me during those darkest times in my life. I hoped my students had the care they needed but wanted to provide them with additional support since they spent time with me almost every day of the school year.

First, I needed to know more about my students to be able to respond with care and create an environment where students could feel safe to express their emotions especially after experiencing trauma (Silver & Zinsser, 2022). I also wish I was more familiar with the empathy theory at that time. Kristie J. Fleckenstein explains in her critical work on empathy that it "enables a person simultaneously to identify with and evaluate the suffering of another" (702) before responding or undertaking any of the steps. Some of the students may need a stronger support system and possibly professional counseling. The only school counselor on that school site was always busy with standardized testing, ACT or SAT prep, and college applications, and I didn't have the professional expertise to do that. All I had was my compassionate heart and words.

Words can heal—I read it somewhere before. More precisely, there is a concept and practice of poetry therapy, the "use of language, symbol, and story in therapeutic, educational, and community-building capacities" (Gorelick, 2005). Since writing was one of the major academic goals in this class, writing to get through difficult times sounded like a viable option as well. It would not interfere with learning because the healthier my students were, the more likely their young minds would perceive other lessons. I came to the next class with a new prompt and provided a poetry option response to it.

My students were not exposed to poetry much in the previous grade, and while I included reading and discussing poems quite a bit during the fall semester and often added this choice to the daily journals, students seldom wrote poems in response. Sincerely, I did not write much poetry at that time myself. After moving to the United States in 2005, I focused all of my efforts on getting my teaching credentials transferred to a MA degree here and obtaining a Louisiana state teaching certificate to be able to teach in a public school. Because English was my second language, preparing for classes took more time and effort compared to the local teachers. I also thought I wasn't skillful enough to write poetry in English. In other words, poetry wasn't at the forefront of my priorities.

Intuitively, however, I decided that there was no better time to begin, so my prompt for that day read:

> *Please, tell us how you feel today. What makes you feel this way? Is there any event in the past or anything that is going to happen soon affecting how you feel? You may tell as much as it makes you feel comfortable and safe. If you prefer not to discuss your feelings, write about anything you would like to share with us today. Your journal entry today may be constructed in a paragraph or poem form. You may also draw a picture and write a couple of sentences or poetry lines if you choose to do so.*

I wanted my students to turn to poetry because writing poetically means leaving blank spaces for things that are difficult to name, using less words to describe and process than in a regular paragraph form. To encourage responding in a poetry form, I spent a few minutes reminding students that the easiest way to express oneself through a poem is to try one of the forms of an "I Am" poem format, which was familiar to students. I projected on the board a couple of templates of the poem from the web sites.

I also pointed out that instead of going through a prescribed template, they could use a more flexible approach and choose fewer verbs that might help telling their story and finding the words to describe what they feel. For example, each stanza could begin with "I see," "I know," "I remember," "I understand," and so on until they could actually articulate their "I feel" statement. Or they could choose one line that will repeat the beginning of each stanza, e.g., "I am strong" or "I feel lost."

The two examples I modeled for that day were to help the adolescent writers in my class craft their poems. I chose short poems to eliminate intimidation and show that poetry was not beyond or above us: it belonged to our daily lives, and each one of us was capable of creating a poem. The first poem utilized an "I + verb" structure and was about the loss of my first husband when I was young. I projected the poem on the board and read it out loud.

I Feel Sad by Leilya A. Pitre

I see your picture on my desk,
Taking me to fond memories
We shared together.

I know your presence in my life
Was a generous gift
Anyone would be happy to have.

I remember your smile,
And the way your mouth curled upward
When you brought me flowers.

I read the words of comfort
That are meant to heal me,
But they make me cry.

I feel sad.

I told students what happened to my husband, how old I was at the time of his death, and how difficult it was for me to cope with that loss. Immediately, I heard several students say: "I am sorry, Mrs. Pitre." One of them came up to me asking: "Do you need a hug?" I held back tears responding to the hug and felt sad but not alone.

To create my poem, I chose the verbs "see," "know," "remember," "read," and "feel." I wanted my students to understand that before we named our feelings, we had to reflect on our experiences and do some inner work: to see, to know, to remember, and even to read. Some of them may want or need to do other things: to listen, to hear, to witness, to cry, to relive, and etc. By doing so, we process pain, grief, or other traumatic experiences; we also admit that bad things happened and somewhat accept them. This may not be the healing itself yet, but certainly seems like one of the first steps toward it.

The second poem with "I Am" structure was in response to the students' journal entries, which I mentioned earlier. In the poem, however, I intentionally avoided addressing their stories in particular to respect their privacy:

I Am Anxious by Leilya A. Pitre

I am anxious:
    Worries swirling in my mind,
    Clinging to me like a heavy cloak after the storm.

I am anxious:
    The world's unrest, injustice, and hatred
    Pull me to a breaking point.

I am anxious:
    My heart aches for those
    Who suffer and cry.

I am anxious,
    But I push forward and face reality.
    I will see a new day and a new hope.

That second poem was more straightforward beginning with the way the speaker felt at the moment—being anxious. Modeling this poem, I explained that I sometimes use spacing as a placeholder for some things that were difficult or painful to disclose, things I was still holding back. I also drew their attention to the final line of the poem: "I will see a new day and a new hope." I wanted them to understand that the traumatic experiences did not define our future and that we were able to cope with struggles and losses toward a better tomorrow, even if it is a tiny step at a time.

Setting a timer for ten minutes that day, I also wrote with my students. It had a repeating line, "I am soft-spoken and strong," and I wanted my students, especially the timid and quiet ones, to relate and learn to hold onto their inner strength. After the time was up, I asked for volunteers to share. A couple of students shared their journal entries. Devin was angry with the administration's push enforcing the dress code. His main complaint was about students restricted to uniforms, but teachers wearing whatever they wanted. Another student, Maggie, was frustrated with school lunch "healthy" choices. We discussed both issues briefly. I inquired if anyone wrote a poem and immediately saw at least two students who looked down. Without insisting to share, I suggested that if someone felt a little shy to read a poem out loud, they may, if they want, post it to our work board on the wall, so the others can read.

To encourage students even more, I shared my poem asking what they thought about it:

I am Soft-Spoken and Strong by Leilya A. Pitre

I am soft-spoken and strong.
I wonder if the quiet voices are ever heard.
I hear the whispers of my heart hitting the silence.
I see the beauty in calm and gentle strength.
I want people to understand my silent power.
I am soft-spoken and strong.

I pretend to be unshaken, a steady rock in the storm.
I feel the weight of grief, yet I stand tall.
I touch the wounds of my soul with tender hands.
I worry that my quiet strength is misunderstood.
I cry in the darkness, finding strength in my tears.
I am soft-spoken and strong.

I understand that silence is not weakness.
I say that healing comes from within.
I dream of a world that values the soft-spoken.
I try to show my strength through my actions.
I hope to inspire others with my gentle resilience.
I am soft-spoken and strong.

That poem allowed me to show my students that despite all the grief and sadness I carried, I was able to move on with my life, to see hope, and to heal. My students recognized my hidden abilities and even joked about my "superpower." They seemed to understand the main message too: silence or being soft-spoken was not weakness; it was my inner strength that helped me cope.

When I said goodbyes to my students on that winter day, I hurried to my desk and got into reading and writing. (Honestly, I just wanted to "disappear," so my kids could post their poems). It worked, and I saw two poems on that board in a few minutes. Both were sobering. The first one, written by Michelle, allowed me to humbly witness her vulnerability:

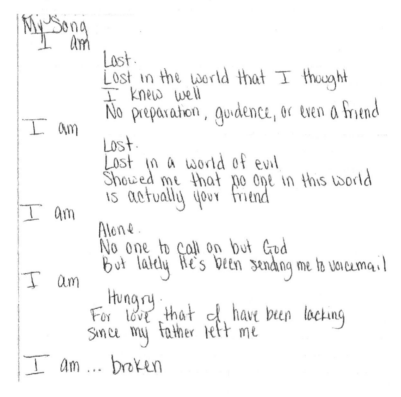

My Song
I am

Lost.
Lost in the world that I thought
I knew well
No preparation, guidence, or even a friend

I am

Lost.
Lost in a world of evil
Showed me that no one in this world
is actually your friend

I am

Alone.
No one to call on but God
But lately He's been sending me to voicemail

I am

Hungry.
For love that I have been lacking
Since my father left me

I am ... broken

Michelle was always quiet in class, very polite and so very quiet. She never complained about the classwork, her home life, or relationships with others. The line "No preparation, no guidance, or even a friend" revealed how lost she might have been "in the world." Further, she expressed loss of trust in people and their goodness calling that same world "evil." Finally, she disclosed that her hunger for love began after her father left. The final line, "I am...

broken," allowed her to name how she felt at that moment. I wanted to think that writing the poem helped her in some way to process her situation, and maybe even to begin her journey toward healing. She knew that if no one else would, I would read her poem: sharing it and allowing me to witness her experience made her feel seen and heard. What if it were the first time she had been offered space and time to express her feelings in a public setting? Poetry turned out to be less intimidating because she did not have to write long paragraphs or have sensitive conversations. She was able to use the white spaces to leave things unsaid the way she chose to do it.

I had no idea Michelle was hurt so deeply. I remember thinking: "How am I going to deal with this? What can I do for this child?" I could only love and care for her. I could let her know that I heard her, and I genuinely valued her. I also wanted her to see good in people, to experience kindness and love for which she longed in her poem. That poem was her opportunity to think more, to be seen, and I was glad she took a chance and posted it on the board. For me and other students in class, it was an act of bravery, but also a tiny peek into Michelle's soul. I wanted to see hope in that act of writing and sharing, but mostly, I wanted Michelle to see hope for herself.

The second poem came from Desiree, the girl by her dad's bedside who I mentioned earlier. Unlike Michelle, Desiree was more vocal. She often participated in class discussions; she loved to read out loud and always volunteered when I asked for readers. She made jokes and laughed. Yet, she never shared about her dad's illness before that day. The poem below is the one Desiree wrote:

Dad's Final Days by Desiree

I see
>   a man lying under white hospital covers
>   with a face exhausted by pain
>   and as white as the walls in his room.

I know
>   he is my Dad, my favorite person in the world,
>   who read me countless bedtime stories
>   and taught me to read when I was five.

I remember
>   him tall and strong, funny and kind,
>   reliable, protective, and loving.

He brought me treats from every trip he made.

I read
>> stories to him now,
>> for he has numbered days left,
>> I want him to know I can do it through pain.

I feel
>> scared, sorrowful, sad.

In this poem, Desiree expressed all her love to her dying father showing us how much he had meant to her and how grief-stricken she was. Choosing the verbs — see, know, remember, read, and feel — allowed her to create a thread, in which she attempted to describe the sad and imminent reality of her life. Her poem's structure closely imitated my first model poem and worked well to help Desiree organize her thoughts. The brevity of poetry allowed her to put her feelings into manageable pieces. I also noticed how she utilized spacing from the second example I provided for them. The spacing after the verbs made me pause and wonder about things she left unsaid; I also thought it could have been for her a chance to take a breath and gather strength to continue the poem. Desiree skillfully adopted from both the mentor poems elements that served her purpose and message.

Desiree's poem helped us observe her sadness, but also strength. In the second stanza, she described him as "my Dad, my favorite person in the world," a touching tribute to a loved one. She was devastated by the fact that her Dad, once "tall and strong, funny and kind, / reliable, protective, and loving," was fading away in front of her eyes. The line, "I want him to know I can do it through pain," signals her determination to stay by her Dad's bedside till the end. That line demonstrated her incredible ability to offer compassion under her tragic circumstances.

I consider the two poems gifts to me and those who read them on the classroom wall later that day and in the following days. Because students' work was often showcased in the classroom, it became a habit for many of my students to walk around and read what was posted on the walls. I saw students reading Michelle and Desiree's poems, spotting their slight nods and compassionate eyes. Reflecting back on those days, I am wondering whether I had to revisit the poems and somehow bring them back into a class discussion. Maybe, in the end, I wasn't ready for more discussions yet, but I do not regret assigning that prompt and the poems it produced.

What I learned from that experience was that both, Michelle and Desiree, wanted to share their stories. They wanted someone to notice them — to be seen and heard. They chose to post their poems to the writing board, and, hopefully, it helped them in their long journey toward healing. Those girls might not come to full acceptance of their situation yet, but at least they opened up and shared their pain in our classroom community. They made the first step toward recovery publicly, and poetry helped them do it. Those students realized that they were able to process their experiences and use poetic art with its possibilities to tell a story without saying a lot. Poetry served as a much needed outlet for putting thoughts and feelings into the words.

Another observation that stayed with me from that year was that people, and adolescents in particular, felt more comfortable to engage in emotional release through writing than through conversation or public discussion. One of the leading experts in poetry therapy, Gillie Bolton asserts that "a piece of paper is much more private: it can't answer back, interrupt, embarrass, or worst of all — remember" (p. 120). It is for this reason many find writing poetry stress-relieving and cathartic. More than that, when writing poetry in the classroom to address students' lives and experiences, we have to emphasize that there is no "good" or "bad" poem when we write to explore our feelings. This poetry is not judged on its literary merit. Instead, "there is only what each person creates out of himself for himself" (Leedy and Rapp, p. 145). We strive to represent our internal emotions, images, and struggles in the way we experience, understand, and interpret them.

Your Turn

Leilya Pitre has a way of making writing enjoyable, accessible, and effective, which you will discover with her prompt. She teaches at Southeastern Louisiana University, and coordinates the English Education Program. She loves to learn about people, culture, and rich traditions all over the world. Leilya's love for poetry is reflected in her recent book, *Where Stars Meet People: Teaching and Writing Poetry in Conversation.*

Short Prompt

Assist students in expressing their feelings and thoughts through poetry composing by introducing or reminding them of the use of the "I Am" poem format as an accessible way to write about one's experiences. To introduce the prompt, you may use the following wording or adjust it the way you find more fitting for your students:

Please, tell us how you feel today. What makes you feel this way? Is there anything that is bothering you and affecting how you feel? Tell as much as it makes you feel comfortable. If you prefer not to discuss your feelings, write about anything you would like to share with us today. Your journal entry today may be constructed in a paragraph or poem form. You may also draw a picture and write a couple of sentences or poetry lines if you choose to do so.

Full Prompt

Inspiration: As English teachers, we have countless opportunities to learn about our students from their writing, especially daily journals where they often share views on the topic at hand, connecting it to their life experiences. To be effective, we have to know our students better to tailor our teaching to their individual strengths and challenges. Thus asking them to craft a poem using the "I Am" form opens up a possibility for the teacher to learn about them and for students to learn about each other and connect, as well as establish a community space where everyone feels welcomed, supported, and safe, but most importantly seen and heard.

Process: To support students' writing, you may follow these instructional steps that work for most daily journaling activities in my classroom, and specifically in connection with poetry writing:

Introduce the journal prompt:
- Read the prompt aloud to the class. You may adopt my prompt provided earlier in this chapter or refine it for the needs of your students.
- Emphasize that students can write about their feelings or any other topic they wish to share.
- Encourage creativity and reassure students that their entries are private and will be respected.

Introduce the "I Am" Poem Format:
- Explain that one way to express feelings in poetry is

through the "I Am" poem format.
- Show examples of "I Am" poems to the class (these can be printed or projected).
- Discuss the structure of the "I Am" poem using one or two templates.

Provide Examples and Templates:
- Share a few examples of completed "I Am" poems with the students. You may use the examples of my poems from this chapter.
- Provide blank templates for students who might need a structured format to start.
- Provide students with a list of adjectives to describe feelings and a list of verbs, in addition to the verbs in the templates, they may use in their poems.
- Model crafting a poem for your students: show your thought process, explain how you follow the template, use spacing, and/or choose words.
- Encourage Expression and Creativity:
- Remind students that their poems do not have to rhyme and that they can be as personal or imaginative as they wish.
- Allow students to illustrate their poems if they choose, providing art supplies as needed.
- Encourage students to write freely and not worry about perfection.

Sharing (Optional):
- Offer students the opportunity to share their poems or journal entries with the class, if they feel comfortable.
- Create a safe and supportive environment for sharing.
- Designate some space in the classroom for posting students' work.

Leilya's Suggestions for the Classroom
Finally, to help your students succeed, please keep in mind these suggestions too:
- Do not offer this prompt at the very beginning of the school year. Get to know your students first, and it will help you frame the prompt considering your students and their life experiences;
- Do not assign grades or any form of evaluation for this work; in other words, do not turn this opportunity for sharing and healing into an assignment;
- Be supportive and positive in your feedback.

- Respect students' privacy and allow them to keep their entries private if they wish.
- Celebrate the creativity and effort of each student.
- By using these instructions, teachers can help students engage with the journal prompt and explore their emotions and thoughts creatively through the "I Am" poem format. Exercises, similar to this one, are beneficial for building a community in your classroom, improving not only students' writing skills, but, hopefully, their emotional state, sense of belonging, and coping abilities.

References

Atwell, N. (2015). *In the middle: A lifetime of learning about writing, reading, and adolescents*. Heinemann.

Bolton, G. (1999). "Every poem breaks a silence that had to be overcome": The Therapeutic Power of Poetry Writing." *Feminist Review, vol. 62/1*, 118-133.

Dean, D. (2010). Teacher as writer: Encouraging students through modeling and participation. *English Journal*, 100(1), 21-26.

Duane, A. & Venet, A. S. (2022). Thirteen ways of looking at trauma: Possibilities and considerations for ELA teachers. *Special Issues, Volume 2: Trauma-Informed Teaching: Toward Responsive, Humanizing Classroom*. NCTE, 13-23.

Dunn, M.B. & Garcia, A. (2020). Grief, loss, and literature: Reading texts as social artifacts. *The English Journal, 109*(6), 52-58.

Elbow, P. (2000). *Everyone can write: Essays toward a hopeful theory of writing and teaching writing*. Oxford University Press.

Fleckenstein, K. S. (2007). Once again with feeling: Empathy in deliberative discourse. *JAC, Vol. 27, No. 3*(4), 701-716.

Gallagher, K. (2011). *Write like this: Teaching real-world writing through modeling & mentor texts*. Stenhouse Publishers.

Gorelick, K. (2005). Poetry therapy. *Expressive therapies*, 117-140.

Leedy, J. J. & Rapp, J. (1973). Poetry therapy and some links to art therapy. *Art Psychotherapy, vol. 1/1*, 1973, 145-151.

Murray, D. M. (2004). *A writer teaches writing*. Heinle & Heinle.

Pitre L. (2019). A circle of trust: Creating a community of writers. *The English Journal, 109*(1), 59-66.

Rodgers, C. R. (2002). The benefits of teachers writing with students: An analysis. *Journal of Teacher Education*, 53(5), 382-390.

Silver, H. C., & Zinsser, K. M. (2022). Lessons for the future: Supporting the social-emotional needs of children, families, and educators in Head Start during the COVID-19 pandemic. *Translational Issues in Psychological Science, 8*(3), 362–374.

Whitney, A., & Lensmire, T. (2016). Writing together: An inquiry with students. *English Education,* 48(2), 131-151.

Poetic Reflection by Jonathon Medeiros

When I am found out as a teacher, after the "Oh, I could never do that" and the "Wow, summers off!", people inevitably get around to asking: "What do you teach?" When they do, I can barely force an answer.

In my mind are ideas and feelings that swirl around, wordless, or waiting for words.

Out loud I might say that "I have Language Arts classes" or that "I learn about language with high school students." Sometimes I give in and say that "I teach 11th Language Arts and Rhetoric." I know that "I teach English" is not the right response for me. For one, people relish the chance to exclaim "I hated English!" as if we might bond over that, as if I might not actually love my job.

But more importantly, my students have different languages and have brilliant ideas in those languages. I do not want to raise up one language as more correct than another. Instead, I want us all to learn about the power of language, especially the power of reflective writing, of struggling to find words for our thoughts. This is a powerful way to help us process our world, our lives, the texts and conversions around us, and to connect across the void to each other. Poetry writing can be a simple avenue for this kind of work.

I've realized that many of my students do not have, are not given, the time and space to reflect on themselves, their own ideas and values, to even realize where they are, the communities they are part of and consequently the responsibilities they have to themselves and each other. When faced with questions like "Who are you?" or "What do you believe?" or "Why this and not that?" many students come up blank or point to some other source, like a book of faith or a coach. But I want us to slow down, to reflect, to look at ourselves, and to process what we see by writing and talking.

To do this kind of work, we first look to other people and struggle through their ideas, not to take them wholesale as our own but to follow their lead, to explore, reflect, and discover our own feelings and ideas. For example, we start the year by looking to Aunty Puanani Burgess and her amazing text "Building the Beloved Community," itself responding to Martin Luther King Jr. She is a voice that sounds different from the typical ELA text and we begin to realize that ideas can be important and serious and not sound like "proper" English. But also we follow her lead and turn her ideas towards our own lives, in an attempt to process what she is saying and to explore who we might be right now.

Burgess's work centers storytelling to build and heal community. The first of these stories is the story of our names. She explains her process in prose but she also teaches us in verse. Burgess explores her name in a poem called "Choosing My Name." This poem becomes our teacher and so we ask, what is this poem teaching? We read, reread, and discuss the text. Students practice typical Language Arts skills like analysis and textual response, but they also go further by exploring their own names. Ostensibly they are proving they know what she did by doing it themselves, but really they are doing the work of reflecting and exploring themselves. This poem is teaching us how to know ourselves, our names, and our connections to family, community, and each other.

The poems the students create are poignant, funny, insightful, and remain as one of the most memorable things we do, even months and years later. We also stage a poetry reading, reminding the students that their ideas matter too, just as much as Aunty Pua's, just as much as Walt Whitman's, more so even. In the Burkean parlor, these students are equal guests, they belong there too.

Truthfully though, the presented poem is not the point. The work leading up to it is what matters. That exploratory, reflective work, is where the discoveries are, where the learning really is. This is the one truth that I know: the work matters, the work is where the learning is; the final product is a carcass.

So, when someone asks me "What do you teach?" I think about reflection, about using writing to help us process, our names, our ideas, our worlds. I often do not know what I think until I write or talk or both. Struggling to find words changes us; poetry can be a purposeful and powerful processing tool for each of us, a lifelong healthy habit, like stretching, breathing, drinking water.

> The sand at the beach
> Depends on the beach
> It is leftovers, the end of the circle of matter,
> Just crushed shells,
> Houses of beings who have long ago moved on
> It is recycled, ground coral,
> Broken pieces of spines or bone or tooth
> Piled up on the sea floors, on the edges of land, not quite land itself
> It is fine, or coarse, like yellow or white silt or multicolored

pebbles
Some sand shows you what it was
Allows you to peer into the ages
And places it came from, the edge of that reef
Or an island long eroded under the waves
Some sand shakes off when you stomp
Your foot at the car door
And some stays with you for hours,
Days,
Appearing when you clean an ear,
Or run your hand through your hair,
Wipe your palm across your eyes,
Or when you sweep the floor of a room that is far from the
shore
How much sand have I swallowed,
Tumbling in the sea? Sitting on a towel,
Eating a picnic of chips, dip, peanut butter and veggies, and
sand, of course
How much has disappeared into my clothes,
Towels, the floors of cars?
The sand at the beach
Depends on the beach
I was raised on an island of them,
On a planet of beaches fringing the specks of land that rudely
Interrupt the sea
I was raised by the shore,
The shore raised us, tempted us into jumping from tree limbs
And dunes,
Warmed our backs as we found respite from the wind, the
water,
It caked the corners of our eyes,
Polished our skin
And it says to us "I am moving. Are you?"

Jonathon Medeiros, former director of the Kaua'i Teacher Fellowship, has been teaching and learning about Language Arts and rhetoric for nearly 20 years with students on Kaua'i and he frequently writes about education, equity, and the power of curiosity. He believes in teaching his students that if you change all of your mistakes and regrets, you'd erase yourself.

CHAPTER 15

Write Along With Me: An Invitation Accepted
Margaret Simon

> *Poems are like prayers, sent out into the world to help us endure challenges and ultimately, make our world a better place.*
>
> –Georgia Heard

There's a new coffee shop in town connected to the gift shop of Cane River Pecan Company, an inviting space of high ceilings and ambient lighting, tall windows, a mural of Bayou Teche snaking through this very place, "You are Here." We sit on the sofa and side chair, not as teacher to student, but as writers together making sense of the world.

Kayla sent me persistent emails from September to February asking me to lead an after-school poetry group. I finally said, "Can we meet at the Pie Bar?"

Francisco, a 26 year old violinist who was visiting our town, told me he wanted to write poetry. I invited him to join Kayla and me.

I have been teaching for a long time, 36 years. I use poetry as a teacher showing students the way to imagery and figurative language in their own writing. I teach gifted elementary students in two rural schools in New Iberia, Louisiana. I travel from school to school with a notebook for each setting and write when my students write. I freely share my writing with my students—the good and the not so good drafts. I never expected to build a relationship with a student through this practice.

Meet the Student

The year 2020 was hard on everyone. Losses were huge. Loss of loved ones. Loss of learning. The messages of the pandemic kept us all worried and anxious, not to mention our tender students.

I held daily meetings with a small group of students remotely. These students were slipping from my grasp. The district had set up remote learning through an online program that most of them just wouldn't do. More and more of them turned their cameras off when we met. Their grades were dropping, and I felt helpless.

In October, Kayla came back to in-person school. She was in 5th grade. She was the only gifted student in her grade and in her school. Giftedness in the state of Louisiana is determined through testing: an IQ test and 2 academic tests for reading and math. A student qualifies for special education classes if they meet the criteria of 6 points or higher on a matrix that leans heavily on these test scores. At some schools there are few who qualify. Kayla was one out of her whole school of 500+ students, so she was isolated and alone. We met for her morning ELA block, masked and 6 feet apart.

Building a Relationship Using Side-by-side Writing

Kayla was lost, sad, and resistant to help. I tried each day to draw her out of her shell. There were days I couldn't reach her, and we sat in silence. But there was always poetry.

Poetry became a safe space for us to talk to each other. We would read a poem that I selected as a model poem. We'd discuss the elements and what we thought the poem was trying to say and then we would write together.

Kayla did not always share her writing. But as the year progressed, she became more confident. In the fall of 2020, her grandmother had died suddenly. Both Kayla and her single mother were devastated. Neither one could speak about it. Until Kayla wrote a tribute poem to "Honey," her dear grandmother.

Honey by Kayla

Her smile that brightened up the room and everyone's day.
Optimistic and unique, she was.
Never frowned or had open emotions, she just kept her beautiful smile
    on her face as always.
Ever since I first even laid my eyes on her, I just knew she'd be my best
    friend forever and always. And now....
You know about the woman that I loved with my whole heart, named
    Honey.

Finding Form

Using the acrostic form gave Kayla a space to honor her grandmother. This form is easy to teach. Using the letters of a word going down the page on the left margin, write a word or phrase using each letter of the word. "Honey" was Kayla's grandmother. The letters gave her a structure to work from. Using simple forms, such as acrostic, haiku, cinquain, can hold space for a student to say what they want to say.

By January 20, 2021, Kayla and I had built a trust for each other around poetry. Together we watched the amazing Amanda Gorman present her poem "The Hill We Climb" at the presidential inauguration. Amanda Gorman is a black poet who became the first National Youth Poet Laureate in 2017. President Biden asked her to be his inaugural poet, and she delivered a spectacular poem as the youngest poet to have written and performed as an inaugural poet.

Kayla immediately felt the rhyme and rhythm in her soul. Rhyme became part of her healing poetry about her grandmother.

Nirvana by Kayla

Honey was like nirvana on Earth
Paradise she was, all since her birth
August 21st, a brand new soul
Is the birth of a soul who makes our family whole
Sad to see her gone, preciousness now only expressed in pictures
But her life goes on in our hearts, and when our hearts are broken, she's our little fixer.

Kayla and I looked for everything Amanda Gorman had to offer. We watched video after video. One of these was recorded by the Library of Congress[1] when Amanda Gorman read "In this Place (An American Lyric)" written for Tracy K. Smith's inauguration as Poet Laureate in 2017. Amanda Gorman's poem and a lesson plan are available at Poets.org.[2] The poem uses the literary device of anaphora (a repeated phrase) to capture the reader. "There's a poem in this place." Anaphora is a device used by Martin Luther King, Jr. in his famous "I Have a Dream" speech. Kayla adapted the line as a title for her poem.

As Kayla listened to the poem, she wrote. And after class that day, she sent me two more poems by email. Amanda lit a fire in her, a flame for words.

There's a poem in this place by Kayla
after Amanda Gorman

Not here nor there
But there's no need to look everywhere
tug and pull on my hair
Hoping that this poem, has time to spare
There's a poem in this place
While i'm in disgrace
Of finding my lyric
That belongs in this place
There's a poem in this place
Still not being found
Is it in a dog hound?
No, it weighs more than that one pound
There's a poem in this place
While the wind is hitting my face
Being withdrawn due to lack of space
Without leaving any sign of a trace
There's a poem in this place
Where could it be?
Wait, I have found it!
It's in YOU
and ME.

Our writing together became a conversation. The model poem would serve as a jumping off place, and then we were two writers making sense of the world using poetry.

"The simple and powerful act of creating a deep relationship with words you love can be a medicine—igniting healing and awakening in you and those around you" Kim Rosen (2009, 19).

In *Poem Central: Word Journeys with Readers and Writers* (2014, 90), Shirley McPhillips writes, "Being invited into someone's inner life can be disconcerting, even disturbing. We can turn away. Or we can enter into a relationship with the poem, perhaps better to understand the human condition we share with others the world over."

I didn't turn away from Kayla, from her sorrow or from her words. I allowed her to bleed on the page with me beside her, honoring each new poem, showing her that someone cared.

Poetry Connects Us

In the spring of her 7th grade year, Kayla contacted me through email with an invitation to her birthday party. I couldn't attend her party, but I wrote back and shared a poem I had written about my father who died in April, 2022. Because she had shared so much of her grief in our time together, I felt I could share my most vulnerable poems as well. I wrote in response to Allison Berryhill's prompt "What You Missed"[3] on Ethical ELA: "What have you missed? What might you have missed by skipping/avoiding an activity or situation? What have others missed that you wish they'd experienced? I invite you to explore "something missed" in a literal or imaginary sense."

What you Missed the Year You've been Gone by Margaret Simon

Since you've been gone, spring sprang again with bright
cypress green and pops of buttercups along the roadway.
Baby June was born on winter's solstice. She's blooming,
too.
You'd want to make raspberries on her strawberry cheeks.
Since you've been gone, we've moved Mom twice
finding better and better care for her. We think you'd
approve
because I walked beside a woman with a dog
who told me about her mother. We talked and talked
then she said her name was Beverly like your favorite niece
whose southern drawl comforted like a soft pillow.
I miss you on days like this, when the birds sing opera,
the sun hides behind the clouds. I kiss your great
grandson.
He's forgotten you died and says, "Where's Pop?"
I haven't forgotten, but I think I see you in his smile.

Kayla was moved to write another poem about her grandmother, Honey.

(Untitled) by Kayla

Since you've been gone, intrusive thoughts compelled me
convincing me I was the reason you aren't here

Elijah was born, and so was Chandler
I see you when I look in Chandler's eyes, so they wonder
why I don't look at him often

Since you've been gone, things have been going well
Moving houses, Having kids and getting promoted in
workplaces

I haven't been making the best of friends
Friends you wouldn't approve of

because your definition of a friend is to grow old
and have kids that'll call each other "cousin."

I miss you on days where the clouds are white
Where the sky is bright, and no spite in Honey and Miss
K's world

We Are Poets

To be a teacher of writing, you have to make yourself a student
sitting beside them, reading together, writing together, sharing
your own life with each other. Kayla's willingness to share her grief
with me showed that even on the darkest days when she wouldn't
turn her camera on or put her head down on her desk, she was
listening and learning the healing power of writing poetry. She has
carried that lesson with her and it will sustain her for the rest of her
life.

Today, we meet at The Pie Bar, drink an iced tea or lemonade,
talk about a poem, open our notebooks and write. Kayla has come
back to me. Not all students will do this. I am honored that she has
kept me in her life, and I have kept her. She chose to call our small
writing group *The Three Pecans* since we are three who meet at a
Pecan Company's Pie Bar, but the name stuck. We laugh about it.
We laugh a lot. Kayla wrote about our special bond in a poem, of
course, because she is a poet. She will always be a poet. I am sure of
that!

(Untitled) by Kayla

The three pecans
with each meeting,
grow from orchards
speak upon themselves
about flores, raíces,
and things that are "dumal"
French styled books
& broken down pens
with tiramisu & cake
that looks like shamrock
the presence of each pecan
blessed with the other.

Your Turn

Margaret Simon has been an elementary school teacher for 36 years, most recently teaching gifted students in Iberia Parish. She published a book of children's poetry, *Bayou Song: Creative Explorations of the South Louisiana Landscape*. Margaret's poems have appeared in anthologies including The Poetry of US by National Geographic and Rhyme & Rhythm: Poems for Student Athletes.

In 2017, Amanda Gorman became the National Youth Poet Laureate. In this role she broke ground with young African American poets. She immediately became a national role model when she became the youngest person to write and perform a poem at a Presidential Inauguration. She read "The Hill We Climb" which has since become a book.

Short Prompt
"A Poem in this Place" by Amanda Gorman makes use of anaphora, a repeated line: "There's a poem in this place." Play a video of Amanda Gorman reading this poem. Write using the line "There's a poem in this place."

Full Prompt
    Inspiration: The idea that someone who died would actually miss things came to me in a poem by Ted Kooser, former Poet Laureate of the U. S. In his poem "Mother," he explores all the things his mother is not present for, such as wild plums

blooming, three rains, and other things found in nature.

Mother
by Ted Kooser

Mid April already, and the wild plums
bloom at the roadside, a lacy white
against the exuberant, jubilant green
of new grass an the dusty, fading black
of burned-out ditches. No leaves, not yet,
only the delicate, star-petaled
blossoms, sweet with their timeless perfume.

You have been gone a month today
and have missed three rains and one nightlong
watch for tornadoes. I sat in the cellar
from six to eight while fat spring clouds
went somersaulting, rumbling east. Then it poured,
a storm that walked on legs of lightning,
dragging its shaggy belly over the fields.

The meadowlarks are back, and the finches
are turning from green to gold. Those same
two geese have come to the pond again this year,
honking in over the trees and splashing down.
They never nest, but stay a week or two
then leave. The peonies are up, the red sprouts
burning in circles like birthday candles,

for this is the month of my birth, as you know,
the best month to be born in, thanks to you,
everything ready to burst with living.
There will be no more new flannel nightshirts
sewn on your old black Singer, no birthday card
addressed in a shaky but businesslike hand.
You asked me if I would be sad when it happened

and I am sad. But the iris I moved from your house
now hold in the dusty dry fists of their roots
green knives and forks as if waiting for dinner,
as if spring were a feast. I thank you for that.
Were it not for the way you taught me to look
at the world, to see the life at play in everything,
I would have to be lonely forever.

Ted Kooser, "Mother" from Delights & Shadows. Copyright © 2004 by Ted Kooser. Reprinted with the permission of The Permissions Company, an LLC on behalf of Copper Canyon Press.[4]

Process: Begin with the line "You have been gone for (insert time, a month, a year, etc.) and have missed..." What would you want to tell your loved one about? Is it nature, a change in your life, or a new understanding? Write in the first person using *you* for the one who is missed. Include sensory details as evidenced in Kooser's poem.

Margaret's Suggestions for the Classroom
- Do not shy away from a deep dive into a poet's work. Every poet has their own voice. Students can find their own voice by experimenting with lines and poetic devices from other poets.
- Students need to know that their teachers are writers, too. Write with your students every time you ask them to write. Do not ask your students to do something you are not willing to try yourself.
- Performance poetry can be powerful. Encourage your students to share their writing in a public space. Encourage poetry readings at your school.
- During National Poetry Month, my students secretly post poems in the hallways. These can be original poems posted anonymously, or poems by authors. The more students read poetry, the better the world will be.

Links

[1]https://blogs.loc.gov/loc/2021/01/amanda-gorman-selected-as-president-elect-joe-bidens-inaugural-poet/

[2]   https://poets.org/lesson-plan/teach-poem-place-american-lyric-amanda-gorman

[3] https://www.ethicalela.com/what-you-missed/

[4] https://www.coppercanyonpress.org/

CHAPTER 16

"That Could Be a Poem!" Poetry and Student Engagement
Wendy Everard

Laura and Eveyln strode into our last-period-of-the-day Creative Writing class and announced: "Mrs. Everard, we came up with a new saying. Whenever *anything* happens...we look at each other and say, 'That could be a poem!'"

Their gleeful announcement captured the spirit of our Creative Writing class which has encouraged students to bend writing rules, think outside of the box, and write from their hearts. These post-Covid days at school have seen their fair share of tears, anxiety, and depression, and part of my job as an English teacher has me acting in the role of mentor, coach, and counselor as well as educator. Regardless of whether these roles are in my purview, the vulnerable emotional state of students right now is hard to deny, and teaching is hard to do if we aren't dealing with the challenges of student mental health. Creative writing—and poetry, in particular—has served as a needed emotional balm for my students.

I launched our inaugural Creative Writing class in the fall of 2020, amid masks, quarantining, and the revolving door that our hybrid school year became, with some students learning at school, some from home, and many instances of entire classes periodically quarantined at home. The year before, I had discovered Sarah Donovan's Ethical ELA website and had begun to write poetry again on my own, after a respite of many years to focus on teaching and parenting, as a way to heal from my father's long illness from COPD and to express my feelings about motherhood. Our Creative Writing class gave me the opportunity to pass this gift of "poetry as healing" on to my students.

One way that I did this was to open the door to participation in Ethical ELA to my students. Teachers were invited to contribute prompts to the site, and one month I developed a prompt on the poetry form called the ghazal, an Arabic poetry structure with an inventive but fairly structured form. Students were intrigued and challenged by the form, but rose to this challenge.

As I believe in writing with my students, I shared a poem that I had written, reflecting on my dad's recent passing. He was difficult to communicate with, a Vietnam veteran and a man of few words concerning his feelings and his wartime experiences. Conveying my feelings through poetry really seemed to help me with the grieving and healing processes as I worked through my feelings about our relationship:

Ghazal by Wendy Everard

The silence appalls me now,
Signaling, finally, the end of his life.

Given the choice, I would have had noise,
Rounding, with him, this very last bend in his life.

It happened so suddenly, breathtaking utterly, watching the monitor
Tracing the very last trend in his life.

Time seemed to slow, but speed up as well,
The space seemed to swell, and God seemed to send for his life.

His hands fluttered — pale birds! — yet I uttered no words
Unsure what he heard, as he groped for one final friend in this life.

I also asked one of my Creative Writing students, Ali, if he wouldn't mind sharing (on the Ethical ELA site) a ghazal that he had written during class. Ali was pleased and excited at the prospect of sharing a poem in a form that was perfected by one of his favorite poets, Rumi. Ali was visiting from Pakistan, and this was his first journey from his home in Peshawar to the United States. He eagerly embraced creative writing and poetry:

Ali's Poem

It's the deepness of his eyes
That kept me captive for so long

It's the sensation of your presence
That makes every moment so long

Today the wine also stopped pouring
That healed me for so long

Walking on the shores of life
I waited for you so long

Surrounded by sorrows and pains
I called for help so long

Every known has become unknown
Heart has been abandoned for so long

After the end of your company
I cried for you for so long

He is surprised by your presence, Ali
Where were you for so long?

An exchange student, Ali was finding it difficult to make friends. Intelligent, quiet, and thoughtful, he was observant and a bit shy. He'd found his niche a bit in soccer, but he struggled to find companions who were like him. During Creative Writing class, poetry (and personal narrative) gave him the opportunity to blossom, expressing his feelings and playing with English expression in a forum that encouraged experimentation with language. Ali and I would talk frequently, both in person and through his running Google doc, about how his writing was progressing, about writing itself, and about his ideas. Sometimes he was much more forthcoming on the "Comments" section of the Google Doc that contained his writing pieces than he was in person. I would comment on an idea or an instance in his life that he expressed in a poem or in a piece about his life, and he would open up like a faucet, happy to share his experiences with a friendly and receptive ear. As much as Ali learned from our class, I learned from him about his life in Pakistan and the differences from (and similarities to) his life here, in the United States.

Ali wasn't the only student to experience the pleasant and satisfying release of self-expression through verse; another student,

Betty, embraced poetry writing with fervor and found, in self-expression, some profound catharsis as she wrote often about her identity and how it affected her relationship with her family. In a response to my "Mosaic Poem" prompt on Ethical ELA, Betty wrote about her internal struggles:

(1/3) - Mosaic Poem by Betty

my mosaic used to be beautiful,
but now,
it's tearing at the seams.

it used to glow, it used to
be polished,
shiny,
pristine, but now…

now it's cracked.

the pieces that were carved from her,
her,
or him:
those pieces are
falling apart.

they've faced the end of
a sledgehammer too many times.

slowly, but surely,
despite how beautiful they used to be,

i'm learning to
let go.

because it's not those pieces that
define me.

and when the little workers,
with their hard-hats and their construction tools,
come to get rid of those pieces,
my mosaic will be whole again.

it'll make a new picture!

a brand new,
shiny,
beautiful picture.

one where i get to flourish.

one where everyone will look
and say,

"wow, they're strong;
look at what they've
accomplished."

my new mosaic will withstand

the floods,
the hail,
the hurricanes,
and the tornadoes.

we are a mosaic of everyone we've ever loved,

but which pieces
we want to keep...

that's up to us to decide.

Betty was going through a rough patch during her time in our class. As a young, openly gay woman, Betty struggled with family members who were resistant to her acceptance of and burgeoning openness about her sexual identity. In particular, Betty found herself caught between her dad, who was supportive of her journey, and his mother—her grandmother—who struggled to accept that the granddaughter that she'd always thought she'd known possessed a facet of herself that was difficult to accept. Betty was candid about this struggle in class, expressing her feelings through her poetry and prose. In particular, Betty found poetry a cathartic experience, using the form to express her feelings about her dad, her grandmother, herself, and the struggle that they were enmeshed in. Having a supportive group of class members in which to express herself was critical in helping Betty to embrace her identity, attempt to understand what her family members were feeling, and become comfortable expressing how she felt about the situation. There were times that Betty offered to read a poem to us, though it made her emotional; her classmates proved to be a loving and supportive cohort of friends and companions, helping Betty to come to terms with her feelings through her poetry.

Not only were the students in our Creative Writing class eager participants while in class, but many volunteered to be student mentors when I formed a Middle School Creative Club after school. They showed up once a week, after school, to write with younger, emerging writers, serving as positive writing role models for them and taking the lead in drawing them out of their shells and encouraging them to assume the mantle of young writers.

Creative Writing class opened the door for Ali, for Betty, for me, and for all of my students to express and share our words, experiencing some catharsis and comradeship, together. On the heels of a world-upending pandemic and in the midst of strife and struggle, students and teachers alike were emotional deeply and daily. It was occasions such as this that brought— and continue to bring—students and teachers together as writing partners to engage in authentic, heartfelt, productive dialogue with one another.

Your Turn

Wendy Everard's role as mother and teacher gives her plenty to write about since she started writing personal narrative and poetry, lifelong hobbies that were reignited when she joined a summer institute with the Seven Valleys branch of the National Writing Project a few years ago and began mentoring student teachers. She is a high school English teacher and writer living in central New York.

Short Prompt
To begin, journal a bit about people who have influenced — who, in your opinion, have built the mosaic that is you (for better or worse!).
Add some reflection on what facets of you have come to being as a result of these influences.

You may begin writing in your journal right away to continue your healing. If it feels that you are not ready yet for a poem, you may just jot down some of your thoughts, write a narrative paragraph about your experience, or record these thoughts on your phone. You may always come to it later — you've already made the first step.

Full Prompt
If you would like more support, the full prompt is printed below for you to follow along with Wendy Everard's Mosaic Poem.[1]

The Inspiration:
In the midst of 2021, one of my students shared this with me:
"There was an internet trend a little bit ago that was based on the saying 'We are all mosaics of everyone we've ever met' meaning that every part of us, all our quirks, are something we do because someone we know or love influenced us to. I don't like my mosaic. I don't like most of the people who influenced it. I want to build a new mosaic." –Mica, Grade 12

The Process:
- Write a poem about the mosaic that comprises you, for better or worse.
- Write a poem about the mosaic that you'd like to be.

- Write a poem about someone you know who is a mosaic, composed of people or experiences.

NOTE: A useful approach is to start with prose, reflecting about the influences that have built us (or someone close to us). Then draw from the ideas and language in your prose to build your poem. Use whatever form you wish for this poem. This article[2] by writer Fatimah Alayafi may serve as inspiration. As always, feel free to write on a topic of your choice today if you have a poem that just needs to be written!

Wendy's Suggestions for the Classroom
Finally, while this chapter is for you, dear teacher, we'd love for you to invite students to write. If you want to try a version of this prompt with your students, here are a few things to keep in mind:

- Offer the option of writing from a different persona if the topic is too close to home — remind students that they can write about someone else who is a mosaic of others and that this can be someone that they know personally or even a celebrity, athlete, or writer who has been influenced by those who came before them.
- word the prompt appropriately for your students' age;
- include a mentor poem. The more students read, the better they write. It helps expand their vocabulary as well.
- spend a few minutes modeling how to approach the poetry composing. Show them your writing process. Notice that you also may struggle with phrasing or finding the most fitting word.
- allow students to reject your prompt completely and write something they choose to create on their own.

Extending this writing activity to your students may result in developing closer connections with your students, their lives, and experiences. It might be that little nudge they need to open up, discover a way of sharing their inner emotional state, and find a path to healing with poetry in a safe space of their classroom.

Links
[1] https://www.ethicalela.com/mosaic-poem/
[2] https://medium.com/change-your-mind/we-are-a-mosaic-of-everyone-weve-ever-loved-74b1556a3b51

CHAPTER 17

Finding Home
Jennifer Guyor Jowett

Dear Mrs. Jowett,

When I first entered this school, I didn't understand what a poem really was. I thought writing was meaningless scribbles on paper. I never put too much thought into writing. I never understood how a debate worked, how to give a proper speech, or how to just write. Of course, I knew how to write back then, but not in the same way. Not only has my writing style changed, but I have too. I have learned how to put true depth into my writing. I hope you continue to inspire students the way you have inspired me.

Sincerely, Misa

Throughout that year, Misa was on a journey, both literal and figurative. She arrived in our junior high classroom, sharing a room with 20 other students in our suburban Catholic school, after having spent a lot of her life in Palau, an archipelago country I'd heard of but wouldn't have been able to accurately identify on a map. Her school experience, her whole life experience really, differed drastically from that of our students. She was quiet, observant, thoughtful, and a fast learner.

Misa began teaching me words from her language, Palauan, during our daily walking breaks. I hoped to get to know her by finding spaces where we shared an interest, and conversations about culture and language were a starting point. Reaching another person through words is one way to make them feel at home, and I wanted her to feel we could be a home too. Granted, we didn't get very far in our altered role of teacher/student. School is a busy place and my brain is a sieve under the deluge of things to do, but one word took hold quickly, *daob*, which means sea.

She wrote of the sea, her home, continuously throughout the year during our 15 minute daily writes. I could sense the yearning behind her words, the loss of a place and what it meant to her. Poetry about the sea began popping up almost immediately. Here's a piece from early in the year:

Art by Misa

When I create art
I move my pen along paper
Long lines
Like the wind blowing along
The   earth
Small wavy lines s t r e t c h across the paper.
More and
          More.
I have created a sea.
With spots calm and rough.

Big curved lines

     Islands
A place to explore and a home to many.
I have created something,
I have created a world.
From my imagination
All
   In   one
Small piece of paper.

Her play with space is intriguing, (we'd explored poems from Kwame Alexander's *Crossover*, noting the artform of word placement), especially in conjunction with the topic of home: the separation between *the* and *earth*, the word *island* sitting all alone on a line, and the word *one* isolated and distanced from all. Misa clearly had something to voice, and the arts became an outlet.

Writers have a tendency to return again and again to meaningful topics as they try to work through and better understand them. This return is an exploration as much as it is a healing. In a class of only forty some students, our junior high staff of five gets to know each of them pretty well. As Misa and I talked throughout the year, I found that she came more alive when she spoke of Palau, and while she may not have been homesick, there was a calling for her islands. Michigan, for most of the school year, differs greatly from Palau, and she yearned for the warmth and the water.

Her writing was most alive then too.

We begin our English classes with a Daily Fifteen where we explore a poetry prompt, read mentor poems, and write in sustained quiet for fifteen minutes. Students select the piece they feel most connected to and most strongly about to share with me in their journals or with the entire class in an optional open mic setting at the end of the week. Giving students prompts that guide and allowing them to have topics of their choosing enables them to find their voice and to delve into writing that often has autobiographical themes.

Shortly after, Misa wrote this from a Snapshot Poem prompt:

Snapshot Poem by Misa

A brown rocky path back home
The thumping of tiny feet
A small child carries a silvery-blue fish
Laughing as she catches up to her parents

She throws the fish onto her shoulder
Touching its silvery scales
Brown hair tangled from running
A big smile from fishing

This poem has a sense of joy in laughter and smiles, a sense of energy in the thumping, throwing, and running. There's a grounding of both the land and the people. While snapshot poems give us just a glimpse, they allow us to see beyond the image and into the person.

Later, Misa's sense of yearning for home returns, more strongly, from a "What I Want Is" prompt. Based on C.G. Hanzlicek's poem of the same name, this writing focuses on two line stanzas while reinforcing prepositional phrases. It allows students to continue to refine their voice by declaring a want and furthering imagery through adjective and adverb phrases.

What I Want by Misa

What I want is
An ocean

Sometimes calm
Sometimes waves break the shore

What I want is
The familiar sound of waves roaring in the distance

The tide rising and falling
Day after day

What I want is
Another chance to

Dive into the deep blue water
After rolling in the sand

At that time of year, we were in the cold months of Michigan. Most students were wishing for tropical vacation spots to escape the snow and ice. But Misa was wishing for her home, the familiar, for a day to day that rose and fell with the tide. Just as place can shape us, we can shape place in the writing of poetry.

One of her final pieces was a Location Poem modeled after a selection from Elizabeth Acevedo's *Clap When You Land* and mentor poems written by previous students and me. In the introduction of the mentor pieces, we focused on noticings: line breaks, interesting verbs, sound words, and internal rhyme.

Misa's poem not only shows the development of her writing over the course of the year (notice the word choices, figurative language, and the play with placement in onomatopoetic words), but this poem also highlights her voice.

From Palau by Misa

I can tell you a lot about rain

I know when the tin roof above beats in an endless tune
And when the sky darkens to a soft gray and blue mix,

217

Because rain is our way of knowing the sky.

I know the cold breeze that comes
With the endless flow of misty droplets that fall to the ground.
When rain comes, the world becomes still and silent.

The rain is the sky's way of speaking.
Its way of telling stories of the past and words of the future.

I know too the dangers that follow,
Typhoons beat at the wood walls of home,
The trees rumble with excitement from the cold breeze.

Branches are thrown at homes
Like candy in parades,
The storm is still marching through the sky

And beating its tin drum.

I long for warmth and comfort,
Alone at home.
I long for the safety and heat of the sun.

But still,
The drum goes on.
Tap!
   Tippity-
      tap!

One of the lines that speaks most to me is "The rain is the sky's way of speaking." Not only is the line beautiful in its personification but it mimicked Misa's journey. Poetry was Misa's way of speaking.

Water is still present (mentioned in at least five ways), as is home (note the words connected to it). She mentions that rain is the sky's way "of telling stories of the past and words of the future." She first writes of her home with typhoons beating at the wood walls and ends with longing for its warmth and comfort, the safety and heat. It's a transformation, symbolic of her journey. There's a sophistication that developed throughout her writing this year. That finding of voice. But that's not all that's happening here. The writing she'd done told stories of her past while her words, and the healing that came through them, allowed her to see into her future.

Misa had discovered that reaching another person through words not only makes them feel *like* home but makes them feel *her* home. And that is one way to feel *at* home.

Your Turn

Susan Ahlbrand knows quite a bit about relationships. With over 36 years as an 8th grade English Language Arts teacher in a small southern Indiana town, she is experienced at forging connections with her students and continues to celebrate life with six BFFs who have supported one another for 53 years. Her prompt offers us a place to make a connection too.

Short Prompt
If you are ready to write, here is a short prompt to get you started: Select a photo from your past that you are drawn to. You might choose one that has strong memories associated with it or the first one you find on your phone's camera roll for a quirky, lighter mood. Craft a poem in any form that feels right to you.

Go to your journal or device. Explore your voice there. If you are feeling so overwhelmed that you are not sure how to begin, remember that sharing your words is a way to make you feel at home.

Full Prompt
If you'd like a little more support, the full prompt is reprinted below. For now, open your notebook or device and follow along with Susan Ahlbrand's inspiration in Snapshots in Time.[1]

Inspiration: Snapshots. A frozen moment in time. Ones from film that we used to take with a camera and send off to be processed, often finding their way into a scrapbook or photo album. Digital ones that sit on our phones, in our camera roll, or on a social media site such as Instagram. These frozen moments in time have a whole lot of context around them. Today, we are going to find a picture and use it to inspire a poem. You could drift toward a pure description of the image; you could write about the context of the still shot. You could use the image to ponder what happened before, what happened after.

Process: Find a picture. Any picture. Some places to look . . .
- Open a photo album.

- Open your photo stream.
- Search the walls of your home.
- Resort to Google images.
- Go to Instagram and select the first picture you see (on your feed or from your own account).
- Look for details and for the backstory.

Your poem can take whatever form you would like. You could revisit some of the poetry forms you've written in the past. You could toy with a new one that you've wanted to try out.

Jennifer's Suggestions for the Classroom

Finally, while this chapter is for you, dear teacher, we'd love for you to invite students to write. If you want to try your own Daily Fifteen with your students, here are a few things to keep in mind:

- We begin our year with an Identity unit where students write about themselves. This is a topic for which they have a wealth of information, and stories can be found here.
- Autobiographical writing can evoke strong emotion for students. They may write about difficult topics or personal experiences. It's important to let them know that they do not have to share everything they write. Allowing options for topics and choices for sharing helps them establish a space for autonomy.
- We spend a lot of time creating a respectful environment from the very beginning of the year. I show them how to respond to one another's writing by focusing on the positives in my feedback. I ignore my editing voice and help them grow confidence by commenting on what I love so that they build upon what's working more intuitively. I respond to them verbally in the same way and by offering them stem sentences for feedback: I was really drawn to… One thing I noticed that worked well was… I love how you…
- Much of my focus during mentor poems involves noticings — especially of craft: word choices, interesting placement and the use of negative space, noteworthy figurative language, etc.
- Students are not bound to a rubric during this independent writing time. If there's a craft move I want them to try, I'll nudge them toward it or ask them to include it. But if they have an idea they feel could work, they have the agency to try it. That's how they discover whom they are as writers.
- By offering 4 weekly writing prompts and encouraging students to explore them, they find what works and what doesn't. This makes their end of week choice for the pieces they share with me in their journals or with the class in an Open Mic

> not only more refined but also self-selected with an eye for voice and elevated craft.
> - Allowing Open Mic to be optional helps create a comfortable space. Some students love to share their writing, others love to share feedback, and others love to listen for ideas, for noticings, for pondering.

Link
[1] https://www.ethicalela.com/24-30-snapshots-in-time/

Part III

why we write poetry with students across our communities

Part III: Community Nurturing

In Part III, we extend our work beyond the walls of the classroom to imagine how our poetry can live in public and digital spaces to serve others. We feel such joy when our poetry can serve others, and by turning our lines and verses over to an anthology publication or a spoken word event or a public poetry celebration, we can witness the poetic healing in new spaces. If you are looking for small and large-scale ways to try poetic writing that's engaging and authentic, your own community likely has a wide range of spaces, so we share our experiences to help you imagine possibilities with others.

In "Poetry Slams: Welcoming a Community of Voices," Barbara Edler tells about her experience (after over 40 years of teaching) in her first Poetry Slam in Iowa.

"Writing Poetry as Literacy Advocacy in Belize" is an interview with Belize educator Melissa Bradley, who shares the impact of poetry in her teaching and community with Sarah Donovan.

With Denise Krebs, Kim Johnson, and Margaret Simon, "Opportunities to Extend Our Community (and to Write More Poetry)" explores several ways you can stretch your writing community into an amazing writing network.

CHAPTER 18

Poetry Slams: Welcoming a Community of Voices
Barbara Edler

When I learned via a Facebook post that the Iowa Poetry Association was sponsoring a poetry slam at the Public One Space in Iowa City, I immediately signed up. Iowa City is a 90-minute drive from my home and much closer than the other venues slated for the competition, Perry and Des Moines. Only twelve Iowa poets would be able to perform so registering in advance was a must. The top three performers from each region would then advance to the state level where they would compete to become the state representative for the BlackBerry Peach National Poetry Slam, hosted by the National Federation of State Poetry Societies.

I was so excited. Then realization kicked in, and I had to acknowledge the fact that I really wasn't a slam poet because I basically write short poems. Slam poets have poems that are generally over two minutes in length and often employ a rapid-fire delivery. I am a huge fan of *Button Poetry* and many of these poets do not deliver their poems in this rapid-fire style, yet I thought I should still compete. However, due to my experiences, I believe that the Iowa judges I have encountered at the state level prefer poets who can deliver lines quickly using a kind of "rap" style technique. I am also a mature white woman. Slam poetry is rooted in giving voice to people of color who have felt marginalized.

Construction worker and poet, Marc Smith, is credited with beginning poetry slams. He began the trend during a reading series at the Get Me High jazz club in Chicago. Soon slams became popular and spread about the country. According to Smith and Kraynak's book *Take Me to the Mic*, a successful slam includes five ingredients: "poetry, performance, competition, audience interaction, and a sense of community" (2009). One of the key points to remember about a slam is that the judges are culled from the audience and the audience is in control by showing their enthusiasm for a poem/performance.

Basically, I perform my poetry with emotion, memorizing the lines so that I can use facial expressions and eye contact to engage the audience, although memorizing poetry for a slam is not required. I kept asking myself, "What were you thinking, Barb, signing up for such an event?" Nevertheless, I was determined to go through with my commitment and felt compelled to stretch myself as a writer and performer.

After I emailed the coordinator that I was interested, I felt even more committed. If I say I am going to do something, I try my very best to follow through. I anxiously waited for the date of the slam to be announced, hoping that I would not have a conflict that would prevent my attending. Finally, the date was set, and I received word that I would be one of the performing poets. I realized I did not have any other commitments or personal obligations to prevent my attending the competition.

Now that I knew I was definitely going to perform, I started reviewing my poetry that I had saved in Google folders or Word folders on my computer. Although I had been writing poetry since high school, I had only recently begun to write more consistently, trying hard to keep track of my recent poetry by utilizing electronic folders. Most of my older work is either in a literary magazine, completely lost, or stuffed in an old writing folder.

Unfortunately, as I reviewed my work, I did not find much that I thought would be suitable. Many poems were too short and awkward. One of the key things I was focused on was trying to have poems that would be at least two minutes in length as each performance could be up to three minutes long. I began to wonder if I could even perform a two-minute poem. I had to have three poems because the slam had three rounds. Memorizing all three poems was challenging to say the least, but I have been on stage before so I knew the importance of memorization and engaging the audience through eye contact and physical presence. Therefore, I was determined to not only write or revise my poems but to also commit them to heart. Generally, I write for myself, but knowing I would be in front of an audience which would include some of my peers, I did not want to look like a fool.

Trying out for high school and college plays as well as community theater has been a passion of mine although I haven't performed on stage for several years so I really wanted to re-experience the thrill of performing in front of a live audience. As I continued to reread my poems, I began to think of ways to combine a few so they would be longer. I looked for my most emotionally charged poems that I thought would move the audience. My go to person for feedback is often my sister. She will tell me which words she does not like or will offer a revised line or two to help with fluency. My sister definitely has more ability with writing poetry that is lyrical whereas I struggle with composing ending rhymes.

After I revised by elaborating and combining poems, I began to memorize the pieces. I have studied lines before, usually chunking the sections until I have each part memorized, and then I begin practicing aloud at home in my bedroom or as I drive down the road. This often helps me to hear when I need to change something or when the flow of the poem is off kilter. It is also wonderful to be able to practice in front of a friend or family member which can be difficult for me to do as I will still become nervous. Practicing my poems aloud often led to more revision as I found it difficult to vocalize a line so that it moved smoothly or I tended to forget a certain line and consequently decided to drop it even though I often wished I could have held on to it.

Finally, I decided on three poems: one was about my older sister Pam. I had written a poem about seeing her ghost on Facebook. For this poem, I added more information about her and how she had impacted my life.

I Saw Your Ghost on Facebook Today by Barbara Edler

"Be quiet! I'm trying to read the *Bible*," you screamed
trying to silence our constant bickering
your newfound faith had you
wearing an AGAPE cape
burning your albums and
constantly praying—
you, who used to wear red hot pants and white Gogo
boots,
a guitar strap for a belt,
who once got kicked out of a high school band concert for
wearing
       bloomers
our Great Aunt Grace shipped all the way from
Long Beach, California.

you were my awesome older sister
who introduced me to the fantastic flavors
of fast food like sanchos at Taco Kid
food I never even knew existed —
who took me all the way downtown

to Armstrong's Department Store
to buy me my own pair of crushed velour bell bottom
pants,
purple with white piping,
just like yours—
who gave me her own black bib overalls
covered in sweet white daisies.

You were the coolest dresser ever
until you found the light
loved the Lord
and him.
Jeff, I remember,
Jeff was his name.

Did you know that one night our father
gathered all of us into the kitchen
to break the news that you tried to end your life—
silent and stunned, we couldn't believe
you'd turn on yourself because of a lover's break.

I saw your ghost on Facebook today
bronzed and beautiful, lying on a Puerto Rican beach,
it's really your daughter,
a gypsy at heart—
she's everything you wanted to be
fiercely independent, gorgeous, and free.

Another poem was a found poem that I had created during Ethical ELA's VerseLove from April 2022. This prompt asked participants to borrow lines from other poets. I borrowed a line from Stephenos, a VerseLove writer, who wrote "On my front stoop/I dropped your ashes." I changed this a bit and opened my poem with "I dropped your ashes on the front stoop today." I also borrowed an image from Susie Morice's poem "made in frayed bell bottoms/with our embroidered peace signs." Because of the peace signs, I focused on the idea that the subject was a Vietnam war veteran. Basically the poem is about losing a loved one to mental health, and I worked on extending this poem a bit further by including a few more tunes which included "Jump in the Line," one of my son's favorite songs he would perform at karaoke bars.

Shellshocked on the Front Stoop by Barbara Edler

I dropped your ashes
on the front door stoop today
ashes are heavy, you know

once you were light-
a beautiful breeze,
free as the peace signs
embroidered on your frayed
bell-bottom bluejeans

remember the time you told me
you were born to be wild
a true nature's child
you'd break all the rules
wherever you roamed, would be your home

but war swallowed you whole
spit you back broken and bruised

I ached to piece you back together
like grandmother's broken fine china
shattered across the floor
impossible to fix

I played our favorite tunes
"Whiter Shade of Pale"
"Not Fade Away"
"The Weight"
"Jump in the Line"
"Let it Be"

but stars nor tunes
could bring you back to me
my compass, my sail

I dropped your ashes on the front stoop today
ashes are heavy you know

My final poem was titled "I Sip Coffee and He Smokes the Green" which was about my son's death. Losing my son Alex has been extremely difficult, especially since I have numerous questions about the way he died, something the local authorities were not willing to investigate. He's been gone for almost six years now, and I still have difficulty accepting this loss. Alex was a gifted musician, actor, speaker, writer, and athlete. He was endearing and very entertaining; he had a beautiful voice and wonderful stage presence. I wanted to honor him by telling a little about his story. Of course, anytime that I write a poem about losing my son it is cathartic, but at the same time it can be difficult to share. I try not to sensationalize my grief or be overly sentimental. Controlling my emotions while performing is also challenging. I certainly did not want to feel rejected by the audience.

I Drink Coffee and He Smokes the Green by Barbara Edler

I rise reluctantly
too tired to sleep
too tortured to lie still

I look at my face in the bathroom mirror
aged with grief
it appears blue in the morning light
dark lines shadow the contours

I pour myself a cup of coffee
sit outside to watch
the Mississippi turn pink
feel my dead son
smoking the green beside me

I cannot let him go

after prison he returned home
his feather-flight fractured
his addictions uncured
a walking corpse among the living
not even 30

I longed to see him heal

hoped he'd find happiness
ached to mend him

five months later he ended his life
or so **they** say
was he tortured with regret
murdered
driven to madness by meth

afterwards I heard his voice
calling from the dining room lights
flickering above me

I didn't do this, I didn't do this, I didn't do this

but who's going to believe an old woman like me
someone too blue to breathe
unable to purge guilt or grief
drowning beneath a sorrowful sea

so I keep him here beside me
while I sip coffee
and he smokes the green

The evening of the slam arrived. Since I wanted my poems to be the focus when performing, I wore black slacks and a black blouse with a gold scarf, which also showed my Iowa Hawkeye pride. At this time I did not know who my audience would be, but they would include other poets, and I imagined people who tend to support writing or poetry events.

As I drove to Iowa City, I practiced my poems. I had made a hotel reservation because the event started at 7:00 p.m.. Unfortunately, I had some difficulty finding the venue and then locating a place to park which enhanced my anxiety. Fortunately, once I arrived, I was warmly greeted by Kelsey Bigelow, an amazing spoken word poet. Kelsey is the Slam Poet coordinator for the Iowa Poetry Association and offers writing workshops as well as traveling nationwide to perform her poetry. Her most recently published book is titled *Far From Broken.* Since she was the coordinator for the event, she asked me to draw a slip of paper which would determine my turn to "slam." I drew number eight.

The slam was to have twelve different poets and the top eight would advance to the second round. After the second round, the final four would perform and all would be invited to the state competition in Des Moines. The poetry slam was the opening event for a three-day poetry extravaganza in April appropriately titled *Poetry Palooza.*

Kelsey was also the emcee for the state competition. I heard her perform with Rainy the Negro Poet and Charlie/Hannah Hall, two other spoken-word poets, at the Englert Theater in Iowa City a few weeks prior to the slam. This viewing experience helped me gain a better understanding of how a spoken word/slam poet performs. Rainy's poetry shared the experience of a black man in the United States. Charlie/Hannah Hall wrote about being unaccepted by his father for being gay, and Kelsey's poetry captured the pain of losing her mother. All three poets shared personal poetry so I felt confident about my poetry selections for the slam.

When I took my seat at the Public One Space, I felt self-conscious and believed a couple of the women looked at me like, "Okaaayyyy, you're going to slam?" Of course, this could have just been my perception as I was three times older than any of the other slam poets. I did feel out of place and a bit uncomfortable, but I've experienced feeling awkward a thousand times, so I tried to keep a smile on my face and remain composed.

To begin the Poetry Slam, a "sacrificial lamb" is chosen to perform a poem. This is a standard way to begin a poetry slam and is the term that was used for the evening. Laura Johnson warmed up the audience by sharing her poem, and the judges rated her. This warm-up activity helps the poets gain a better awareness of the judges and how the event operates. Kelsey then discussed the appropriate etiquette for a poetry slam. For example, during a slam you can make guttural sounds, deep groans of approval or snap your fingers. This group of poets also had a chant that they would often loudly repeat, "We Love You Poet, We're Gonna Let Everyone Know It." Hey, I found this a bit different, but I tried to embrace it throughout the others' performances by making grunting noises of approval or by snapping my fingers. Still, this type of behavior was a bit out of my comfort zone.

After each performance, Kelsey asked the judges for their scores. They would hold up a card with their handwritten score on a piece of paper. Kelsey would read each score aloud so the performers had an idea how they were faring. These scores were then tallied to determine who was moving on to the next round.

Suddenly, it was my turn to perform. I began with my poem "I Saw Your Ghost on Facebook Today," which started with my sister's voice screeching: "Stop fighting, I'm trying to read the *Bible*." Since I was trying to capture her yelling, I yelled, which was a little too loud for a microphone. Yikes! This threw me off a bit, but I was able to continue and ended with some fairly good scores but definitely not fantastic ones.

Since I was near the end of the round of poets, it did not take too long for me to find out who was advancing. I was somewhat surprised to hear my name called. I thought to myself, "Yes! At least I was moving on to one more round."

During the second round, the order was reversed so I was one of the earlier performers. I may have forgotten a line in the second poem "I Dropped Your Ashes on the Front Stoop Today" but I felt that I paced myself well and was able to effectively convey the emotions. After the second round ended, I realized I was actually moving on to the final round. I felt validated. I hadn't wasted time practicing and memorizing. I was proud of myself for competing and not being totally rejected. One thing that helped was that I was the only advancing poet performer who had all my poems memorized, which is not a requirement for a slam, but hey, I thought it gave me an edge.

I'd saved my final poem which was the most personally important one for me. It focused on my son's death that was ruled a suicide. Dawn Terpstra, president of the Iowa Poetry Association and a judge during the evening, shared that several people had shed some tears while listening to my poem. One of the judges actually gave me a ten, the best score a poet can receive. Thankfully, I performed my poem without having a breakdown.

Scores were recorded and I received second place overall. I believe this was due to my final poetry performance, one of the most personally honest poems I have written. Writing this poem and sharing it with others has allowed me to purge my complicated feelings. I wanted people to consider another side of his death and that sometimes it can feel impossible to accept what authorities tell you. More importantly, after his death, I felt Alex's presence, an experience others may understand.

Several people spoke to me after the event and complimented me about my performance. One couple expressed their congratulations and noted that my poetry was different from the other performers. The other poets/performers were vibrant young people, sharing compelling stories. Their performances were faster paced, but they also shared personal poems that included homosexual themes, suicide and rejection. I was deeply impressed by the talent demonstrated throughout the evening.

Afterwards, I knew I would want to have some new material for the state competition. For this event, my sister and niece came to watch me perform. The venue was larger, a middle school auditorium in Des Moines. I felt a bit more comfortable at this event because I wasn't the only person with some age. Again, I drew a number, and I performed near the end of the round. All twelve advancing poets attended the event from the four regional contests, and they were all amazing!

Prior to each slam, I practiced in front of my niece and sister. They were great supporters behind the scenes. Two other friends also listened to me perform. One via Facetime and the other listened to me while I was driving to Des Moines. Although I practiced enough, I probably did not begin preparing for the slams soon enough. Performing personal poetry in front of a wide audience is thrilling but also daunting.

As I listened to the other performers that night, I was awed by their content and performances. I had planned to perform my poem "The Burning Field," which detailed a part of my childhood and a sexual assault I experienced as a young teen in the woods where my friends and I always played. I began the poem expressing the joy and wonderful moments of my childhood that I shared with my neighborhood pals and how that part of my life felt almost magical until the assault. At the last minute, I changed my mind and decided to perform "I Sip Coffee and He Smokes the Green." I thought I had to come out with my strongest poem to advance, but I did not make it to the second round. Afterwards, I regretted not going with my original plan. Never second guess yourself, right?

My scores were very good, but not high enough to advance to the second round. I was disappointed, but happy for Charlie/Hannah Hall and the other Iowa City poets who all made it to the second round. By the end of the evening those same three performers who I competed against during the first slam were the top three poets, and Sam, a young Asian woman, once again received first place.

The remarkable thing I observed was that the two who did not win first place had all their poems memorized. They were all incredible poets with powerful poems, but I believed I had a little influence with how they prepared for the event. Charlie/Hannah Hall was also sitting next to me during the event, and he whispered next to me that he did not think I received the scores I should have. "Ahhh," I appreciated his comment and his kind words. Spoken-word poets are very supportive of each other.

Will there be a next time?

I think poetry slams and open mics are becoming very popular. People need to be heard. It's a perfect avenue for creating a community of writers. If you think you might want to explore more about slam poetry, check out *Button Poetry* on *Youtube*. Here you will find amazing videos of poets sharing their poems aloud.

Will I do this again? I am not sure, but I would love to record some of my favorite poems so my family has access to these. I definitely want to organize a slam for local poets this April, the national poetry month! Witnessing a variety of voices sharing their individual stories is not only rewarding, it is also a way to establish a community of writers who will gain a deeper understanding of each other.

One of the best compliments I received after performing was from a woman who was closer to my age. She said she really enjoyed my poem and that I inspired her to believe that she could also compete at a Slam Poetry event. I hope she does and that I will see her on stage next year.

If you are interested in creating your own slam event, I suggest checking out the Women of the World Poetry Slam (WOWPS). Each year the National Federation of State Poetry Societies offers a slam poetry competition called the BlackBerry Peach National Slam. The Poetry Foundation also provides samples of slam poetry.

Remember that Marc Smith's five key ingredients for a poetry slam include: "poetry, performance, competition, audience interaction, and a sense of community." Establishing a sense of community is a vital ingredient. Kelsey Bigelow emphasized that point when sharing her expertise as a slam coordinator. She said, "Remember that your job is more than just running a slam; it's also building community. As a slam master, you need to have the structure clear for the poets and the logistics sorted out. But it's also important to facilitate a space where the entire room feels welcoming and to lead the effort in building the community." A slam poetry event should be respectful, celebratory, with an open invitation to individuals of all ages, race, and sexual orientation. It is a perfect opportunity to witness our collected stories that connect us through our shared experiences of joy and grief, etc. Poetry slams can lead to healing the wounds we silently carry by giving them voice and a moment to be heard.

Your Turn

Are you ready to try your hand with your own poetry slam or presenting a spoken word poem? This prompt comes from Dr. Sarah Donovan who taught junior high in Chicago and is now a teacher educator. This prompt is written for students, but we hope you will write one, too and maybe, just maybe, compete in your local poetry slam (or start one for your community).

Short Prompt

This is a list-poem of "reasons why" or "responses to." Any topic will do, but we suggest you find a topic that you'd like to advocate for change. Reasons why I love X (and give reasons to join your or see your perspective). Responses to people who say or do Y (and show them how to do better or understand the impact). Try to count up or count down to the most important reason. This poem is a chance to make an argument for that change (or for greater awareness or recognition).

Full Prompt

If you'd like a little more support, the full prompt can be found on Ethical ELA[1]. I have also included the prompt below, so for now, open your notebook or device and follow along with educator Sarah Donovan's inspiration: <u>Reasons Why and Responses To</u>.[1]

> **Inspiration:** Our students have a lot to say about what's going on in their lives. We don't always give them a forum to voice their views, in part because we don't know what they'll say or may not trust that what they say will matter. We may not want to hear the raw truth (and sometimes we may think it is not "school appropriate"). I have found that spoken word offers a meaningful framework for organizing ideas around a strong point of view and welcoming students who may feel more comfortable using their voices than their fingers to express their views.

Today's inspiration is called "Reasons Why and Responses To." To begin, common text structures in spoken word include a list, countdown, and counting up. Listen to a few of these spoken word performances. Just a heads up, a few have strong language: Brian Yu's "Reasons Why I Hate Student Loans"[2]; Kevin Yang's "Come Home"[3]; Alex Dang's "Times I've Been Mistaken for a Girl".[4]

Using the count-down or count-up structure, I taught junior high students to blend poetry, research, and argument in order to share their passion and expertise about a subject or issue of interest to them. Here are a few of the spoken word titles that emerged:

- Eight Responses to People Who Say Girls Can't Code
- Six Response to Those Who Can't "Feel" the Beat
- Eight Responses to People Who Say Renewable Energy is Not Sustainable
- Eight Responses to People Who Say They Want to Play Football
- Eight Responses to People Who Say Animals Are Dumb
- Eight Responses to People Who Say Photo Prints Are Useless
- Eight Responses to People Who Ask "What's Human Behavioral Sciences?"
- Eight Responses to People Who Say Making a Movie is Easy
- Eight Responses to People Who Say They Want to Learn Karate

Today, let's play with this spoken word text structure. How can we access our expertise, passions, and even commentary about the world using the rhythm of spoken word? Today's poems will likely look different— more text heavy and less dependent on white space or line breaks — we'll see.

Process:
Select a topic based on a hobby, expertise, passion, or issue about which you already know a lot or want to learn more about.
- Everyday: flossing, the perfect cup of coffee, eyebrow grooming, loading the dishwasher, toast, snoozing the alarm clock

- Expertise: an instrument, perfect running shoe/yoga mat, the beauty of BBQ, planting a garden, birdwatching, a recipe/cooking technique, art technique/period, lesser known, undervalued author/activist/historical figure
- Activism: a cause you know well or volunteer for that most people don't know about, an experience you've had that others need to understand better

Select a framework:

- Responses to people who ask…Reasons to try…What I'd say to people who…What everyone needs to understand about…
- Count up or count down. Some of the examples start at 8 and work down to 1 while others start at 1 and go from there.
- Address the person or group of people directly and use the language they'd understand, i.e., if your audience is new or ignorant/novice to the topic.

Any number is fine — you do not need 8 responses or even 3—maybe you want to make a single statement.

Try a technique: YInvite students to try some craft moves with their draft for a quick revision strategy.

- Anaphora is the repetition of a word or phrase at the beginning of successive lines or a refrain, make this bold.
- Polysyndeton is a literary technique in which conjunctions (e.g. and, but, or) are used repeatedly in quick succession, often with no commas, even when the conjunctions could be removed. Try this with italics.

Sarah's Poem "Reasons Why I Hate Grades"

Five. Because they suck.
Four. As a kid, I never liked competition, comparison as though your A identity made you more worthy of love, attention, a hug than my B identity. Sure, I skipped a few blanks, failed to match terms, only partially shaded a bubble or two, but my story was beautiful. It's not my fault creativity is only worth 10%.
Three. When it comes time to grade an essay, I read. I am transported into the heart and mind of a writer. I notice doubt in parentheticals, certainty in periods, excitement in fragments, and trust-distrust of

their words in my hands. I cannot slash prepositions, scribe "awk," count typos — the being on the page defies such measurement. It feels wrong to conflate it all to a letter, number, score.

Two. What they don't advertise in teacher job descriptions is that the reason you came to teaching— to be the change, to make a difference — will be reduced to the humanity of our students by measuring, ranking, and sorting bodies into tracks of classes, access to opportunities, beliefs of possibilities because of

One test or grade that cannot possibly define worth, should not factor into identity. So the A can do school, comply with rules, lacks wi-fi excuses, doesn't need to be after school child care. So the C is subversive, resists meaningless homework, won't tolerate packets, doodles in the margin of the Cornell notes. So what? Who are they? What do they know? Who do they want to become? See, our students are not letters. We know that. And yet grades drive assignments, phone calls home, eligibility lists, high fives, and disappointed glares. So the next time your student asks, "Miss, what grade did I get?" Change the topic and say, "I'd rather talk about your poem."

Barbara's Suggestions for the Classroom

If you think you are ready to host your own poetry slam event in your community or school, here are a few ideas to consider.

- First establish your rules. Identify how many poets will be performing and the time limit for each round which is usually three minutes with a 10 second grace period. Props, instruments and costuming are not allowed although one can occasionally sing a line in their poem.
- Secondly establish how many judges there will be. Judges at poetry slams are chosen from the audience. If this does not feel comfortable for you, then have your judges chosen prior to the slam who you believe will be equitable. Judges will listen and rate each performance/poem on a scale of 0-10 that can include decimal points. So a judge could give a 7.9 score, etc. All scores are based on personal opinions and whether or not they liked the poem and how they felt about the performance. Judges write their scores on paper and these are recorded after each performance. Someone will have to be recording the scores. The more transparent you can make the scoring, the better. Each score is recorded with the top and the bottom scores dropped to determine the overall score. If you have a white board available in the room, this could be a great place to record the scores.
- Prep your audience. Make sure they understand they are an essential part of the poetry slam. Encourage them to influence

the judges with their vocal enthusiasm. Audience members can show their support by making grunts of approval or making sounds such as "mmmmmm" or "oopf" and by snapping their fingers. Remind audience members that they should also never boo at poets. Sharing one's poetry takes bravery and this must be honored.

- Finally, also share that sometimes poetry can trigger emotions. Establish that each member of the audience takes care of themselves. If someone needs to leave the room due to the content of a poem, be sure to make that clear and acceptable. Every member in the room should feel safe and loved.

Resources

BlackBerry Peach Poetry Slam. (2023). *National Federation of State Poetry Societies.* National Federation of State Poetry Societies - BBP National Poetry Slam. https://nfsps.net

Poetry Foundation. (2024). *Poems of Protest, Resistance, and Empowerment.*
https://www.poetryfoundation.org/collections/142296/poems-of-protest-resistance-and-empowerment

Smith, M., & Kraynak, J. (2004). *The complete idiot's guide to slam poetry.* Alpha.

Smith, M., & Kraynak, J. (2009). *Take the mic: The art of performance poetry, slam, and the spoken word.* Sourcebooks.

Womnx of the World Poetry Slam. (n.d.). *Women of the World Poetry Slam.* https://wowpsfest.com

Links

1 https://www.ethicalela.com/26of30verselove/
2 https://youtu.be/odCrgq5Po8c
3 https://youtu.be/oK-rytupr0o
4 https://youtu.be/U2i-i8k6AbQ

Poetic Reflection by Sally Donnelly

Writing Poetry with Jack

I came to be a writer of poetry a little late. Probably because in high school, I never felt I understood what the poems being discussed in AP English meant. Why did so much depend on that red wheelbarrow? I rarely was asked to write poetry, only to analyze it. Because of this, I avoided poetry as a genre to read or write myself or to ever explore with students, once I became a teacher.

Then I read *Love That Dog* by Sharon Creech. I immediately connected with the main character, Jack, who wrote in his journal, "I don't understand / the poem about / the red wheelbarrow"! As I experienced poetry writing with Jack, I learned it was okay to just enjoy the sounds in a poem and the placement of the words on the page. Finally, Jack taught me how to use the poems his teacher shared as inspiration. Following Jack's lead, I started to write my own poems.

That year, as a 4th grade teacher, I also bravely embarked on a poetry writing unit with my students. First, I gathered poems following the same form (ex: shape poems, list poems, haiku). Daily, I picked one form and read those poems aloud, just to be heard and enjoyed. Next, I stood at the white board and tried to write in the same form. I asked my students to watch and help if I got stuck. Douglas Florian wrote list poems about what he loves about each of the four seasons. After reading these aloud, I announced I would try to write a list poem about what I love about my favorite sport, swimming. First, I brainstormed some specific swimming words - goggles, dive, kicking. Students called out more words. Then I created this list poem in front of my students:

What I Love About Swimming by Mrs. Donnelly

Goggles new
Bathing suit blue
Lane lines strong
Eight lanes long
Backstroke
Breaststroke
Butterfly
Free
Diving
Streamline
Stroking and kicking
Flip turns quick

Back and forth
Back and forth
Reaching hard for the wall
Watches stop
Best time ever
Hurrah!

Afterwards, I asked my students to write. All, inspired by poet Douglas Florian, wrote at least one list poem. Then, day after day, I followed the same process. I gathered poems by published poets, read them for enjoyment and bravely stood in front of my students and wrote. I never practiced the night before. I drafted my poem in the moment. Then, I gave worktime to my student writers.

My students that year learned important lessons from my poetry writing approach. They learned poems come in many forms. And that poems don't need to rhyme. And that poems can be about objects in their life, like legos and pet lizards. Some even learned to express strong feelings by including important objects as symbols, just as William Carlos Williams does in "The Red Wheelbarrow." And I learned that so much does depend on time spent writing poetry.

Sally Donnelly, NCBT, is in her 32nd years as an educator, currently a Reading Specialist in Arlington Virginia.

CHAPTER 19

Writing Poetry as Literacy Advocacy in Belize
Sarah J. Donovan with Melissa Bradley

In Chapter 1, we shared data from our research study about teachers writing poetry as healing. In that survey, we invited educators to contribute to this book stories of healing. In this interview, we talk to Melissa Bradley.

This interview delves into the transformative power of poetry in the context of literacy advocacy in Belize through an insightful interview with Melissa Bradley, a dedicated educator and poet. Melissa shares her deeply personal journey of using poetry as a means of healing and expression, particularly during challenging times, such as coping with her mother's illness. Her reflections on how poetry has provided an escape and a safe space for self-expression highlight the therapeutic benefits of writing. Melissa's experiences underscore the potential of poetry to serve not only as a creative outlet but also as a powerful tool for emotional resilience and personal growth.

Melissa discusses the broader implications of poetry and literacy in the educational landscape of Belize. She offers a candid look into the struggles her students face, from peer pressure and identity issues to parental expectations and societal taboos. Through her work with the Literacy Club, now rebranded as Literary Luminaries, Melissa has championed the cause of literacy by encouraging students to embrace their voices and stories through poetry. Her commitment to fostering a love for reading and writing, while promoting Belizean culture and language, demonstrates how poetry can be a vital component of literacy advocacy, bridging the gap between personal expression and cultural preservation.

SJD: What is the role of poetry in your life?

MB: Poetry represents many things in my life. It transports me to imaginary dimensions; it is an escape from my reality and a place to be me without judgment.

SJD: In the survey, you wrote that you found writing poetry about your mom to be healing. Can you tell us a little bit about that process, and, if you will, share the poem?

MB: Over the past four years, my mother has been sick. She is in and out of the hospital and this was a new experience for me. Because the strongest person I know is in a vulnerable state. It is hard to watch her struggling to speak and walk at times. She is no longer able to do everything for herself. I never imagined the day would come when I would see her like this. What hurt me most, is the fact that I know she had a hard life but always smiled through it and this sickness came and stole her joy. I battle daily with the thought of losing her as the hospital visits become more frequent and her brain continues to shrink.

Mamma by Melissa Bradley

I have not seen you smile for a while
I miss your cheerfulness
This surgery
Has drained your energy

Tell me
Does it hurt to smile?
I know you are still there
Let me see you

Do you have control
Over your facial expression?
Does it only allow one emotion?
Mama

I see you
You are different
Your eyes strain to smile
Your soul spoke to mine

You have accepted your fate
Please don't concentrate
So hard on the pain
God hears your cries

I see your attempts to smile
They are still beautiful
Your smile still lights up the room
I see you mama

You are not gone
Your situation is different now
But you are still you
Strong and beautiful

Blitz Poem by Melissa Bradley

They say when it rains it pours
They say a mother is her child's first hero
First hero, I need you forever
First hero this cannot be the end
The end my heart is not ready
The end no please I have known you all my life
My life has never experienced a day without you
My life will never be the same
The same love I have for you
The same love you lived for me
For me can you please continue to live
For me and all those who treasure you
Treasure you for all eternity
Treasure you in the past now and in the future
The future will wait
The future you can't be my enemy
My enemy I thought I had none
My enemy, I don't claim you
Claim you let me have her there
Claim you NO this is what I fear
I fear who I will be without you
I fear not knowing how to live without you
Without you, I would not be the woman I am today
Without you where would I begin
I begin with wanting to appreciate the time spent with you
I begin praising God for creating you
Creating you is one of His greatest joys
Creating you a priceless work of art

Of art, I do admire
Of art, you are a strong fort
Strong fort stay strong for me
Strong fort this cannot be your destiny
Your destiny is His will
Your destiny I must accept
Must I accept it now
Must I accept Your plan
Your plan is bittersweet
Your plan makes me feel helpless at times
At times I wish I was a healer with superpowers
At times I imagine you living a better life
Better life than this you would disagree
Better life no no no you lived your life
Your life not your way but as much as possible His way
Your life is a beacon for generations to come
To come to know you is to love you
To come to this realization that I need to celebrate you
Celebrate you is my continuous prayer
Celebrate you now and always
Always you remain, my heroine,
Prayer works I believe so I offer up for you today my forever
love

SJD: Tell us a little about your school and students. In the survey you wrote: "Students are experiencing peer pressure because they want to fit in. They are also battling with finding their identity because of what they are told is expected of them as a male or female. Additionally, some students are still not allowed to choose a career path for themselves. Their parents are the ones forcing them to choose a path that leads to prestige and wealth." Can you tell us a little more?

MB: My school is a government high school located in Belize City. It is a coeducational institution that has four form levels. The school follows the national curriculum for Belize. It is known as one of the top high schools in Belize and the best government school in Belize.

In my years of teaching, many students have confided in me about their feelings and experiences. When it comes to peer pressure, fitting in is most important. Some students will ignore their values and beliefs just to be accepted in a clique. I think back on two

Hispanic male students who denied their culture because they identified as Creole. They refused to speak Spanish in their Spanish class and intentionally failed the subject. I later found out that these boys were teased about their spiky hair and Spanish accent.

Another identity problem facing students in Belize is their battle with sexual orientation. As a teacher, I often try to sensitize the classes I teach to respect individuals for their choices. It is a hard topic to discuss because Belizean society still views this as a taboo subject. I have had students crying or becoming depressed because they cannot tell their parents how they feel and the school environment makes things worse when their peers reject them and call them nasty names. Sometimes these students end up fighting to defend themselves.

In reference to the career path of students, they are not the ones who are choosing the jobs they are interested in. Their parents are the individuals who decide what career their children must take. This is another problem because while some students obey their parents and pass to move on to higher studies, there are many who do not pass. Instead, they give trouble in school to spite their parents. Oftentimes, I would hear students say they feel stressed because their parents keep pressuring them. They know their parents want to live vicariously through them.

SJD: In the survey you wrote: My Literacy Club is presently working on a poetry compilation and we are hoping to publish by October of this year. At first, some of the members were unsure if they wanted to participate because they were afraid of being judged. Some participated because they want their work to be published. *How did that turn out? How did you navigate the process?*

MB: The Literacy Club was formed as a requirement for teachers. Each teacher had to supervise a club at our school. I chose the literacy club because I saw it as an avenue for students to express themselves through various forms of expression. I realized how much writing has helped me to cope with various circumstances throughout my life and believed it could also help these students.

I mentioned that some students were skeptical about joining the club because they did not understand what literacy meant. They thought the club was for individuals who had problems reading or those who struggled with learning. To clarify this, I started putting up posters about activities the club would be involved in, such as poetry and short story writing and publication, creating and managing the school's newspaper, developing posters, and completing community service.

There was a setback in the publishing of the document as all the students did not provide their short biographies and pictures. Club time was often canceled to support some other event at the school. Some students submitted their poems late and eventually, everyone got busy with academic expectations of the school.

I had to decide to work independently of the school since we were not getting enough time to meet. So now, the literacy club has been changed. The name is **Literary Luminaries**. The majority of the students who were a part of the club graduated already. However, some are still a part of this group. We are now opening up the group to anyone who is interested in promoting literacy. The compilation has not been completed as yet however it is almost finished.

SJD: You have written a book or several books. Can you talk about literacy in Belize and your goals as a scholar and creative writer? Tell us about your latest book.

MB: In Belize, literacy is something that is evolving. People used to associate literacy programs with poor reading. So they often thought that the individuals who these programs aimed to help are those struggling with reading. However, over the last four years, educators have been promoting programs that go beyond the negative connotations by highlighting activities that look at building on what participants already know.

As a scholar, my goal as a literacy activist is to ensure that I add to the body of literature that mirrors the lives of the students and people in Belize. While I strongly believe it is important to learn about the world, other people, and their belief systems, I also strongly believe we must not lose our culture, history, and traditions in the process. Schools in Belize use far more foreign text to teach students than they use Belizean text. This has implications.

It makes me question what we are teaching our students. We continue to perpetuate the saying, "What is foreign, is better."

My latest book *Mahagni Gyal* was published on May 29, 2024. This book is set in the early 1990s and it covers the coming of age of Melony, a 13-year-old girl who grew up in Belize, a young independent country. The book is the first part of the series to be completed as there are only two chapters in this book. Inspiration for this fictional book came from my childhood experiences. I wrote this book because there is a shortage of YA books in Belize written by Belizean authors. Most of the books written by Belizean authors are for children and the majority of these are folklore stories. I wanted to do something different. So I wrote a book for teenagers and the young at heart. The book includes Kriol dialogue. I am passionate about the Kriol language and want to promote the reading of Kriol since Kriol is still an oral language. It was surprising to find out that a lot of people in Belize did not know that Belize Kriol has a dictionary created to standardize the spelling of Belizean Kriol words.

SJD: What else do you want to say or share about writing poetry and the role of writing poetry in schools?

MB: Writing poetry should be encouraged more in schools so students can express themselves in various forms. Writing poetry plays an important role in schools because it gives students a voice, and a safe place to write, and makes their wants, needs, and identities visible.

CHAPTER 20

Opportunities to Extend Our Community (and to Write More Poetry)

Sarah J. Donovan with Kim Johnson, Denise Krebs, & Margaret Simon

As you can see throughout this book, our writing and our community has evolved over time and together, with trusted distant online colleagues witnessing our lives one poem at a time.

But many of the chapter-authors here and the poets we cite within have rich writing lives beyond this community and some beyond poetry.

In this chapter, we want to share a few other ideas to spark your engagement in your local community and/or other physical and digital spaces. To explore this dynamic landscape of poetry writing in community, we sat down with several chapter authors who have rich experiences in both digital and print environments. In this interview-style chapter, these educators share their insights and strategies to extend your writing community. From leveraging social media platforms to participating in local writers' groups, to publishing memoir and teacher resources, their stories offer valuable perspectives on how to enhance your craft and connect with teacher-writers.

SJD: What book(s) have you published? And can you tell us a little story about what prompted this book? Why you wrote it?

Denise: I've been connecting with other educators online since 2010 through blogging. My online writing and publishing has been a great way to meet like-minded educators and collaborate on a number of projects. One project was with my friend, Gallit Zvi when we explored and practiced Genius Hour together with our middle school students—her in Surrey, British Columbia, and me in a small farming community in Iowa. Our experiences led us to write *The Genius Hour Guidebook* together. The first edition was published by Routledge and MiddleWeb in 2016. In the last five years, though, I've been doing a lot more with poetry. Some have been printed in various anthologies, which has been rewarding. However, my proudest poetry publications are ones I've printed just one copy of. Last Christmas I made one for my daughter. It was called *I Believe You*. After reading it, my daughter wrote in a thank you, "This is the most beautiful gift I've ever gotten. It has already brought me to tears several times and I feel like I know you better than I did before. Thank you so much. I will cherish it forever." I wrote another book of daily couplets for my grandson's first year. Now I am working on one for my first granddaughter. I'm really enjoying this one-of-a-kind publication now.

Margaret: Each book carries with it a story from idea to publication. What were the seeds that were planted that came to fruition? In 2012, I published a middle grade novel, Blessen. I first began thinking about this story on a drive to a writing workshop. As I drove I looked at the surrounding landscape. I passed a street named New Friend Rd. and imagined a child living there with her mother and grandfather in a trailer. She was not wealthy but was happy with who she was. The bits of a character began to form. At the workshop, I had the opportunity to write the first chapter. After that, I worked with a writing critique group and they suggested I try self-publishing. I knew someone who was running her own publishing house and for a fee, she published Blessen. I kept writing about Blessen and published the sequel, Sunshine, in 2019. In the meantime, I connected with an online writing group I met through blogging and making connections at NCTE.

As I shared more poetry on my blog, I became part of Poetry Friday, a weekly link up for poetry bloggers. Through these connections, I was given the opportunity to write a poem for the National Geographic's *Poetry of US* curated by J. Patrick Lewis. I wrote a poem about living on the bayou in Louisiana, *Bayou Song*, which became the title poem of a collection published by UL Press in 2018.

I have two forthcoming books with UL Press, a local university press. One is poetry I wrote alongside a historian's prose about the first African American woman to get a medical degree in Louisiana. Phebe Hayes, my co-author, did the research for this book and asked me to write poems from the point of view of our heroine, Emma Wakefield Paillet. This book will be out in the fall of 2024 titled *Were You There: A Biography in Poems about Emma Wakefield Paillet.*

I am really excited that UL Press is publishing their first baby board book with my manuscript "What's That Sound: The Birds of the Bayou" in 2025. The idea for this book came to me after spending time with my grandson. He played a game with me that he created, "What's that sound?" he asked, then he would mimic an animal sound. The words for this book flowed out as a poem. A working relationship with a local university press has been helpful in my journey to publication.

The more I write for children (and now having grandchildren) the more I want to write for children. They are the best audience. My experiences as a teacher of elementary aged children as well as my connections with poets and writers have nurtured the writer in me.

Kim: I wanted to write before I ever wanted to read, so I wrote the color names of my crayons in the front covers of all the books in the house when I was five. I learned to read from learning the letter sounds as I wrote in my father's collection of rare books. As a preacher's kid, I was never far from trouble, and writing in these volumes was my first *serious* trouble (there was much more to come)! Through the years, I collected my stories and shared them in a memoir entitled *Father, Forgive Me: Confessions of a Southern Baptist Preacher's Kid* (Tate Publishing, 2012). Although this book is out of print, I keep rewriting parts of it in different forms of poetry. I have also written poems that appear in two poetry anthologies — *Rhyme and Rhythm: Poems for Student Athletes* (Archer Publishing, 2021), and *Bridge the Distance: Teacher-Poets Writing to Bridge the Distance: An Oral History of Covid-19 in Poems* (Sarah J. Donovan/Oklahoma State University, 2021) — and in *English Journal*, a publication of National Council of Teachers of English. This book you are reading is a mosaic of the years of writing alongside those who know me better than the friends and colleagues I see daily. Our experiences writing together, gaining a sense of trust and family, and feeling the nudge to share our journey with other teachers to highlight the difference that a writing group has made in our own lives is what prompted this book. We know the power of relationships and writing to change lives, and we want to share the magic.

SJD: What advice do you have for teachers wanting to write a book or publish a book of their writing or about their teaching?

Denise: Have patience, if you are looking to publish a book through traditional means. Gallit and I wrote our book as an e-book in 2013. We had a publisher, but the plan ended up falling through. Fortunately, we had a good partnership with John Norton, who worked at partnering with Routledge to get our book published in print. We had to rewrite it in a different format and it took some extra time, but it was worth it. However, today, there are so many options for publishing without a traditional publisher. Kickstarter, Kindle Direct Publishing and Ingram Spark are available to anyone who wants to publish, so go for it! Sometimes traditional publishers will pick up self-published books later. Also blogging was (and still is) a great way that I share ideas with a small group of readers. You can test the waters first. Gallit and I wrote on our blogs about Genius Hour before we decided to write a book about it.

Margaret: Don't wait! If you want to write, write. Begin. Find like-minded writers and surround yourself with their support and guidance. Writing does not have to be a solo practice. Even if what you write doesn't get published in the traditional sense, there are many other ways to write. I highly recommend beginning a blog and finding ways to connect with other writers. I connected with Two Writing Teachers who hold a March Slice of Life Challenge each year. So many connections can be made through blogging round-ups.

Kim: I would urge a teacher planning to write a book to make a commitment to the habit of daily writing to build stamina for the task. Set a timer if necessary, and produce something—a list of words, a sentence, a paragraph, a page, a chapter. Sometimes, the idea for a book comes in a pre-packaged theme and purpose where a writer has a clear vision of the finished book and embarks on the task with an outline and a plan. Other times, though, a book emerges throughout the writing process as pieces of writing work their way into a book, much like pieces of a jigsaw puzzle that connect to create a picture. I'm reminded of an interview with AdaLimón[1] in which she describes her poems as seeds. She writes poems and puts them aside for a period of time, and then returns to see which ones have taken root, which ones will bloom. This book is a prime example of that type of writing process. Poems that members of our writing group have written over the years ultimately came together, but we had no idea as we wrote each one that a book or two would be part of our journey. This book is a bouquet of poetry seeds that bloomed. Teachers who may not have planned to write a book may, through the process of daily writing, notice that seeds have taken root and are calling them to write a book.

SJD: What is one writing event that you can recommend to teacher-poets new to writing poetry online?

Denise: So many poetry writing opportunities exist online. How can I mention just one? A few I've come to appreciate are VerseLove and the monthly Open Writes at Ethical ELA. I'm also part of the Poetry Friday community that meets weekly. Participants share poems by other poets or poems they have written themselves. In Poetry Friday, I have discovered opportunities to publish my poems in anthologies published by others in the group. There are annual events like the two-day poem contest at Contemporary Verse 2 and The Poetry Marathon, and the year-long daily Stafford Challenge to name a few. If you are interested in writing with an online community, you can find a group for you.

Margaret: During the month of April, I coordinate a Kidlit Progressive Poem. The sign up is on my blog reflectionsontheteche.com in March. The poem progresses from blog to blog each day with a different person adding a line. This is low stakes community writing.

Kim: The monthly Open Write at www.ethicalela.com[2] is an online writing event that nurtures craft by meeting poets wherever they are and helping them grow by writing five days out of each month. This group was born from VerseLove in April, when poets celebrate National Poetry Month by writing a poem each day for 30 days. When I first joined VerseLove, I was intimidated by all the ornate words and knowledge of poetry forms that I didn't have. It felt a lot like I'd painted a red dot on a page and offered it up for comment among the masterpieces of art gallery works painted by far more colorful and accomplished artists. What I found was a group of writers who found something encouraging to say about my writing and fostered growth by stretching my creativity into new forms. By reading their poems and feedback on others' poems, I discovered new techniques and styles. The feedback and commenting from this community of writers has been the single most powerful contribution to my growth as a writer. I would recommend the Open Write as a place for a teacher-poet to begin to nurture a writing life. If VerseLove is a poetry writing marathon, the Open Write is the 5K of writing that gives a writer just enough of an introductory experience to feel a tremendous sense of success in building poetry stamina.

SJD: Do you have any ideas for teachers wanting to host a poetry event in their community?

Kim: Yes, it's called a progressive poetry walk culminating in an open mic night. A popular trend popping up along walking paths is Storywalks. These weather-proof posts feature picture books that are read in sequence from a starting point to an ending point in incremental distances along a trail or path. A children's book is cut apart and displayed in each of the stands so that children read a book as they walk.

To introduce the concept to our community in rural Georgia, we planned a Progressive Poetry Walk on our town square during National Poetry Month. As part of a statewide Literacy Grant, we ordered stands for the poetry walk and kiosks for poetry stations where community members could write poetry and then come to our Open Mic night to share their poems.

The System-Wide Teacher of the Year for our school district, Clayton Moon, well known as a poet in our small town, wrote a poem for our celebration of National Poetry Month. Using our theme, Bloom!, he wove specific places in our rural county into the lines of his poem. Next, we sectioned the poem onto 12 pages and asked a recent high school graduate to illustrate the pages of the poem before we laminated each page as an added weatherproof measure. Finally, we placed them in the stands in order so that citizens could stroll and read the poem from beginning to end by walking around the town square. On the final stand, a QR Code scan featured a video of our poet reading his poem.

We promoted this event on social media, through our local newspaper, and by going live on the air during the morning show at a local radio station to talk about our National Poetry Month celebration. Here are Clayton Moon and me (foreground) with Bill Bailey of Fun 101.1 in the radio station studio in Thomaston, Georgia.

Clayton Moon's poem, illustrated by a recent high school graduate, was broken into twelve stanzas and displayed on stands, then placed around the Zebulon, Georgia square so that visitors could start at the Chamber of Commerce and read in small sections all the way around the square. We placed a QR Code at the top of each stand letting readers know how the Progressive Poetry Walk worked; on one stand, we placed a code with Clayton Moon reading his poem, *The Kiss of a Flutter's Eye.*

Our local bookstore featured an author signing for Clayton Moon during National Poetry Month. Here we are at A Novel Experience on the downtown Zebulon, Georgia square. Clayton published a book, *The Kiss of a Flutter's Eye*, featuring his title poem.

Clayton Moon read his featured poem, *The Kiss of a Flutter's Eye*, during an Open Mic night in our local coffee shop at our culminating event during National Poetry Month. Clayton Moon's Poem:

The Kiss of a Flutter's Eye by Clayton Moon.[3]

Morning rays dance with Elkin's dogwoods,
As a butterfly glides clockwise from the backwoods.
Anticipation of a lively spring,
Blooming, blooming, what will spring bring?
Oh, how this county bursts with color,
Brushed by the butterfly's faintest flutter,
Round and round our springy town
Over cobble streets and back down.
Meansville, Molena, Williamson, and Concord,
All the flowers line-dance towards,

Words That Mend

A beautiful square adorned with pansies,
Where citizens stroll enjoying the fancies

Sweet tea, coffee, and pastries,
While conversing under shade trees.
Butterfly on a rose, you rest,
Spread your wings so we can picture the rest:
Tilting to the wild of rural,
The dandelions corner milkweed in a countryside mural.
Daffodils blooming on forgotten homesteads,
Snapdragons awakening in the neighbor's bed.
Black-eyed Susan waving by nineteen,
Clovers patching bare spots in-between.
Wisteria twisting around the loblolly pines,
Coffee shops nested in the captain's vines.
Magnolias guarding the courthouse,
Cherokee roses remembering native scouts.

Camelia and Iris welcoming all to the neighborhood,
Tucked in red mulch, surrounded by Maplewood.
Gardenia, ferns, and lilies border porches,
Daisies sprouting to tango with horses.
All the way to Hollonville,
Where sunflowers crowd into fields.
Through rows of planted crop,
To the majestic hardwoods on Hagan's Top.
Down low in scrub oak valleys,
Through the begonia's in Pike alleys.
Amongst flowered briars in the swamp,
Darting through peach orchards, where whitetails stomp.

High in the clouds for an aerial view,
Oh, how the colors soak through,
Every corner and crevice,
Colorful, blooming, Pike's so precious.

As late light retreats from Lithia Springs,
Enchanted buds remain nestled but prepare to bring,

More blooms in the morning mist,
Fluttered by a butterfly's kiss.

Before heading back to center,
On a Cosmos wave to enter,
The spirit of Pike,
On a cozy petal to rest tonight.

Sailing back to the square
to nest above the pink azalea in the cool air.

A young girl has the butterfly in her sight,
And she imagines what it sees during its flight.

So, she wishes a wish, of vibrant bliss,
Opening her eyes to a fluttered kiss.

Denise: I'm beginning to use Kim's inspiration, working with a local group of poets in my community to plan something for next April!

Margaret: I haven't done a community event in a long time. Years ago, I would invite the current poet laureate of the state to come to our town to present. These events were held at an art gallery. I've also participated in a Word Crawl in which different poets were stationed at different businesses along a main street. Each poet had a period of time to read. The time slots were advertised ahead of time.

SJD: You have all led various professional development for teachers. What tips do you have for teachers reading this book for sharing their experiences at local or national conferences? How can teachers become leaders in their communities to advocate for writing poetry?

Denise: Keep connecting with and collaborating with like-minded educators. I've had the opportunity to present at three NCTE conferences with small and larger groups of educators, through Ethical ELA. I can't imagine ever being able to do this on my own. I would suggest that you become a part of a poetry writing community, and you will find ways to develop leadership and advocate for writing poetry.

Kim: I echo all of Denise's suggestions. Building community is the key to success, with a focus on making a difference in small but powerful ways. Being a leader in a community is much like being an orchestra conductor and not a soloist. It's about starting small, forming relationships, and gaining trust before choosing the sheet music and playing the instruments. In my community, I met partners face to face and asked about their mission statements, their current initiatives, and their planned events. My goal was to suggest ways that I could take what was already happening and build on it rather than creating something new, since the new would emerge from the now. For example, our Chamber of Commerce's display window had an opening for two weeks in April, so we featured poems written by local poets on brightly colored canvases and invited people to come into the local shops to write their own poetry at kiosks, then upload their poems to a community Padlet. As our coffee shop considered events to celebrate National Poetry Month, we held three Open Mic nights, featuring two local poets and our Georgia Poet Laureate as main speakers for those evenings. Prior to the Open Mic nights, two other local poets and I invited those who wanted to write to meet downstairs and write at a poetry station or to select a favorite poem to read at the event. Making poetry accessible and offering guided steps are the keys to successfully advocating for writing poetry. Suddenly, the flutes are joined by other woodwinds and brass, strings and drums, and the symphony of poetry graces the town!

The Chamber of Commerce welcomed a springtime burst of colorful poetry in its window display for two weeks in April during National Poetry Month on the Zebulon, Georgia courthouse square. I created these by using colors associated with our theme, Awakenings, painted onto canvases using arced brush strokes. Once they were dry, I used vinyl letters to create the words after I tried a paint pen and discovered that handwriting and paint pen lettering are not the same skill set.

Here, a poetry kiosk in one of our stores welcomes shoppers to stop and write a Cento poem by arranging the magnetized lines of existing poetry into their own original poem. On one side of each stick is a line of poetry, and on the other is the title of the poem and the poet's name. Even the most reluctant poet will find success with Cento poems; they never have to lift a pencil to create a poem! Writers scanned the QR code at the top for a YouTube video on how to write a Cento poem, and then scanned the bottom to upload their photo of their poem to a community Padlet to share with others.

Here is an example of a Paint Chip poem in one of our community kiosks. By leaving a mentor poem so that writers can see how to write the poem using paint chip colors, it allows every writer to experience success.

References

Donovan, S. (2021). *Rhyme and rhythm: Poems for student athletes.* Archer Publishing.

Donovan, S. (2021). *Bridge the distance: Teacher-poets writing to bridge the distance: An oral history of COVID-19 in poems.* Oklahoma State University.

Johnson, K. (2012). *Father, forgive me: Confessions of a Southern Baptist preacher's kid.* Tate Publishing.

Moon, C. *The kiss of a flutter's eye.* BookPatch.

Limon, A. (n.d.). *The hurting kind* [Video]. YouTube. https://youtu.be/yxnms7ZNSYA

Links
[1]https://youtu.be/yxnms7ZNSYA
[2]https://www.ethicalela.com/
[3]https://youtu.be/8jG6JoWO-k4

EPILOGUE

The Healing Power of Poetry in Education

As we come to the end of this book, we reflect on the journey we have taken together through the transformative power of poetry. The stories and poems you have encountered in these pages have offered glimpses into the lives of teachers, students, and communities who have found solace and strength through the written word. We hope that, as you have read these narratives, you have felt a sense of connection and healing, and that the words have offered a space for your own experiences to mend.

You have met educators like Jennifer Guyor Jowett, who introduced us to The Daily Fifteen, a poetry writing routine that has profoundly impacted her students in a Catholic school in Michigan. You've read about Susan Ahlbrand's student Andie, whose journey through the early days of COVID-19 and mental health challenges was supported by the power of poetry. Leilya Pitre shared how her students took their first steps toward recovery by expressing their feelings through the "I Am" poem format. These stories, among many others, have illustrated the diverse and meaningful ways poetry can be integrated into our lives and classrooms.

Throughout these chapters, we have seen how poetry provides a sanctuary for teachers and students facing the challenges of burnout, compassion fatigue, and the myriad pressures of modern education. The human lives behind the roles of teacher and student are rich with emotions, struggles, and aspirations, often overlooked in the busyness of daily routines. Poetry offers an outlet for these inner experiences, allowing us to articulate our deepest feelings and find comfort in shared expression. Sarah J. Donovan's experience with terzanelle poetry in a new town, Leilya Pitre's journey of grieving her mother, and Denise Krebs' discovery of emotions through combining music and poetry are just a few examples of how poetry has served as a healing tool.

We hope this book has provided not only inspiration but also practical ways to bring the healing power of poetry into your own life and work. Whether you are a teacher, student, or someone who values the written word, we encourage you to create spaces where writing and being are cherished. Let the stories of Melissa Bradley, Barbara Edler, Denise Krebs, Kim Johnson, and Margaret Simon remind you of the importance of community and the profound impact of sharing our voices.

As you close this book, may you carry forward the lessons learned and the healing found within these pages. May the words you have read continue to mend and strengthen you, creating a foundation for resilience, compassion, and joy. Together, let us build communities that are enriched by the beauty and strength that poetry brings, ensuring that every voice is heard, every story is honored, and every heart is healed.

Appendix

Table of Forms

Students can paste this into their notebook so they can try different poems as they are inspired to do so. They can also use this table to imagine their own form, drawing on various features from a range of options.

Form	Stanza	Lines	Meter/ Syllable	Typical Topic	Rhyme Scheme	Pattern of Repetition
4X4	4	4	4	any	no	The first line is repeated 4 times in lines 1, 2, 3, and 4 of each stanza.
acrostic	varied	varied	consistent	any	no	Relies on the repetition of initial letters to convey a message related to the word those letters form
The Arabic	any	any	any	any	any	Write the poem from right to left
blackjack	1 or more	3	7	any	no	Uses enjambment; typically one complex sentence; can be repeated to tell a story
blitz	1	50	short	any	no	Intense and quick progression, each line begins with the last word of the previous line; no punctuation

Form	Stanza	Lines	Meter/ Syllable	Typical Topic	Rhyme Scheme	Pattern of Repetition
bop	3	6-10	varies	personal or social issues	yes	ABAB - CDCD - E includes refrain
cinquain	1	5	2-4-6-8-2	any	no	There is a merging then a topic switch in line 6 (see didactic and American within the chapter)
decima	1	10	varies	any	yes	ABBAACCDD C or ABBAACCDD C
diamant e	1	7	word count	two objects	no	Involves a pattern of words, progressing from one subject to another
duplex	1	14	couplets	any	yes	AB bC cD dE eF like the sonnet and ghazal;the second line (or some variation of the couplet becomes the first line of the next couplet
elegy	any	any	any	grief, death	no	Reflecting on a person or something that died
etheree	1	10	increment al	any	no	Match the syllable count to the line line 1, 1 syllable

Form	Stanza	Lines	Meter/ Syllable	Typical Topic	Rhyme Scheme	Pattern of Repetition
extended haiku	varies	3s	5-7-5	any	no	Multiple haiku that work together to explore a topic in multiple ways or as a narrative
ghazal	5-15	couplets	same meter per line	loss, mysticism, love	yes	AA BA CA and so on, the second line of each couplet rhymes; repeated rhyming word
Gogyohka	1	5	5-7-5-7-7	any	no	Liberating the structure and themes of haiku and tanka
gogyoshi	1	5	varies	any	no	Concise expression
haiku	1	3	5-7-5	nature	no	A pivot from observation to aha
hay(na)ku	1	3	varies	any	no	First line has one word; second has 2 words, third has 3 words
lazy sonnet	1	14	one word	any	yes	ABAB CDCD EFEF GG
monotetra	1	4	8	any	yes	AAAa, with the fourth line using the rhyme of the preceding 3 lines
nocturn	varies	varies	varies	night, darkness, contemp-lative	varies	Includes repeated images or themes
nonet	1	9	incremental	any	no	Start at 9 syllables in line 1 and decrease to 1 syllable in line 1

Form	Stanza	Lines	Meter/ Syllable	Typical Topic	Rhyme Scheme	Pattern of Repetition
pantoum	multiple	4 per stanza	consistent	any	yes	ABAB, each line is repeated in a specific pattern for a weaving effect
rondeau	3	8 or 10	varies	love, nature, light themes	yes	ABbaabAB with capital letters indicating repeated lines
skinny	1	11	word count	any	yes	The 1st and 11th line are the same words rearranged; lines 2-6-10 repeat single words; other lines are single words, too
sonnet	1	14	10	love	yes	ABAB CDCD EFEF GG
tanka	1	5	5-7-5-7-7	nature, humanity	no	A pivot line that shifts focus or tone
tricube	1	3	3-3-3	any	no	Syllable count
tritina	3	9	10	any	yes	ABC, CAB, BCA, end words of the lines repeating in a specific pattern

Glossary of Terms

This is another resource that students can paste into their notebooks. We imagine many are familiar to students already, but there may be some new ones. Again, students may want to check off which ones they try or play with during the school year and refer back to this list to develop their repertoire of craft moves. to paste in notebooks.

Term	Definition
Alliteration	The repetition of the same consonant sounds at the beginning of words that are in close proximity.
Allusion	A brief and indirect reference to a person, place, thing, or idea of historical, cultural, literary, or political significance.
Anaphora	The repetition of a word or phrase at the beginning of successive clauses or lines.
Enjambment	The continuation of a sentence or clause across a line break in a poem, without a pause or punctuation.
Figurative Language	Language that uses figures of speech, such as similes, metaphors, allusions, personification, hyperbole, oxymoron, anthropomorphism, and apostrophe.
Form	The structure and organization of a poem, including its length, stanza arrangement, rhyme scheme, and meter.
Hyperbole	An exaggerated statement not meant to be taken literally, used for emphasis or effect.
Imagery	Descriptive language that appeals to the senses, creating vivid mental pictures for the reader.
Innovative	Writing that is unexpected or non-cliché, often involving a fresh approach to form, structure, or conclusion.
Jargon	Discipline or content-specific language that shows expertise or knowledge in a particular field.
Logos	Persuasion through logic, using facts, details, examples, research, reasoning, and explanations.
Metaphor	A figure of speech that directly compares two unlike things by stating that one is the other.

Term	Definition
Meter	The rhythmic structure of a poem, determined by the pattern of stressed and unstressed syllables in each line.
Onomatopoeia	A word that phonetically imitates the sound it describes, such as "buzz" or "sizzle."
Pathos	Persuasion by appealing to the audience's emotions, using powerful phrases or ideas to evoke feelings such as disgust, sadness, joy, laughter, urgency, or compassion.
Personification	A figure of speech where human characteristics are attributed to non-human things or abstract ideas.
Repetition	The deliberate use of the same word or phrase multiple times in a text to create emphasis or rhythm.
Repetition (General)	The act of repeating words, phrases, or structures for emphasis, including forms like anaphora, epistrophe, asyndeton, polysyndeton, analepsis, alliteration, assonance, and consonance.
Rhyme Scheme	The pattern of rhymes at the end of each line of a poem, typically described using letters to denote which lines rhyme.
Sensory Language	Descriptive language that appeals to the senses (smell, sound, taste, touch, sight) to create vivid imagery and bring the setting or characters to life.
Simile	A figure of speech comparing two unlike things using "like" or "as."
Stanza	A grouped set of lines in a poem, often separated by a space, that usually follows a specific pattern of meter and rhyme.
Syntax	The arrangement of words and phrases to create well-formed sentences, including varied sentence structures such as gerunds, infinitives, subordinating conjunctions, asyndeton, anaphora, parentheticals, appositives, and parallelism.
Transitions	Words or phrases that show changes in time, place, or ideas, including subordinating conjunctions (when, while, after, before) and conjunctive adverbs (thus, however, therefore).
Translanguaging	The process of using multiple language varieties in a single conversation or text, allowing speakers to draw on their entire linguistic repertoire.

VEEPPP: Public Speaking Guide

Students can paste this into their notebook for reminders about how to read aloud and perform their poem (or other writing) in a more formal setting like the open mic.

VEEPP	Public Speaking
Volume	We can hear you in the back of the room. You may make your voice louder or softer in certain parts to emphasize something, show passion/emotion, or make the audience lean in, but it is related to content. Your volume does not distract from your message.
Eye Contact	We can see your eyes at different points of the performance to show you are trying to connect with us — your audience. You can hold eye contact with 3 angles of the room, so you are showing you know your content well.
Expression	The way you say the words and phrases show you are interpreting the mood and content to communicate to the audience. You may change expression in different parts as the mood shifts or ideas become more serious or light-hearted.
Pace	You stay within the time allowed. You perform with a pace that matches the content and mood; it is slow enough for us to hear and process the words and fast enough for us to feel the rhythm. You may slow down to emphasize certain parts or to let an important idea really resonate with the audience.
Pronunciation	You clearly practiced and know the words you've written, especially technical ones. The audience is not distracted by phrasing or unclear pronunciation.
Professionalism	You clearly prepared for the performance. You stand strong (no swaying), say "thank you" at the end to signal closure, stay for a moment to accept the applause, and your demeanor treats the topic and audience with respect.

Poetry Listening Handout

Listener's Name: _____

Something to celebrate about the author's writing!
- o **Jargon:** discipline or content-specific language: fancy words and words specific to the subject/topic (shows expertise/knowledge)
- o **Figurative language:** simile, metaphor, allusion, personification, hyperbole, oxymoron, anthropomorphism, apostrophe
- o **Repetition:** anaphora, epistrophe, asyndeton, polysyndeton, analepsis, alliteration, assonance, consonance
- o **Sensory language:** smell, sound, taste, touch, sight-colors, shapes, textures, movement— the setting/place comes alive, can imagine characters
- o **Logos:** facts, details, examples, research, reasoning, explanations, logic
- o **Pathos:** emotional, powerful phrases/ ideas that cause disgust, sadness, joy, laughter, sense of urgency, outrage, compassion, sympathy
- o **Innovative:** unexpected lead, twist, ending, non-cliche; form: inserting an epistle, poem, mixing genre forms; the conclusion was fresh (something we haven't heard)
- o **Transitions:** subordinating conjunctions (when, while, after, before) show time/place/idea changes; conjunctive adverbs (thus, however, therefore, on one hand, on the other hand)
- o **Syntax:** starting with a gerund, infinitive, subordinating conjunction, asyndeton, anaphora, parentheticals, appositives, parallelism; long, short, one-word sentences.

Name	Feature to Celebrate	Text Evidence Check if you complimented the author.→	
Sarah	Sensory language – **smell**	"rotting stench of a fish left in the garbage for days"	❑
			❑
			❑
			❑

Compliment Giving (look at the person): *(Name), when you read, "QUOTE," I thought it was a (vivid, effective, thoughtful, creative, innovative, moving, brave) example of (TECHNIQUE) because (REASON).*

Example: *Julie, when you read, "rotting stench of a fish left in the garbage for days," I thought it was a powerful example of sensory language because fish in the garbage is offensive and lingers.*

Compliment Receiving (look at the person): *Thank you* (looking at the person.)

Peer Conferring Protocol

Peer Conferring Protocol for the Writer

Writer's Name:_____

Listeners' Name(s): #1_____ &

#2_____

Instructions: Before you read or ask for feedback let your listener know what you need from them: *One thing I really want your feedback on is (my opening, closing, organization, transition, etc.).*

Now, read your writing to the listener. If you notice anything you'd like to change as you read, feel free to stop and make that revision.

When you are done reading, ask the listen some questions and write notes of their responses to help you with your revisions:

    1. What stood out to you as a reader/listener?

#1

#2

    2. What feedback do you have based on my initial request?

#1

#2

    3. What are you still wondering about, would like to hear more about, or would you like me to make it more clear/or less obvious in my revision?

#1

#2

Thank the listeners. Invite them to share their writing with you.

Bonus Poems

Welcome to the bonus content section of our book, where we've gathered an eclectic array of poetry prompts that have sparked creativity and joy in our classrooms. These prompts, cherished and refined through years of teaching, offer a diverse mix of themes and styles to inspire writers of all levels. Whether you're looking to explore personal reflections, experiment with new forms, or simply find a starting point for your next poetic endeavor, you'll discover a treasure trove of ideas here. And for even more inspiration, be sure to visit www.ethicalela.com, where hundreds of additional prompts await to fuel your poetic journey.

1. Whimsical Science
2. Marcher or Leaper: Forging Your Own Destiny
3. Kennings Atmospheric Atoms
4. Rewrite, Redo
5. Ode
6. Postcard Poetry
7. Try a Triolet
8. Fibonacci Poem
9. Pile Poem
10. Etheree
11. Nocturn
12. A Moonlight Experience
13. I Dream a World
14. Hands
15. Places We Call Home
16. Burrows & Seeds
17. A Container for Worries
18. A Night Poem
19. The Morning After
20. Solving a Problem: The Bop Poem
21. Tricube
22. Abecedarian Poem
23. Haiku Photographs
24. Gogyoshi
25. Ekphrastic Poetry

About the Editor

Sarah J. Donovan is a former junior high English language arts teacher of fifteen years and an Associate Professor of Secondary English Education at Oklahoma State University. She has edited other collections of literature: *Rhyme & Rhythm: Poems for Student Athletes, Teacher-Poets Writing to Bridge the Distance, 90 Ways of Community: Nurturing Safe and Inclusive Classrooms One Poem at a Time, and Just YA: Short Poems, Fiction, & Essays for Grades 7-12.*

About the Authors

Susan Ahlbrand is in her 36th year of teaching 8th grade English/language arts in the small southern Indiana town of Jasper. When not preparing lessons or grading papers, she enjoys reading and writing, binge-watching shows with her husband, exercising, attending sporting events, and heading off to visit one of four kids who are scattered across the Midwest and South.

Tammi Belko serves as a District Gifted Intervention Specialist for Cuyahoga Falls City Schools. As a former middle school teacher and Power of the Pen writing coach, Tammi has spent over seventeen years sharing her love of reading, writing and poetry with her students. Tammi resides in Cleveland, Ohio with her husband and youngest daughter. When she isn't absorbed in reading young adult literature, she can be found listening to music, hiking or enjoying a musical performance with her daughters. She is the author of the young adult verse novel, *Perchance to Dream.*

Barbara Edler has taught English for forty-plus years in Iowa, the last thirty in Keokuk where she encouraged students to find their own voice while taking risks, coaching speech participants, and supporting NHD competitors. During the last few years of teaching, Barb worked with talented and gifted students and honed her technology and engineering skills. Keokuk is located in the very southeast tip of the state where she enjoys watching the Mississippi roll by, reading, writing, playing cards, watching birds, and basically appreciating the simple things in life.

Wendy Everard has taught English for 27 years in Central New York and has taught grades 7-12. She currently teaches English 12, Creative Writing, and AP English Language. She is a consultant for the National Writing Project and recently participated in an NEH Summer Institute on Abolition and the Underground Railroad. She spends her time at home with her husband and two daughters, writing for pleasure and creating curriculum, walking country roads, birding and adoring her dog and two cats.

Kim Johnson, Ed.D., lives in Williamson, Georgia, where she serves as District Literacy Specialist for Pike County Schools. She enjoys writing, reading, traveling, and spending time with her husband and three rescue schnoodles—Boo Radley (TKAM), Fitz (F. Scott Fitzgerald), and Ollie (Mary Oliver). You can follow her blog, *Common Threads: patchwork prose and verse.*

Jennifer Guyor Jowett has been a middle grade ELA instructor for over thirty years. She enjoys helping students rediscover their voices and their love of reading. Her students write frequently with her during The Daily Fifteen. Jennifer is the author of *Into the Shadows*, a middle grade novel inspired by true events set during WWII, and her poetry can be found in *Bridge the Distance: Teacher-Poets Writing to Bridge the Distance: An Oral History of Covid-19 in Poems.* She is the creator of the Dog Eared Book Awards, a word celebrator, and a mitten state dweller. Discover more about her at this site: jenniferguyorjowett.weebly.com

274

Denise Krebs has a master's degree in elementary education with a concentration in teaching reading. She taught in Arizona, California, Michigan, Iowa, and the small island Kingdom of Bahrain in public and private schools and recreation centers for nearly 40 years (with a ten-year sabbatical when her children were young). She loves to cook, bake, create, write, tell stories, and spend time with her grandchildren. Follow her on Instagram at @mrsdkrebs. She blogs regularly at *Dare to Care* and has had some of her poems published in anthologies. She co-authored *The Genius Hour Guidebook*, published by Routledge Eye on Education and Middle Web, now in the second edition.

Leilya Pitre lives in Ponchatoula, LA, which is known as the Strawberry Capital of the World. She teaches at Southeastern Louisiana University and coordinates the English Education Program. As teacher educator, she is passionate about helping her students to become nourishing, devoted, and effective teachers in the classrooms. She is one of the co-editors of Study and Scrutiny: Research on Young Adult Literature and one of the curators of Dr. Bickmore's YA Wednesday Weekend Picks. She loves to learn about people, cultures, and rich traditions all over the world. In her free time, she reads, writes, listens to music, visits her children and grandchildren, or travels with her husband.

Margaret Simon lives on the Bayou Teche in New Iberia, LA. Margaret has been an elementary school teacher for 36 years, most recently teaching gifted students in Iberia Parish. Her first book of children's poetry was published in 2018 by UL Press, *Bayou Song: Creative Explorations of the South Louisiana Landscape*. Margaret's poems have appeared in anthologies including *The Poetry of US* by National Geographic and *Rhyme & Rhythm: Poems for Student Athletes*. Margaret writes a blog regularly at *Reflections on the Teche*.

Links
[1] https://kimhaynesjohnson.com/
[2] https://jenniferguyorjowett.weebly.com/
[3] https://mrsdkrebs.edublogs.org/
[4] https://reflectionsontheteche.com/

Words That Mend: The Transformative Power of Writing Poetry for Teachers, Students, and Community Wellbeing is a book written by teachers for teachers. It offers poetry as a powerful transformative agent to service teachers, their students, and community. The authors candidly share their personal stories of trauma, pain, and loss, as well as stories from the classrooms and community events. They emphasize that processing traumatic or tragic events through poetry writing has become a step toward recovery and rediscovering hope. Moreover, writing it in a community where they connect and support each other is even more helpful. This text recognizes the need for continuous healing for teachers who then will be able to support their students and communities. With this goal in mind, teacher-poets extend their invitation to foster spaces that allow including poetry in teaching and learning practices for academic achievements, for restoring emotional wellbeing of teachers, students, and their families, and for a centering of creative writing in ELA. The book includes practical ways for teachers to engage in poetry writing for self, students, and community by providing prompts, instructions, and a space to share their poems.

ALSO AVAILABLE
FROM ETHICAL ELA CONTRIBUTORS

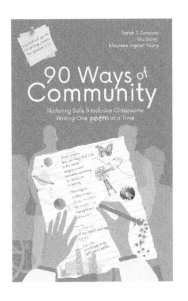

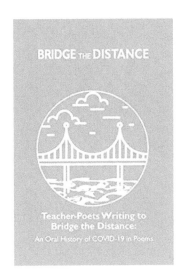

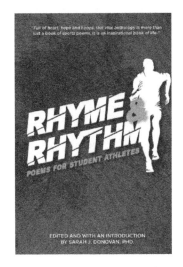

Made in the USA
Monee, IL
01 December 2024

71318208R00157